LAW, CORPORATE GOVERNANCE
AND PARTNERSHIPS AT WORK

Law, Ethics and Governance Series

Series Editor: Charles Sampford, Director, Key Centre for Ethics, Law, Justice and Governance, Griffith University, Australia

Recent history has emphasised the potentially devastating effects of governance failures in governments, government agencies, corporations and the institutions of civil society. 'Good governance' is seen as necessary, if not crucial, for economic success and human development. Although the disciplines of law, ethics, politics, economics and management theory can provide insights into the governance of organisations, governance issues can only be dealt with by interdisciplinary studies, combining several (and sometimes all) of those disciplines. This series aims to provide such interdisciplinary studies for students, researchers and relevant practitioners.

Recent titles in the series

Ethics and Socially Responsible Investment
A Philosophical Approach
William Ransome and Charles Sampford
ISBN 978-0-7546-7581-5

Improving Health Care Safety and Quality
Reluctant Regulators
Judith Healy
ISBN 978-0-7546-7644-7

Idealism and the Abuse of Power
Lessons from China's Cultural Revolution
Zhuang Hui-yun
ISBN 978-0-7546-7208-1

Integrity Systems for Occupations
Andrew Alexandra and Seumas Miller
ISBN 978-0-7546-7749-9

Promoting Integrity
Evaluating and Improving Public Institutions
Edited by Brian W. Head, A.J. Brown and Carmel Connors
ISBN 978-0-7546-4986-1

Law, Corporate Governance and Partnerships at Work
A Study of Australian Regulatory Style and Business Practice

RICHARD MITCHELL
Monash University, Australia

ANTHONY O'DONNELL
La Trobe University, Australia

SHELLEY MARSHALL
Monash University, Australia

IAN RAMSAY
University of Melbourne, Australia

MEREDITH JONES
State Service Authority, Victorian Government, Australia

Routledge
Taylor & Francis Group

LONDON AND NEW YORK

First published 2011 by Ashgate Publishing

Published 2016 by Routledge
2 Park Square, Milton Park, Abingdon, Oxfordshire OX14 4RN
711 Third Avenue, New York, NY 10017, USA

First issued in paperback 2016

Routledge is an imprint of the Taylor & Francis Group, an informa business

British Library Cataloguing in Publication Data
Law, corporate governance and partnerships at work : a
 study of Australian regulatory style and business practice.
 -- (Law, ethics and governance series)
 1. Corporate governance--Australia. 2. Partnership--
 Australia. 3. Capitalism--Australia. 4. Corporation law--
 Australia.
 I. Series II. Jones, Meredith.
 338.6'0994-dc22

Library of Congress Cataloging-in-Publication Data
Law, corporate governance and partnerships at work : a study of australian
regulatory style and business practice / by Richard Mitchell, Anthony
O'Donnell, Shelley Marshall, Ian Ramsay and Meredith Jones.
 p. cm. -- (Law, ethics and governance)
 Includes bibliographical references and index.
 ISBN 978-1-4094-2106-1 (hardcover)
 1. Corporate governance--Law and legislation--Australia.
 2. Industrial relations--Australia. I. Mitchell, Richard, 1946-
 KU956.3.L39 2011
 338.60994--dc23

 2011021121

 ISBN 13: 978-1-138-27712-0 (pbk)
 ISBN 13: 978-1-4094-2106-1 (hbk)

Contents

List of Figures and Tables

Figures

Tables

Preface

This book is the result of a five-year Australian Research Council funded project (DP0343080) on the relationship between corporate governance, corporate ownership structure and the management of labour. The project, carried out under the general title of the 'Corporate Governance and Workplace Partnerships Project' was based in the Centre for Employment and Labour Relations Law and the Centre for Corporate Law and Securities Regulation in the Law School at the University of Melbourne until 2007, and since then has been carried out by those two Centres in association with the Department of Business Law and Taxation and the Department of Management at Monash University. Although the project commenced officially in 2003, earlier work had been carried out by a group of collaborators in preparation for a similar project, and we wish to thank the following colleagues for their help and support at that earlier stage: Michelle Brown, John Buchanan, Sean Cooney, Christina Cregan, Simon Deakin, Peter Gahan, Pamela Hanrahan, Tim Lindsey, Jill Murray, Geof Stapledon and Veronica Taylor. In particular we owe a great deal to Michelle Brown, Chris Cregan and Peter Gahan for their work on a research strategy, much of which was carried over to the present project.

Various smaller projects have paved the way to some degree for this study. These have included studies on employee decision making in enterprises, and the content of various forms of agreements made pursuant to the *Workplace Relations Act 1996* (Cth). We extend our thanks to Michelle Brown, Christina Cregan, Anthony Forsyth, Glenn Patmore and Lea Waters in respect of the first group of projects, and Kamillea Aghton, Andrew Barnes, Donna Buttigieg, Rebecca Campbell, Kate Creighton, Joel Fetter, Peter Gahan, Emma Goodwin, Anthony Forsyth, Samantha Korman, Tanya Josev and Nicole Yasbek in respect of the second group. Some colleagues, including Jarrod Lenne, Ann O'Connell, Cameron Rider, Andrew Barnes and Tanya Josev, have worked on an associated project focussing on employee share ownership schemes, and we are grateful to them for the contribution that their work in this regard has made to our core project.

To some extent also, this project has evolved from an earlier collaboration between the Centre for Employment and Labour Relations Law and the Department of Management at the University of Melbourne, and the Centre for Business Research at the University of Cambridge. That earlier work, exploring the individualisation of employment relations, was important in pointing the way to the necessity of undertaking a fundamental reappraisal of the manner in which business corporations are engaging with labour, and the role that law is playing in that reformation. We wish to acknowledge the support of Stephen Deery in that earlier project.

Also involved in that earlier project, and equally important to the present project, has been the support of Simon Deakin. In mid-2003 Simon travelled to Melbourne to take part in a scoping exercise which enabled us, over several days, to plan our project in greater detail. This was an important impetus in getting the project off the ground and we thank him for this major contribution.

Over the five-year life of the project many others have assisted with the work in one way or another. Chief among these have been our colleagues Kirsten Anderson (who helped carry out a number of the research projects), Malcolm Anderson (who provided statistical analysis of some of our data) Jarrod Lenne (who was involved in the early stages) and Geof Stapledon (who was particularly helpful to us as an advisor in the institutional investors aspect of the project). David Merrett generously shared his research in the early years of the project. Similarly, Alan Dignam shared some of his research ideas with us when he visited Melbourne Law School. Others, including Christina Cregan, Harry Glasbeek, Gideon Haigh and Andrew Pendleton, presented seminars as part of the seminar series associated with the project. In particular we wish to acknowledge the important contribution made by Anthony Forsyth, Phillip Lipton and Peter Gahan to parts of what are now Chapters 2 and 5 of this book.

In the later stages of the project we have taken part in various conferences and seminars which have given an opportunity for us to present early results arising from intermediate stages of the research. In March 2005 we took part in the 'Economic Globalisation and Corporate Governance Symposium', conducted under the auspices of the *Wisconsin International Law Journal* at the University of Wisconsin, USA. The results of that symposium are contained in the *Wisconsin International Law Journal* vol. 23, 2005. In early 2006 we took part in another international workshop conducted by the Institute for Technology, Enterprise and Competitiveness at Doshisha University in Japan, under the title 'Re-embedding the Corporation? Managerial, Regulatory and Financial Perspectives on Corporate Social Responsibility'. The outcomes of that programme are contained in *Corporate Governance: An International Review* vol. 15, 2007.

In late 2006, the Corporate Governance and Workplace Partnerships Project organised its own two-day workshop drawing upon our own research, and the work being carried out by other groups of Australian researchers which we felt was, in one way or another, pursuing similar themes or lines of inquiry to that work. The papers presented at that workshop were subsequently published as an edited volume (S. Marshall, R. Mitchell and I. Ramsay (eds), *Varieties of Capitalism, Corporate Governance and Employees*, Melbourne University Press, Melbourne, 2008). We owe the contributors to that volume, Kirsten Anderson, John Burgess, Richard Gough, John Howe, Jim Kitay, Russell Lansbury, John Lewer, Max Ogden, Nick Wailes, Peter Waring and Mark Westcott, our thanks for their participation. Several others, Sean Cooney, Colin Fenwick, Peter Gahan, Leon Gettler, Jarrod Lenne, Jill Murray, Christine Parker and Geof Stapledon, provided commentary, chaired sessions or provided other papers during the workshop, and we thank them for that support.

In the early stages of this project all of the authors were based in the Law School at the University of Melbourne, and we wish to thank the Law School and its research office for their support in varying ways for the project. Richard Mitchell also wishes to thank the Department of Business Law and Taxation, and the Department of Management at Monash University for its support since late 2004, and in particular he wishes to acknowledge the collegial support and assistance he has received from Helen Anderson, Phillip Lipton, Abe Herzberg, Anthony Forsyth, Carolyn Sutherland, Paul von Nessen and Michelle Welsh.

Finally, it is necessary for us to acknowledge the contribution to our research made by the participants who agreed to give up their time and to provide us with information. The project could not have occurred without key personnel from companies and investment funds providing confidential documents about their business processes and strategies, and sitting for hours answering our questions about their relations with employees and shareholders. They welcomed our scrutiny in the spirit of open inquiry and provided us with valuable insights into the ways that regulation shapes their behaviour.

We hope that the body of research reported in this book makes a useful contribution to understanding the role that law plays in shaping business priorities. The material focuses upon Australian businesses and regulation, and aims to paint a thorough picture of the competing motivations and priorities of companies in relation to employees and shareholders in particular from the late 1990s through to the mid-2000s. The research helps to situate the Australian regulatory style and type of capitalism in comparison with other countries. We also understand ourselves to be participating in a broader international investigation of the forces that shape change in regulatory styles and the ways in which markets are governed. Like Australia, many countries around the world underwent rapid reform in the laws regulating companies and workers in the 1990s in the name of market liberalisation, with significant implications for the structures of labour markets and the relative priority given to employees and shareholders. It is necessary to note that at the end of this long period of liberalisation in Australian labour law, which covered virtually the entire period of our empirical research into corporate restructuring and employment reorganisation, the election of a Labor government in Australia saw something of a return to stronger union and worker protection mainly in the form of the *Fair Work Act 2009*. We have not had scope to analyse in detail these most recent developments in this work, although it is important to note that labour markets remain considerably liberalised when compared with the system of two decades ago. This book examines the impact of that liberalisation, and contributes to an international debate about whether, and to what extent, the law matters when it comes to influencing the values and priorities of the most important private institution of contemporary capitalism – the company.

The authors
2011

Chapter 1
Corporate Governance, Employment Systems and Workplace Partnerships in Australia

1.1 Introduction

This book examines the relationship between various factors which shape the manner in which Australian business corporations manage their labour or employment systems. We assume this to be an issue of critical importance to the welfare of Australian society and its economy.[1] In particular our project has been concerned with the task of identifying and examining factors which are of paramount importance in the creation and sustainability of what we have labelled 'Partnerships at Work': that is, situations in which business organisations are seen to work closely and co-operatively with their employees rather than contrary to their interests.

Following upon earlier similar studies,[2] our research has focussed upon the interaction of three factors in particular which are seen to influence outcomes in this area: types of corporate governance, types of ownership structure (i.e. financial capital arrangements), and systems of labour engagement and utilisation (employment systems). Importantly, we have oriented our study to locate the interaction or cross influence of these three core factors within the regulatory environment set by laws and legal institutions.

The work is grounded in several overlapping and intersecting debates which have been underway for the past two decades at least. At the general social level, numbers of major corporate collapses and scandals, most recently and spectacularly in the wake of the financial crisis of 2008, have given rise to concern over how corporations are managed and monitored, and how they may be made more accountable in the public interest.[3] Associated with these general concerns,

---

1 H. Gospel and A. Pendleton (eds), *Corporate Governance and Labour Management: An International Comparison*, Oxford University Press, Oxford, 2005, p. 1.

2 Ibid.

3 The international literature on these matters is extensive. For an account of Australian incidents in the general context of the international panorama see J. Hill, 'Regulatory Responses to Global Corporate Scandals' (2005) 23 *Wisconsin International Law Journal* 367. See also D. Noakes, 'Dogs on the Wharves: Corporate Groups and the Waterfront Dispute' (1999) 11 *Australian Journal of Corporate Law* 27; P. Darvas, 'Employees'

or arising because of them, several key issues have found their way into public debate. These include, for example, the appropriate constitution of company boards (particularly the mix of executive and independent directors);[4] the level of accountability by management to shareholders,[5] and the apparently highly inflated levels of corporate executive remuneration.[6] Other issues in debate have included the domination of a shareholder-oriented perspective of corporate performance,[7] the impact of corporate takeovers and mergers on employees,[8] and the rights of other stakeholders (such as employees and creditors) to be considered as 'insiders' rather than 'outsiders' when it comes to corporate decision-making.[9]

In more specialised ways, several strands of academic literature, grounded in different disciplines and fields of learning, have also contributed challenging

Rights and Entitlements in Insolvency: Regulatory Rationale, Legal Issues and Proposed Solutions' (1999) 17 *Company and Securities Law Journal* 103. Gideon Haigh's book on James Hardie Industries is an excellent study of corporate culture in evolution: *Asbestos House*, Scribe, Melbourne, 2006.

4   Gospel and Pendleton, above n. 1, pp. 3–8; Hill, ibid., pp. 385–400.

5   K. Pistor, Y. Keinan, J. Kleinheisterkamp and M. West, 'The Evolution of Corporate Law: A Cross-Country Comparison' (2002) 23 *University of Pennsylvania Journal of International Economic Law* 791, pp. 795–796.

6   See Hill, above n. 3, pp. 407–414, and also by the same author 'Regulating Executive Remuneration: International Developments in the Post-Scandal Era' (2006) 3 *European Company Law* 64; R. Mitchell, A. O'Donnell and I. Ramsay, 'Shareholder Value and Employee Interests: Intersections Between Corporate Governance, Corporate Law and Labor Law' (2005) 23 *Wisconsin International Law Journal* 417, pp. 443–445; G. Haigh, 'Bad Company: The Cult of the CEO' (2003) 10 *Quarterly Essay* 1.

7   W. Lazonick and M. O'Sullivan, 'Maximising Shareholder Value: A New Ideology for Corporate Governance' (2000) 29 *Economy and Society* 13; J. Armour, S. Deakin and S. Konzelmann, 'Shareholder Primacy and the Trajectory of UK Corporate Governance' (2003) 41 *British Journal of Industrial Relations* 531; Gospel and Pendleton, above n. 1, pp. 6, 14–15; Mitchell et al., ibid., *passim*.

8   J. Froud, C. Haslam, S. Johal and K. Williams, 'Restructuring for Shareholder Value and its Implications for Labour' (2000) 24 *Cambridge Journal of Economics* 771; S. Deakin, 'Workers, Finance and Democracy' in C. Barnard, S. Deakin and G. Morris (eds), *The Future of Labour Law*, Hart, Oxford, 2004, pp. 84–89; Gospel and Pendleton, above n. 1, p. 7.

9   Gospel and Pendleton, above n. 1, pp. 3–4; A. Forsyth, 'Corporate Collapses and Employees' Right to Know: An Issue for Corporate Law or Labour Law?' (2003) 31 *Australian Business Law Review* 81; S. Bottomley and A. Forsyth, 'The New Corporate Law' in A. Voiculescu and T. Campbell (eds), *The New Corporate Accountability: Corporate Social Responsibility and the Law*, Cambridge University Press, Cambridge, 2007. Prior to the rise of the 'shareholder value' paradigm in recent decades, managerial authority and decision-making was probably guided by an implicit (and uncontroversial) 'stakeholder' perspective of the corporation: see P. Osterman, *Securing Prosperity: The American Labour Market – How it has Changed and What to Do About it*, Princeton University Press, Princeton, 1999, pp. 147–150.

and diverse perspectives to the study of the relationship of corporate governance and labour management. These include contributions from management studies, institutional and financial economics, business studies, industrial relations and law among others. These various debates are reviewed in the earlier work of Gospel and Pendleton[10] and are not repeated here. Our following, more selective, coverage of the literature is oriented more directly to accommodate the objectives of the present project.

1.2 The Political Economy of Capitalism

Work carried out on the institutional bases of different types of capitalism and different business systems has posited various styles of, and approaches to, economic organisation within states.[11] As noted, this literature draws on a diverse range of academic disciplines and scholarship. Jackson and Deeg have identified three key 'theoretical innovations' contributed through the comparative capitalisms work.[12]

The first of these is that national economies are 'characterised by distinct *institutional configurations* that generate a particular systemic "logic" of economic action'.[13] These configurations are comprised of associations of institutional variables which constitute each particular system, including such matters as corporate governance, industrial relations, work systems, forms of finance and corporate ownership and so on.[14] The second 'theoretical innovation' identified by Jackson and Deeg is that the comparative capitalisms literature 'suggests a theory of *comparative institutional advantage* in which different institutional arrangements

---

10   See above n. 1, ch. 1.
11   The literature is extensive. Examples include J. Hollingsworth and R. Boyer (eds), *Contemporary Capitalism: The Embeddedness of Institutions*, Cambridge University Press, Cambridge, 1997; R. Whitley, *Divergent Capitalisms: The Social Structuring and Change of Business Systems,* Oxford University Press, Oxford, 1999; P. Hall and D. Soskice (eds), *Varieties of Capitalism: The Institutional Foundations of Comparative Advantage*, Oxford University Press, Oxford, 2001; W. Streek and K. Yamamura (eds), *The Origins of Nonliberal Capitalism*, Cornell University Press, Ithaca, 2001; I. Fannon, *Working Within Two Kinds of Capitalism*, Hart, Oxford, 2003; B. Amable, *The Diversity of Modern Capitalism*, Oxford University Press, Oxford, 2003; R. Boyer, 'How and Why Capitalisms Differ'(2005) 34 *Economy and Society* 509. For a recent review see G. Jackson and R. Deeg, 'How Many Varieties of Capitalism? Comparing the Comparative Institutional Analyses of Capitalist Diversity', Discussion Paper No. 06/2, Max Planck Institute for the Study of Societies, Cologne, 2006.
12   Jackson and Deeg, ibid., p. 6.
13   Ibid. The emphasis is that of the quoted authors.
14   But note that the number and content of the relevant institutions varies in different accounts; see Jackson and Deeg, above n. 11, pp. 30–33.

have distinct strengths and weaknesses for different kinds of economic activity'.[15] The important implication of this is that there may be no single most efficient style of capitalism – different varieties work effectively according to the fit between institutional style and the type of economy pursued. Such a perspective seriously challenges the idea that there might be a global 'convergence' upon a best practice model of capitalist economy.[16]

The third 'theoretical innovation' is that the comparative capitalisms literature is taken 'to imply a theory of *institutional path dependence*'.[17] In other words, as Jackson and Deeg explain further, the fact that there are 'institutional linkages and complementarities' within national systems makes it difficult to introduce changes which can have the effect of transforming 'the overall institutional configuration from one type of capitalism to another'.[18]

The literature on comparative capitalisms tends to explore the interaction between various institutions within larger production regimes. Our focus here is on the interaction effects of two such institutions: corporate governance and industrial relations (other institutions that figure in the literature include systems of vocational training, welfare arrangements and competition policy). With respect to this particular interaction, the varieties of capitalism literature examines at workplace level the interplay of business strategy, shareholder value and employees' interests.

For example, one formative work in this area has identified two separate and distinct sets of institutional arrangements, complemented by legal systems and 'styles' of regulation, which are identified either as 'liberal market' economies or 'co-ordinated market' economies.[19]

'Liberal market' economies (typified in the national systems of the US and the UK for example) are said to be characterised by an 'outsider' form of corporate governance and finance, a dispersed shareholder base grounded in extensive and deep equity markets, strong protective rights for investors, an active market for control by shareholders (particularly through takeovers and mergers) and a

---

15   Ibid. The emphasis is that of the quoted authors.

16   See, briefly, Jackson and Deeg, above n. 11, pp. 33–35. There are many layers to the argument about globalisation and convergence: see H. Hansmann and R. Kraakman, 'The End of History for Corporate Law' (2001) 89 *Georgetown Law Journal* 439; J. Gordon and M. Roe (eds), *Convergence and Persistence in Corporate Governance*, Cambridge University Press, Cambridge, 2004; H. Katz and O. Darbishire, *Converging Divergences: Worldwide Changes in Employment Systems*, Cornell University Press, Ithaca, 2000; S. Jacoby, *The Embedded Corporation*, Princeton University Press, Princeton, 2005; J. Hill, 'The Persistent Debate about Convergence in Comparative Corporate Governance' (2005) 27 *Sydney Law Review* 743.

17   Jackson and Deeg, above n. 11. The emphasis is that of the quoted authors.

18   Jackson and Deeg, above n. 11, pp. 35–36. See also Gospel and Pendleton, above n. 1, pp. 8–9. However, the validity of this proposition is also under debate: see Jackson and Deeg, above n. 11, pp. 36–37.

19   See Hall and Soskice, above n. 11.

business strategy focussed upon short-term financial benefits for shareholders. This 'marketised' style of corporate governance is, in turn, said to be allied to a complementary style of labour management which supports the interests of capital over workers. It is argued, for example, that under the 'liberal market' model, one typically finds a more partial, less protective set of labour institutions and rights. Under such a system there is less employment security, fewer minimum standards of employment for workers, and where such standards exist, they apply to a smaller cohort of workers than in the 'co-ordinated' style of economy.

By contrast, 'co-ordinated market' economies (typified in the systems of Germany and other European countries) are said to be characterised by quite different corporate ownership and governance arrangements. In these economies, shareholding is much less widely dispersed, share markets are less developed, and financing is facilitated more through banks and other large lenders. The argument here is that these arrangements engender an 'insider' form of governance where financiers develop longer term relations with corporate managers and there is much weaker 'market' discipline. With a longer term view of the business able to be exercised by management there is also a longer term view able to be taken of relations with workers. Accordingly, the 'co-ordinated market' style of economic organisation is marked by better protections for workers, greater employment security, more investment in skills and training, and a higher degree of employee involvement in workplace decision-making.

Other comparative studies identify more than two groupings or 'families' of nations.[20] To a large extent, these extended groupings open up Hall and Soskice's catch-all category of 'co-ordinated market' economies and differentiate those economies with greater precision.[21] Less considered in the literature, but potentially important for our inquiry, is the possibility that there are varieties of liberal markets or, at least, significant differences amongst liberal regimes.[22]

Our concern to focus specifically on the corporate governance-labour relations nexus was assisted considerably by a 2005 volume by Gospel and Pendleton. Their collection of national studies specifically examined the relationship between capital, management and labour in order to understand more closely how companies in different national systems are controlled and in whose interests they are controlled. In pushing this study of governance beyond the more typical concerns with the composition of corporate boards and executive pay, the

---

20   For example, Boyer, above n. 11, identifies four regime types; Amable, above n. 11, identifies five; and Whitley, above n. 11, proposes a typology of six 'business systems'.

21   As one commentator suggests, the proliferating ideal types that result tend to be 'nested within each other, related like the famous Russian matryoshka dolls': M. Schroder, 'Integrating Welfare and Production Typologies: How Refinements of the Varieties of Capitalism Approach Call for a Combination of Welfare Typologies' (2009) 38 *Journal of Social Policy* 19.

22   See R. Mahon, 'Varieties of Liberalism: Canadian Social Policy from the "Golden Age" to the Present' (2008) 42 *Social Policy and Administration* 343.

authors sought to draw another important variable, labour, more centrally into the discussion.[23] Generally speaking, the authors were interested to discover how finance and corporate governance influenced or shaped the management of labour.[24] For these purposes 'management of labour' was defined to include three sets of corporate policies: work relations (essentially how work is organised); employment relations (employment rights, recruitment, training and employment security); and industrial relations (voice and representation).

The studies that made up the Gospel and Pendleton collection drew on a broad range of existing typologies of national systems of both corporate governance and labour management. For the purpose of setting up some basic hypotheses regarding the mechanisms that might link corporate governance and labour management, Gospel and Pendleton used a parsimonious two-systems approach, derived from the financial economics literature.[25] Utilising their basic concepts concerning the management of labour, they explored the different ways in which corporate governance and labour management were seen to interact in 'market/ outsider' financial systems and in 'relational/insider' systems. As will already be apparent, this dichotomy between two financial systems overlaps in significant ways with the dichotomy between 'liberal market' and 'co-ordinated market' economies that characterises the varieties of capitalism approach. Gospel and Pendleton noted several contrasting features, including the way that shareholder and employee interests are balanced, the differing time horizons adopted for corporate development, the alternative types of business strategies adopted, the relative use of market-based measures of performance to secure commitment, and the nature of relations between companies.[26]

The insights about differing national systems can be appropriately transposed to an analysis of individual companies.[27] As noted earlier, and is explained more fully below (see section 1.4), we have substantially based our study on the Gospel and Pendleton approach insofar as we have attempted to look closely at the interaction of corporate governance and labour management at the workplace

---

23 Gospel and Pendleton, above n. 1, pp. 3–4.

24 Ibid, pp. 14, 18.

25 See, e.g., C. Mayer, 'Financial Systems, Corporate Finance and Economic Development' in R. Hubbard (ed.), *Asymmetric Information, Corporate Finance and Investment*, University of Chicago Press, Chicago, 1990; J. Franks and C. Mayer, 'Corporate Ownership and Control in the U.K., Germany and the U.S.' in D. Chew (ed.), *Studies in International Corporate Finance and Governance Systems*, Oxford University Press, New York, 1997.

26 Gospel and Pendleton, above n. 1, pp. 14–17.

27 See, e.g., S. Deakin, R. Hobbs, S. Konzelmann and F. Wilkinson, 'Partnership, Ownership and Control: The Impact of Corporate Governance on Employment Relations' (2002) 24 *Employee Relations* 335; and N. Conway, S. Deakin, S. Konzelmann, H. Petit, A. Reberiouz and F. Wilkinson, 'The Influence of Stock Market Listing on Human Resource Management: Evidence for France and Britain' (2008) 46 *British Journal of Industrial Relations* 631.

level, distinguishing between companies which display insider-type governance and those which exhibit a dispersed 'outsider' shareholder base. We have, however, attempted to add to that study by taking particular account of the way that law and legal institutions provide important regulatory grounding in the interactive process. In particular we have drawn on an important stream of literature relating to 'legal origins' which identifies legal variables as key determinants in the shaping of national styles of economic regulation.

1.3 The Law and National Systems of Regulation

As with the literature on comparative capitalisms generally, the more particularised debate on the role of law in shaping national 'styles' in economic organisation is both extensive and complex. We have chosen to simplify and abstract out key aspects of this debate for purposes of the present project. Our main focus is to situate our empirical data in its regulatory context. We hope at the same time to be able to add something to the discussion from an Australian legal perspective, especially the extent to which the Australian regulatory 'style' may or may not 'fit' with the broad theoretical structures contained in the international literature.[28]

The idea that 'law matters' when it comes to explaining patterns of corporate ownership and corporate governance has been extensively explored.[29] The 'law matters' argument has been extended in a more particular direction by the 'legal origins' literature which argues that law is a key determinant in the division of production regimes into different types or styles (i.e. that law is crucial to the way that capital and labour are brought together and used for productive purposes in particular states). This idea owes itself to the important work of Rafael La Porta and his colleagues.[30] Through a series of major publications dealing with cross-national legal indicators on matters to do with corporate governance and finance,[31]

---

28   See, e.g., B. Cheffins, 'Comparative Corporate Governance and the Australian Experience' in I. Ramsay (ed.), *Key Developments in Corporate Law and Trusts Law: Essays in Honour of Professor Harold Ford*, LexisNexis Butterworths, Sydney, 2002.

29   See, e.g., B. Black, 'Is Corporate Law Trivial? A Political and Economic Analysis' (1990) 84 *Northwestern University Law Review* 542; B. Black, 'The Legal and Institutional Preconditions for Strong Stock Markets: The Nontriviality of Securities Law' (2000) 55 *Business Lawyer* 1565; B. Cheffins, 'Does Law Matter? The Separation of Ownership and Control in the United Kingdom' (2001) 30 *Journal of Legal Studies* 459; B. Cheffins, *Corporate Ownership and Control: British Business Transformed*, Oxford University Press, Oxford, 2008.

30   Described as '[a]rguably the most important social science research of the past decade': see D. Pozen, 'The Regulation of Labor and the Relevance of Legal Origin' (2007) 27 *Comparative Labor Law & Policy Journal* 43.

31   R. La Porta, F. Lopez-de-Silanes and A. Shleifer, 'Corporate Ownership Around the World' (1999) 54 *Journal of Finance* 471; R. La Porta, F. Lopez-de-Silanes, A. Shleifer and R. Vishny, 'Law and Finance' (1998) 106 *Journal of Political Economy* 1113; 'Legal

but subsequently spreading out to the regulation of labour markets,[32] the authors have argued that different national economic 'styles' can be explained by reference to the 'legal origin' of the country concerned.

The argument about the importance of 'legal origin' is based on the division of legal systems into two families, those originating in the common law tradition, and those which are based in the civilian legal system. Again, this division maps, as we will see shortly, quite neatly on to the divide already identified between the 'liberal market' style of capitalism, and the 'co-ordinated market' type.[33] Thus La Porta and his colleagues explain that the 'liberal market type' derives from its foundation in common law regulatory forms and concepts, whereas the more controlled European and Japanese style production systems owe more to civil law ideas and concepts. Put in more concrete terms, the extensive empirical studies carried out by the La Porta group suggests that the more liquid capital market structure and shareholder-oriented management systems of the Anglo/American model have their origins in the legal concepts of the common law and the more 'stakeholder'-oriented systems have theirs in the civilian codes. In short, 'the historical origin of a country's laws shapes its regulation of labour and other markets'.[34]

Part of the force of this argument lies in the fact that it is not just positing the view that law is *an* important variable to be considered. Rather, 'legal origin' is being identified as *the* decisive or critical factor in determining the 'regulatory style' of a particular system. That is to say law is the decisive issue, not politics, not culture, not geography,[35] though it should also be noted that this argument is hotly debated in the literature.[36]

Determinants of External Finance' (1997) 52 *Journal of Finance* 1131; 'Investor Protection and Corporate Governance' (2000) 58 *Journal of Financial Economics* 3.

32   J. Botero, S. Djankov, R. La Porta, F. Lopez-de-Silanes and A. Shleifer, 'The Regulation of Labour' (2004) 119 *Quarterly Journal of Economics* 1339.

33   See, for example, K. Pistor, 'Legal Ground Rules in Coordinated and Liberal Market Economies' in K. Hopt, E. Wymeersch, H. Kanda and H. Baum (eds), *Corporate Governance in Context: Corporations, States, and Markets in Europe, Japan and the US*, Oxford University Press, Oxford, 2006.

34   Botero et al., above n. 32, at p. 1340. For an account challenging some of the underlying arguments in the legal origin typology see D. Klerman and P. Mahoney, 'Legal Origin?' (2007) 35 *Journal of Comparative Economics* 278.

35   See M. Siems, 'Legal Origins: Reconciling Law and Finance and Comparative Law' (2007) 52 *McGill Law Journal* 55; H. Spamann, 'Contemporary Legal Transplants: Legal Families and the Diffusion of Corporate Law', Unpublished Paper, Harvard Law School, 2006.

36   Particularly in the work of Mark Roe on the influence of politics, see *Political Determinants of Corporate Governance*, Oxford University Press, Oxford, 2003. See also A. Licht, C. Goldschmidt and S.H. Schwartz 'Culture, Law and Corporate Governance' (2005) 25 *International Review of Law and Economics* 229. Some other authors question

A further important point about legal influence is that it is seen as having *persistent effects*. Thus whilst law in national systems can, and does, change, sometimes in quite radical ways, 'legal origins' theory generally seems to suggest that legal origin sets in place a form of 'social control of business' which will persist over time; in other words the systems become 'path dependent'.[37] Such an approach runs counter to the idea that law evolves in a way whereby legal institutions are efficiently matched with economic conditions over time, discarding inefficient legal rules and institutions along the way.[38] Although there is scope for an argument that a certain degree of functionality applies at the onset of a new system of production,[39] even here, as Ahlering and Deakin's brief historical account of the British experience in early industrialisation shows, there is probably no exact fit between the process of economic evolution and legal evolution.[40] Beyond that point, however, the broad suggestion in the legal origins thesis is that path dependency is likely to play an important role, and that certain 'rules' will remain 'sticky'[41] (meaning basically impervious to change) even at the cost of the retention of some inefficient or suboptimal legal institutions or concepts.[42] Importantly, legal origin also suggests that the concept of path dependency operates in respect of laws transplanted through colonisation and legal transfer.[43] Hence 'legal origin' can account for the 'common law' family of nations, and the 'civilian law' family of nations, and, insofar as these map fairly conveniently on to the divide between 'liberal market' and 'co-ordinated market' regulatory styles, 'legal origin' may be used more broadly to explain the endurance of these two broad 'varieties' of

---

the general importance of law to the emergence of particular corporate governance styles: see Cheffins, above nn. 28 and 29.

37   Botero et al., above n. 32; Pistor, above n. 33. See generally, P. David, 'Why are Institutions the "Carriers of History"? Path Dependence and the Evolution of Conventions, Organisations and Institutions' (1994) 5 *Structural Change and Economic Dynamics* 205; R. Schmidt and G. Spindler, 'Path Dependence, Corporate Governance and Complementarity' (2002) 5 *International Finance* 311. Again the issue is highly debatable: see S. Jacoby, 'Economic Ideas and the Labour Market: Origins of the Anglo-American Model and Prospects for Global Diffusion' (2003) 25 *Comparative Labor Law & Policy Journal* 43, pp. 68–69.

38   See R. Harris, *Industrialising English Law: Entrepreneurship and Business Organisation 1720–1844*, Cambridge University Press, Cambridge, 2000; B. Ahlering and S. Deakin, 'Labour Regulation, Corporate Governance and Legal Origin: A Case of Institutional Complementarity?' (2007) 41 *Law and Society Review* 865, p. 888.

39   See E. Glaeser and A. Shleifer, 'Legal Origins' (2002) 117 *Quarterly Journal of Economics* 1193.

40   See Ahlering and Deakin, above n. 38, at pp. 892–896.

41   Pistor, above n. 33.

42   See S. Deakin and F. Wilkinson, *The Law of the Labour Market*, Oxford University Press, Oxford, 2005, p. 33.

43   Again this idea is widely debated; see, for example, Pistor et al., above n. 5; Siems, above n. 35; Spamann, above n. 35.

capitalism. From an economic perspective, in both originating and borrowing countries, the marginal cost of continuing with an established regulatory 'style' is lower than radically recasting the system principally because the fundamental rules are embedded across regulatory institutions and populations. Alternatively, deeply ingrained cultural and social mores, which are also expressed in legal culture, may lock in a certain regulatory style.[44]

But what do we mean when we speak of legal institutions or concepts which constitute the 'regulatory style' of a national system? In the legal origins literature there is extensive criticism of the reliance by La Porta and his collaborators on measuring indicators derived from formal legal rules contained in a country's legislation. This fails, in the eyes of many, to take account of informal legal incidents, the fact that formal difference obscures functional equivalence, the significance of judicial rulings,[45] the importance of compliance and enforcement and so on.[46] Others condemn the categorisations used as just plain wrong.[47] Leaving all of these criticisms to one side, however, we prefer an approach to legal influence which focuses not merely on specific laws and legal institutions, but also on *legal culture*. In other words, whilst we accept the general argument advanced in the legal origins literature that there is a 'causal link running from legal origin to regulatory style and economic outcomes'[48] we also adopt the view of Pistor and Deakin, that a key to understanding 'regulatory style' lies in the core or ground rules which *guide* legal approach and inform legal interpretation. In short it is the ingrained assumptions and socially grounded values inherent in a system's legal culture, rather than specific laws and legal institutions, which best exemplifies, illustrates and explains regulatory style.[49]

Although the different varieties of capitalism organise their systems of production according to regulatory styles ordered by these different legal cultures, a key point in the general argument is that each system develops *institutional complementarities*. That is to say, the different institutions within national types develop in complementary ways to ensure effective outcomes. This supposes that institutions within one particular context (for example the capital market) evolve in a complementary way with those in another context (for example the labour market).[50] All of this depends not merely upon a level of complementarity between

---

44 See K. Zweigert and H. Kotz, *An Introduction to Comparative Law*, Clarendon Press, Oxford, 1985.

45 Ahlering and Deakin, above n. 38.

46 Pozen, above n. 30; Siems, above n. 35.

47 Jacoby, above n. 37.

48 Ahlering and Deakin, above n. 38 at p. 892.

49 Pistor, above n. 33; S. Deakin, 'Legal Origin, Juridical Form and Industrialisation in Historical Perspective' (2009) 7 *Socio-Economic Review* 35, pp. 42–43.

50 See M. Aoki, *Towards a Comparative Institutional Analysis*, Stanford University Press, Stanford, 2001. In turn this can account for continuing diversity or types in styles of economic organisation; see above nn. 17–19 and accompanying discussion.

formal institutions in the legal system, but also a complementarity between the formal and the informal, i.e. the ground rules and understandings which make up the society's legal culture. However, as Ahlering and Deakin warn, the development of a system of regulation based in complementary institutions is not necessarily the result of planned or functionally devised arrangements. Undoubtedly a degree of functionality must be present in the system or the particular legal system would not persist; but path dependency, as we have noted, rules out a purely functional process of legal and institutional development. Workable 'complementarities' are thus just as likely to arise through 'unexpected contingencies or conjunctions', even accidents, as they are through design.[51]

What then are the relevant legal institutions which characterise the different legal families? The legal origins literature separates the common law and civil law systems by reference to their legal and social histories.[52] The common law regulatory system is argued to rely more on contracts and open markets. It is characterised more by independent judges and judicial discretion. Earlier democratising developments in England reduced the influence of the crown over both the courts and parliament. Property owners were therefore able to protect their private property interests against the crown and this protection was extended to investors.[53] The legal origins literature contrasts this with the historical roots of the civilian law systems. France, lacking the stability of the English state, adopted a system characterised by 'fact-finding ... state-employed judges, automatic superior review of decisions and later the reliance on procedural and substantive codes rather than judicial discretion'.[54] The general point being made here is the tendency in the civil law to empower the state (and thus state-based regulation in countries such as Germany and Japan)[55] as compared with the common law's tendency to support more private forms of regulation in nation states such as the UK and Australia.

Drawing together the material from sections 1.2 and 1.3 it is possible to restate a broad general argument as follows. Nation states belonging to the two different legal families, common law and civil law, tend to have different 'regulatory styles' whereby they organise their economies and production systems in different ways.

---

51   See Ahlering and Deakin, above n. 38. The account of 'legal evolution' offered here, and its interaction with the process of economic evolution is discussed in relation to the British labour market in Deakin and Wilkinson, above n. 42, pp. 26–35.

52   See, for example, Glaeser and Shleifer, above n. 39; S. Djankov, E. Glaeser, R. La Porta, F. Lopez-de-Silanes and A. Shleifer, 'The New Comparative Economics' (2003) 31 *Journal of Comparative Economics* 595.

53   The legal origins literature posits that the common law system provides superior outcomes to those of the civilian systems on a number of counts: see Pozen, above n. 30 and the references cited therein. We are not directly concerned with this issue here.

54   See Djankov et al., above n. 52, p. 605. Again we repeat our note of caution above; these general arguments are strongly debated.

55   See G. Jackson, 'The Origins of Nonliberal Corporate Governance in Germany and Japan' in Streek and Yamamura, above n. 11, pp. 163–164.

These different regulatory styles appear to show different approaches in finance systems, corporate governance and labour management systems. Each of these two models has enduring qualities in the form of complementary institutions which may take the form of particular laws and legal institutions, but are also embedded in certain assumptions and understandings which make up a system's legal culture. The common law style of regulation has been carried over to several countries, including the US, Canada, New Zealand, Malaysia, and Australia. The civil law system has found its way into Western Europe, Spain, Portugal, Italy, North and West Africa and parts of Asia.

It is important to note that our study of the interconnection between corporate governance and the management of labour was not specifically designed to test any of the major ideas or theories dealt with in the comparative capitalisms/ legal origins literature generally. Thus we have not been directly concerned with many of the debated issues briefly touched on in the foregoing discussion. For example our research has not been directed to the question of convergence/ divergence in regulatory styles governing types of capitalism, nor to any of the various methodological problems arising from the legal typologies and associated correlations which inform legal origins theory.[56]

Instead, we have generally taken a 'bipolar typology'[57] distinguishing two varieties of capitalism – and two 'regulatory styles' – as a valid way of orienting our inquiry whilst recognising that this masks many finer distinctions within and between systems, and even within national styles for that matter. Whilst one obvious issue for Australian scholars is the degree of correspondence between the Australian system and this general model,[58] a danger of starting with theoretically derived ideal-typic regimes is that the exercise then becomes one of simply aligning countries to these ideal types, rather than examining nation-specific data and observing what families or clusters of nations emerge on the back of this empirical data.[59] It is also a comparativist's privilege – or burden – to step back from fine detail and use ideal types in order to generalise about the 'big picture'. An empirical analysis of a single country is valuable precisely because it allows us to probe the fine detail, and hence analyse important differences between

---

56   On the latter, especially as it effects labour law, see S. Deakin, P. Lele and M. Siems, 'The Evolution of Labour Law: Calibrating and Comparing Regulatory Regimes' (2007) 146 *International Labour Review* 133.

57   Gospel and Pendleton, above n. 1, p. 7.

58   A set of issues in this general vein is opened up by Brian Cheffins in relation to the corporate governance/corporate ownership structure in the Australian economy: see above n. 28.

59   Arguably, this points to the contrast in approaches between Hall and Soskice, above n. 11, on the one hand, and Amable, above n. 11, on the other: see the discussion in Schröder, above n. 21; C. Crouch, 'Models of Capitalism' (2005) 10 *New Political Economy* 439; and C. Hay, 'Two Can Play at That Game … or Can They? Varieties of Capitalism, Varieties of Institutionalism' in D. Coates (ed.), *Varieties of Capitalism, Varieties of Approaches*, Palgrave Macmillan, Houndsmill, 2005.

countries. We have already acknowledged that there is scope for differentiating a greater variety of ideal types, although the literature up to now has been primarily concerned with differentiating types of non-liberal capitalisms.[60] The value of an empirical study of a country such as Australia, which is usually grouped with the cluster of 'liberal market' economies, is that it may point to significant differences amongst liberal regimes, or yield a picture of a production system which comprises a more complex amalgam of elements from different theoretical types: that is, we allow for the possibility of Australia presenting as a 'hybrid' form.[61]

We would also repeat some of the caveats that Gospel and Pendleton articulated in their earlier study. The first follows on from our preceding observations: although we are attempting to give a broad overview of a national system, there will be diversity within any national system, although perhaps a greater diversity between companies could itself be taken as indicative of a 'liberal market' economy, given the lower level of universal regulation and fragmented collective bargaining which allows for a greater range of managerial strategies.[62] At the same time, there may be sectoral clustering within national systems, whereby co-ordinated market capitalism works for companies within certain sectors, and liberal market capitalism works for other sectors, suggesting it may make as much sense to focus on differences within national systems as on differences between them.

A further observation of our own relates to the role of private companies. Australia pioneered the statutory recognition of private companies, which did not make public offerings of shares and restricted transfer of their shares in return for being exempted from various compulsory disclosure and auditing requirements.[63] Private companies still predominate in Australia, with public companies comprising only about 1.2 per cent of total companies as at 30 June 2009.[64] We would suggest that the dominance or otherwise of the listed or public company sector is itself an important threshold question in thinking how to characterise a national system, as private companies are generally going to exhibit a system of insider-oriented governance: a locked-in semi-closed class of shareholders, and a degree of insulation from the forms of marketised pressure for shareholder value, leading investors to find other, more direct forms of monitoring management. However, the comparative law and finance literature has focused overwhelmingly on the role of regulation in relation to publicly-listed companies. The legal corporate governance framework of non-listed companies will in fact comprise a much smaller core of corporate law default rules but will be supplemented by

---

60   See above, n. 21.

61   Crouch, above n. 59, p. 450.

62   C. Brewster, G. Wood and M. Brookes, 'Varieties of Capitalism and Varieties of Firm' in G. Wood and P. James (eds), *Institutions, Production and Working Life*, Oxford University Press, Oxford, 2006.

63   *Companies Act 1896* (Vic).

64   R.P. Austin and I.M. Ramsay, *Ford's Principles of Corporations Law*, LexisNexis Butterworths, Sydney, 14th edn, 2010, p. 157.

contractual mechanisms such as the constitution of the company (sometimes called the articles of association), investor rights agreements and shareholder agreements.[65] These forms of governance remain largely unexamined in the comparative literature, and we should be guarded about the findings that arise from studies which take as their starting point the legal regulation and governance structures of publicly listed companies rather than a broader examination of a nation's corporate sector.

The final caveat is that although we aim to explore the links between corporate governance and labour management, we do not want to deny that other factors are important in shaping the management of labour, such as product markets or the capital intensity of businesses and so on.[66]

Notwithstanding these points of reservation, our study represents one of the first major investigations of the corporate governance/labour management connection in Australia, and for that reason alone we believe that it contributes to broader issues.

1.4 Corporate Governance and Employment Systems in Australia

As we have noted, the theoretical literature suggests that national systems of regulation have developed, following legal origin, certain complementary institutions which characterise regulatory style. In the liberal market systems, one tends to find an 'outsider' form of corporate governance. These systems have dispersed ownership and a highly liquid capital market through which investors are able to diversify their holdings. This enables capital to spread the risk of being subjected to managerial opportunism. At the same time the development of various legal mechanisms has enabled capital to hold management to account. Investor protection may be secured either through the takeover process or strong legal protection for minority shareholders for example.

In the literature, this liberal market system is contrasted with the differing regulatory style and institutional arrangements of the co-ordinated market economy type. The latter model is said to be characterised by an 'insider' form of ownership which is much more concentrated through substantial mechanisms of block-holding. In turn this concentration allows for a more direct form of monitoring and observation of management performance and decision-making.[67]

The argument also suggests that regulatory 'style' in corporate governance is complemented by national style in the regulation of labour. Ahlering and Deakin

---

65   T. Guinnane, R. Harris, N. Lamoreaux and J. Rosenthal, 'Putting the Corporation in its Place' (2007) 8 *Enterprise and Society* 687; J. McCahery and E. Vermeulen, *Corporate Governance of Non-Listed Companies*, Oxford University Press, Oxford, 2008.

66   See, e.g., the case studies in Deakin et al., above n. 27, and M. Westcott, 'The Market for Corporate Control at Tooth and Co' in S. Marshall, R. Mitchell and I. Ramsay (eds), *Varieties of Capitalism, Corporate Governance and Employees*, Melbourne University Press, Melbourne, 2008.

67   See Ahlering and Deakin, above n. 38, pp. 872–873.

Table 1.1   Complementarities in corporate governance and labour law

	Pattern of shareholder ownership	Protection of minority shareholders	Employee representation at company level	Regulation of the labour market
Liberal market systems	dispersed	high	voluntarist	partial
Coordinated market systems	concentrated	low	integrative	universalist

Source: Ahlering and Deakin, above n. 38.

have noted that the institutions of labour regulation intersect with the mechanisms of corporate governance at two levels: the level of the company (the constitution and governance of the company and the influence of workers in decision-making), and the level of the market (the degree to which employment conditions are centrally regulated across the market generally or are left for self-regulation between employers, unions and workers in particular industries, occupations, sectors or enterprises).[68]

In liberal market (common law origin) systems the predominant form of employee representation within the enterprise, and thus the key instrument of employee influence in enterprise management (corporate governance), is 'voluntarist' in the shape of one or more forms of bargaining. Although there is great diversity in the legal form of these bargaining systems, and in the extent to which employers are obliged to recognise and to bargain with unions and workers, these forms of bargaining have a relatively limited role in relation to key areas of managerial prerogative. Further, this voluntarism tends to be associated with only a partial regulation of the labour market generally. That is to say that outside of the reach of the bargaining systems, the extent of regulation over minimum terms and conditions tends to be uneven and partial amongst and between groups and classes of workers.

The co-ordinated market (civil law origin) economies on the other hand tend to feature the *integration* of employee voice into the decision-making structures of business through legally supported mechanisms. These include employee representation on company boards in some European countries, works councils, and laws requiring employees and their representatives to be informed and consulted about business matters. In addition, the regulation of the employment contract through legislation and/or bargained agreements also tends to be more comprehensive in coverage. As a result many of these minimum employment standards take effect as

---

68   Ibid., p. 874.

a form of social rights.[69] Table 1.1 summarises these two sets of complementary arrangements.

As we have noted, the identification of 'national' styles of regulation, and the mechanisms of corporate governance and labour management within them provide the context for our study of the Australian case. Our most immediate objective was to examine the relationship of corporate governance and labour management. Principally we approached this issue by examining the way corporate governance and corporate ownership structure shapes labour management and employment systems, though we are mindful of the case for a causal link flowing in the opposite direction.[70] This general subject gave rise to several more specific sets of questions and issues.

The Ahlering and Deakin schema refers to minority shareholder protection. Minority shareholder protection serves different purposes depending upon whether one is talking about public companies with dispersed shareholdings or other companies, private or public, with concentrated block-holdings. In the former case, minority shareholders require protections against management; in the latter they require protection against potential abuse by the majority of shareholders. In those cases where the protections work to protect shareholders in listed companies from over-powerful boards, they will correlate with a more general notion of shareholder protection.[71] That is, in these instances the practices associated with minority shareholder protection will work to ensure the company is operated to maximise the value of shareholders' investment, rather than spent or wasted on something else.[72] Overall, then, dispersed shareholding is thought to go hand-in-hand with a system in which shareholders occupy a privileged position within corporate governance compared with other stakeholders. Thus the liberal market version of corporate governance is often said to be characterised by a 'shareholder primacy' or 'shareholder value' norm, with shareholder value being defined with reference to financial metrics such as share price and dividends.[73] Furthermore, in most of the literature that considers the importance of law in structuring patterns of corporate ownership and control,

---

69   Ibid. For another perspective on how the 'style' of labour law may vary as between liberal market and co-ordinated market economies, see M. Freedland and N. Kountouris, 'Towards a Comparative Theory of the Contractual Construction of Personal Work Relations in Europe' (2008) 37 *Industrial Law Journal* 49.

70   See Gospel and Pendleton, above n. 1, p. 18.

71   Deakin, above n. 49, p. 55.

72   P. Gourevitch and J. Shinn, *Political Power and Corporate Control: The New Global Politics of Corporate Governance*, Princeton University Press, Princeton, 2005, p. 43.

73   J. Armour, S. Deakin and S. Konzelmann, 'Shareholder Primacy and the Trajectory of UK Corporate Governance' (2003) 41 *British Journal of Industrial Relations* 531; Mitchell et al., above n. 6. This corporate law question as to whether shareholders are privileged over, say, employees is to some extent the obverse of the labour law question that the Ahlering and Deakin schema poses: is managerial prerogative fettered to any degree by employee voice? This points to a sense in which patterns of corporate law and patterns of

minority shareholder protection is seen as directly linked to the dispersal of share ownership.[74] That is to say, greater legal protection of minority shareholders will lead to a greater dispersal of shareholdings and, conversely, block-holdings will persist where potential buyers have little incentive to take a non-controlling minority stake in companies because of the risk of possible exploitation.

So one set of questions advanced in this study concerns the way in which Australian company directors balance the interests of employees and shareholders, and how that affects the management of labour by companies, particularly in their approach to the development of co-operative or 'partnership' style employment systems. At one level, this concerns directors' perceptions as regards both which set of stakeholder interests are to be given paramount consideration, and what it might mean to be in 'partnership' with employees. In addressing these issues, we sought to characterise our target businesses – rather than the Australian system as a whole – in terms of the insider/outsider governance style typology, and to extend our inquiry beyond the listed company sector to include private companies. At the same time we sought to take account of recently occurring changes in ownership structure (thus where a company had recently privatised, demutualised, become a publicly listed company, undergone a merger with another company and so on). We also sought to discover what role the regulatory framework of corporate law plays in the establishment and sustenance of a system of corporate governance which is supportive of or inimical to co-operative or partnership style employment operations.

A further set of issues for us was to identify and examine the kinds of employment practices which appear to offer the basis for more co-operative forms of workplace relations, the circumstance in which such relations arise, and the pressures that companies face in maintaining them. This required us to investigate and categorise businesses according to various styles of employment systems by measures of what we styled 'partnerships', 'high performance workplace systems' and so on. We also sought to examine the role of the Australian regulatory environment in shaping these employment systems, and whether there has been a correlation between the new forms of labour regulation emerging in the past decade of regulatory reform and the development of particular employment systems.[75]

As noted earlier in this chapter (section 1.2), we have drawn heavily upon the work of Gospel and Pendleton in forming an approach to our workplace-based studies of the corporate governance/labour management link. First, we sought to assess each of our target businesses according to whether it could be categorised as an 'insider' controlled company or as an 'outsider' controlled company. Although

---

labour law might be complementary – although this is using 'complementarity' in a weak sense, akin to 'coherence'.

74   See references in n. 29 above.

75   As explained in the following section of the chapter (1.5) we have employed a combination of research methods to pursue these issues.

Table 1.2   Indicators of finance/governance typologies

Relational finance/insider governance	Market finance/outsider governance
Finance	*Finance*
Private financing	Public finance – equities and bonds
Intermediated finance	Arm's-length financing
Thin securities market	Thick securities market
Patient investors	Impatient investors
Stable owners	Fluid owners
Investors generally have shares in a small number of different companies, shareholdings in individual companies may be large and are maintained over time, interest in company management	Investors generally have diversified share portfolios, individual investors will generally have a small percentage of the total number of shares in each company, little active interest in management
Governance	*Governance*
Board made up of insiders (family, bank, other companies etc.)	Board made up of insiders *and* outsiders
Direct discipline (active shareholders)	Indirect discipline (market)
Active but patient owners	Less active and more impatient owners
Weak market in corporate control	Strong market in corporate control
Voice as an instrument of corporate control	Exit as an instrument of corporate control
Top management more stable	Top management less stable

Source: Adapted from H. Gospel and A. Pendleton, 'Financial Structure, Corporate Governance, and the Management of Labour: A Conceptual and Comparative Analysis' (2003) 41 *British Journal of Industrial Relations* 557.

generally we started with the presumption that the Australian regulatory 'style' would reflect the 'outsider' rather than the 'insider' model, we also hypothesised that there might be scope for an argument about systemic divergence in the Australian case,[76] and that the position might appear more complex when examined on a case by case basis in particular companies. Broad indicators looked for in the case studies in relation to this issue are set out in Table 1.2.

Second, we sought to examine in each of our business case studies the extent to which enterprise employment systems could be said to 'complement' the style of corporate governance within the company in accordance with the suppositions of the comparative capitalisms literature. Here we adopted Gospel and Pendleton's

76   See, for example, A. Dignam and M. Galanis, 'Australia Inside Out: The Corporate Governance System of the Australian Listed Market' (2004) 28 *Melbourne University Law Review* 623 and Cheffins, above n. 28.

Table 1.3   Governance/finance structure and labour management style

Relational finance/insider system	Market finance/outsider system
Employment relations	*Employment relations*
Longer term relationships (permanent over casual)	Arm's-length relationships
More investment in training	Recruitment and layoff according to demand/ more use of contingent labour
Wages fixed according to internal admin principles	Wages fixed by market principles/more variable pay
Company specific incentives	Less investment in company specific training
Compressed wage dispersion (smaller gap between executive and shop floor salaries)	Wide wage dispersion
Work relations	*Work relations*
Greater functional flexibility	Less functional flexibility
Product quality innovation	Radical product innovation
Fewer restrictive practices	More restrictive practices
Industrial relations	*Industrial relations*
More employee voice	Less employee voice
Internal representation systems	If union is involved – bargaining at single business unit and will tend to be adversarial
External multi-employer bargaining	

Source: Adapted from Gospel and Pendleton, ibid.

threefold division of labour management systems as indicated earlier (section 1.2). The hypothesised correlation between corporate governance and finance structure on the one hand and labour management style on the other is set out in Table 1.3.

Third, because we were particularly interested in the *quality* of employment systems (beyond their mere conformity with insider/outsider styles) we went beyond the Gospel and Pendleton typology and attempted to identify more specifically what we thought could be said properly to characterise 'partnership' style relations at the business enterprise level. Our task in respect of this issue was made difficult by reason of the fact that amongst the extensive literature dealing with the idea of 'partnerships at work' there is very little common agreement on what the essential elements of such arrangements might be.[77] The discussion

---

77   See, for example, M. Stuart and M. Lucio (eds), *Partnership and Modernisation in Employment Relations*, Routledge, London, 2005; D. Guest and R. Peccei, 'Partnership at Work: Mutuality and the Balance of Advantage' (2001) 39 *British Journal of Industrial Relations* 207; P. Ackers and J. Payne, 'British Trade Unions and Social Partnership:

around partnership draws from an array of concepts, including the 'mutual gains' work of Kochan and Osterman[78] among others, and the 'high performance', 'high involvement', 'high commitment' workplace literature of human resource management.[79] Generally the literature identifies an assortment of 'principles' and 'practices' which are taken to be indicative, if not definitive, of the presence of partnership relations. In a general sense it is clear that 'partnership' anticipates a new approach to employment relations (a new *form* of relations) based around co-operative rather than conflictual modes of regulation and interaction between the parties. It is also clear that there is an assumption to a degree that 'partnership' properly involves relationships between employers and trade unions (a form of social partnership), although there are undoubtedly partnership models which focus upon 'individualised' relations rather than collective styles.[80]

In seeking to identify broad indicators of 'partnership' we felt it was important to distinguish between a commitment to the idea of partnership in principle, or to the belief that the relationship could be characterised as a partnership in principle, and the actual practice of partnership. Asking questions about partnership at the level of principle allowed us to gain insights into whether the *concept* had any purchase in Australian workplaces. Examination of concrete policies and work systems would establish whether or not this principle was followed through into workplace practice.

At the level of principle, our approach was to ask whether respondents believed the idea was relevant as an accurate description of the approach taken by the company towards its employees. In order to gather information about possible partnership relations in practice, we examined material from the public record as well as internal policy documents such as employee handbooks, where they were made available or existed. We sought to identify the presence or absence of a number of indicators including the use of ongoing consultative mechanisms and the employment of high performance workplace mechanisms aimed at building trust and functional flexibility. Security of employment was an additional indicator that we looked for on the basis that mutual benefit is a significant aspect of stronger forms of partnership. This information is set out in Table 1.4.

Rhetoric, Reality and Strategy' (1998) 9 *The International Journal of Human Resource Management* 529; N. Bacon and J. Storey, 'New Employee Relations Strategies in Britain: Towards Individualism or Partnership?' (2000) 38 *British Journal of Industrial Relations* 407; R. Undy, 'New Labour's "Industrial Relations Settlement": The Third Way?' (1999) 37 *British Journal of Industrial Relations* 315.

78   T. Kochan and P. Osterman, *The Mutual Gains Exercise: Forging a Winning Partnership Among Labour, Management and Government*, Harvard University Press, Boston, 1994; Osterman, above n. 9.

79   J. Knell, *Partnership at Work*, Employment Relations Research Series No. 7, Department of Trade and Industry, London, 1999.

80   See Ackers and Payne, above n. 77; Bacon and Storey, above n. 77.

Table 1.4   Indicators of partnership

Principle
Respondents identify a partnership approach
Practice
Direct participation by employees or employee representatives in decisions about broader organisational policy issues
Alignment mechanisms – employee share ownership, performance pay based on organisational performance
Direct participation by employees or employee representatives in own work/work processes
Flexible job design
Focus on quality
Participation by employees or their representatives in decisions about personal employment issues
Employment security
Performance management

Different combinations of these indicators may suggest different types of partnership, or different levels of 'strength' of partnership relations. One approach would be to think of two extremes in a continuum of possible co-operative arrangements.[81] At one extreme are arrangements which are based on co-operation that is mutual or reciprocal and would involve capital as well as labour making concessions. The aim of such co-operation – or collaboration – would be to bring gains to both workers and management. At the other extreme is a form of co-operation which entails acquiescence to managerial prerogative and a restriction of the range of matters which are jointly determined between the parties. Such acquiescence is presumably to further the business interests of the company, in which employees clearly have a stake. Either of these forms might entail individual or collective representation of employees, although the first type is likely to be more consistent with union representation which seeks to advance interests which at times conflict with those of capital. There may be occasions in which union representation is consistent with an approach which bypasses conflictual issues in favour of a focus on shared interests which can provide the basis for less adversarial and more co-operative relations. However, in most cases this is more consistent with direct, non-union representative mechanisms.

Guest and Peccei[82] provide a somewhat similar categorisation of types of partnership arrangements in their empirical study of partnership in practice. They utilise the relational concepts of 'pluralism' and 'unitarism' to explain approaches based on a 'clear acknowledgement of differences of interest between capital and

---

81   See R. Mitchell and A. O'Donnell, 'What is Labour Law Doing about Partnership at Work? British and Australian Developments Compared', in Marshall et al., above n. 66.

82   See above, n. 77.

labour'[83] on the one hand, and those which 'explicitly seek to integrate employer and employee interests'[84] on the other. They added to these two categories a hybrid approach which 'combines elements of the two previous perspectives'.[85] Each of these approaches is associated with a different set of representative and human resource management practices. A pluralist approach would be more consistent with the use of a representative system, though not necessarily involving trade union representatives and often involving directly elected representatives. The emphasis is on various forms of indirect participation designed to safeguard and ensure an independent employee voice within the enterprise. This might include the use of works councils or other alternative employee representation mechanisms. These are sometimes used in combination with direct forms of representation such as work groups or employee surveys. The unitarist approach, on the other hand, might focus on financial incentives and shared ownership as the main mechanisms for aligning and integrating employer and employee interests within the enterprise, perhaps in association with direct employee participation mechanisms. Alternatively, it may also entail the use of human management strategies which focus on individual employee's 'psychic stake' in the enterprise, reflected in their overall level of attachment, commitment and involvement in the enterprise. Approaches of this nature involve 'high involvement' or 'high commitment' forms of resource management practices.

Beyond this set of issues and themes, other important questions remained which led us back into a more general consideration of how the Australian case might be seen to fit into the broad patterns of regulatory 'style' and type of capitalism suggested in the international literature.[86] Important points to note here are the fact that Australian labour market regulation has long been typecast as essentially different from that of many other members of the 'common law' legal origin group of states, and that the dispersion of share ownership in Australian companies does not seem to align with the fundamental Anglo/American model. Prima facie these indicators would seem to suggest that Australia does not map neatly on to the liberal market/co-ordinated market, outsider/insider governance divide illustrated in Table 1.1 for example. These issues are dealt with in closer detail in Chapter 5.

1.5 Methodology

This study combines two different types of analytical approaches. First, it draws upon data derived from a set of 10 case studies of companies,[87] a survey of

---

83   Guest and Peccei, above n. 77.

84   Ibid., pp. 207, 209.

85   Ibid., p. 210.

86   M. Jones and R. Mitchell, 'Legal Origins, Legal Families and the Regulation of Labour in Australia' in Marshall et al., above n. 66. See also Cheffins, above n. 28.

87   Case studies are an accepted form of research technique in social science and industrial relations: see R. Lansbury and D. Macdonald (eds), *Workplace Industrial*

company directors and interviews with institutional investors to build up a picture of the relationship between corporate governance and employment systems within companies, and how the regulation of that connection is perceived by leading decision-makers in the companies. Second, the study also uses a legal and historical approach to the development of regulatory policy in order to investigate what role law and legal institutions appear to have played in the shaping of the Australian 'style' of capitalism.

In this study we were able to gain access to key senior company personnel (usually the company secretary, the human resources manager and/or other senior management figure) for the purpose of carrying out structured interviews. In relevant cases we also carried out interviews with union officials. At least two interviews, sometimes more, were conducted in each of our cases,[88] with the greater number of interviews being carried out in the larger companies. Prior to the interviews we carried out background research on each company from the public record, including textual analysis of newspaper articles, the company's annual reports, the company's website, and industrial instruments such as awards and employment agreements.

Our interviews were organised around a series of questions through which we were able to explore the core matters of our investigation. These included the company's relationship with its shareholders and with its employees, the nature of its employment systems, and the impact of recent changes in ownership or governance structure, or the impact of regulation, on these relationships and systems. The interviews were conducted from 2005 through to 2007.

The selection of our case study companies was made initially on the basis that the company had undergone a recent change in its ownership and/or governance structure. This was with a view to discovering what difference such change might make to the corporate governance/labour management nexus within the one business organisation. We added other companies to our set of studies in order to broaden the range of ownership and governance types beyond the large publicly listed company model. Table 1.5 describes basic relevant details of our case study companies.

Relations: Australian Case Studies, Oxford University Press, Melbourne, 2nd edn, 1990, pp. 7–8; Jacoby, above n. 16, p. 5. It is also necessary for us to acknowledge the limitations of such research. The case studies carried out for the present project were not longitudinal studies, and thus basically reported only on the time frame around the period in which they were carried out. Consequently, our attempts to detect changes in corporate governance and labour management style occurring after a relevant event affecting corporate finance and ownership structure was to some degree obstructed by the discontinuity in key personnel and the consequent loss of so-called 'corporate memory'.

88   With the exception of one case. This company agreed to participate in interviews for the research project and provided us with an initial interview and several background documents. However notwithstanding numerous attempts to schedule interviews with key personnel, no interviews were conducted. Despite this, we took the decision to include the company in our group of studies, principally because the substantial volume of material about the company and its employment systems available on the public record made it feasible to do so.

Table 1.5   Case study companies

Company	Type	Listed	Event
ResourceCo 1	Public	✓	Merger
ServiceCo	Public	✓	Privatisation
ResourceCo 2	Public	✓	Merger
EnergyCo	Private	✗	Privatisation
CommCo	Private	✗	No event
FinanceCo 1	Public	✓	Demutualisation
BiotechCo	Public	✓	ASX listing
FinanceCo 2	Public	✓	ASX listing
ManuengCo	Private	✗	No event
ManufoodCo	Private	✗	Merger/Takeover

Our survey of company directors and our interviews with institutional investors allowed us to approach our research questions from a different perspective, and thus to round out the study. Corporate directors, rather than human resource managers, were selected as the subjects for this survey, because we considered them to be more integral to our central concern, the relationship between corporate governance and the management of labour.

1.6 The Organisation of the Book

The content of this book is structured as follows. Following the present introductory chapter, Chapter 2 gives an account of the regulatory framework in the context of which Australian companies have developed their corporate governance and labour management practices. Principally this account focuses on the relevant corporate law and labour law statutory and institutional frameworks. The chapter takes an historical perspective,[89] with much attention being devoted to the evolution of legal policy over the most recent decade and a half, which is the period of most direct relevance to our case studies.

Chapter 3 contains the detail of our case study research. Brief accounts are given of our findings in each case. The discussion of each of the cases is generally presented in a common format with similar organisational structure and themes.

---

89   On the importance of taking a historical perspective, see Deakin et al., above n. 56, and G. Herrigel, 'Corporate Governance' in G. Jones and J. Zeitlin (eds), *Oxford Handbook of Business History,* Oxford University Press, Oxford, 2008.

Chapter 4 contains the results of our survey of directors and our interviews with institutional investors, including tables and key findings.

In Chapter 5 we present our analysis of the information we have gathered. This analysis attempts to explain the relationship between corporate governance and employment practices in Australian businesses, and how those practices are shaped and influenced by the regulatory framework set by legal rules and policy. Although, as noted, this project was not designed to deal with many of the broader issues found in the comparative capitalisms literature, our analysis does touch upon some issues of relevance to the international debate.

Chapter 6 is a postscript in which we have located the origins of our research agenda and the direction in which it has taken us over the life of the project. The postscript makes an assessment of some of the key research issues in corporate governance insofar as it relates to employment systems and it offers suggestions for future research in this field.

Chapter 2
Law and Regulatory Style
in Australian Corporate Governance
and Employment Systems

Introduction

As noted in Chapter 1, our aim in this book has been to examine the relationships between three sets of factors: corporate ownership structure, corporate governance and the management of labour, with a view to understanding how they interact within the Australian economic system generally and produce certain types of relations between companies, shareholders and employees. At the same time we have sought to examine the role that the regulatory environment established by law plays in these relationships. Largely, our focus here has been upon the law relating to financial markets and companies, and the law regulating labour markets and employment systems.

The research is grounded in empirical studies of business companies in operation, and the views of company directors, institutional investors, other senior corporate actors and labour representatives. In these studies, which are fully reported in Chapters 3 and 4, and in other publications arising from the project generally,[1] we have sought to identify the presence or absence of certain

---

1   S. Marshall, R. Mitchell and I.Ramsay (eds), *Varieties of Capitalism, Corporate Governance and Employees*, Melbourne University Press, Melbourne, 2008, chs. 4, 5, 7, 8 and 10 in particular; S. Marshall, R. Mitchell and A. O'Donnell, 'Corporate Governance and Labour Law: Situating Australia's Regulatory Style' (2009) 47 *Asia Pacific Journal of Human Resources* 150; M. Anderson, M. Jones, S. Marshall, R. Mitchell and I. Ramsay, 'Shareholder Primacy and Director's Duties: An Australian Perspective' (2008) 8 *Journal of Corporate Law Studies* 161; M. Jones, S. Marshall and R. Mitchell, 'Corporate Social Responsibility and the Management of Labour in Two Australian Mining Industry Companies' (2007) 15 *Corporate Governance: An International Review* 57; K. Anderson, I. Ramsay, S. Marshall and R. Mitchell, 'Union Shareholder Activism in the Context of Declining Labour Law Protection: Four Case Studies' (2007) 15 *Corporate Governance: An International Review* 45; M. Jones, S. Marshall, R. Mitchell and I. Ramsay, *Corporate Governance and Workplace Partnership Case Studies: Research Report*, Centre for Corporate Law and Securities Regulation and Centre for Employment and Labour Relations Law, University of Melbourne, 2008; M. Jones, S. Marshall, R. Mitchell and I. Ramsay, *Company Directors' Views Regarding Stakeholders: Research Report*, Centre for Corporate Law and Securities Regulation and Centre for Employment and Labour Relations Law,

organisational and operational characteristics of companies, and how the kinds of ownership structure, governance and labour management play out in certain sets of circumstances. Thus we have sought to identify situations in which capital and labour might be said to be working in 'partnership'-style relations within a business organisation, and what meaning might be attributed to this by company directors and officers. In addition we have tried to identify situations in which companies might be described as conforming to 'relational/insider' or 'market/outsider' types of business organisation, and how finance arrangements, governance and labour management interact and play out in such categorisations.

With the use of this information we are able to speculate in Chapter 5 on the characterisation of the Australian capitalist system in terms of the 'complementarities' between corporate governance and labour management: in short to evaluate the degree to which Australia has a 'style' of capitalist economy which enables it to be grouped with like economies and distinguished from others.[2]

An important aspect of our analysis, as noted, concerns the role of law. In particular we have tried to examine the problems of corporate ownership, corporate governance and labour management with a view to discovering whether or not law is an important factor in how these various dimensions interact or relate. Does law influence the evolution and outcome of economic and social developments?[3] And, if law is important, is it so critical a variable that a nation's style of economy is largely determined by its 'legal origins', by its membership of a particular 'legal family'?[4]

The 'legal origins' literature is comprised of an empirically dense body of scholarship that examines the relationship between the law on the one hand and the prevailing national structures of corporate ownership and control on the other.[5] At present there is a less developed body of work on the role of law in shaping and

---

University of Melbourne, 2007; R. Mitchell, A. O'Donnell and I. Ramsay, 'Shareholder Value and Employee Interests: Intersections Between Corporate Governance, Corporate Law and Labor Law' (2005) 23 *Wisconsin International Law Journal* 417.

2   As a general guide here, we have used the simplified table set out in B. Ahlering and S. Deakin, 'Labor Regulation, Corporate Governance, and Legal Origin: A Case of Institutional Complementarity?' (2007) 41 *Law and Society Review* 865 at 876. The Ahlering and Deakin table is reproduced as Table 1.1, in Chapter 1.

3   See, for example, B. Cheffins, 'Does Law Matter?: The Separation of Ownership and Control in the United Kingdom' (2001) 30 *Journal of Legal Studies* 459; B. Black, 'The Legal and Institutional Preconditions for Strong Stock Markets: The Nontriviality of Securities Law' (2000) 55 *Business Lawyer* 1565; B. Cheffins, 'Comparative Corporate Governance and the Australian Experience' in I. Ramsay (ed.), *Key Developments in Corporate Law and Trusts Law: Essays in Honour of Professor Harold Ford*, LexisNexis Butterworths, Sydney, 2002.

4   E. Glaeser and A. Shleifer, 'Legal Origins' (2002) 117 *Quarterly Journal of Economics* 1193; R. La Porta, F. Lopez-de-Silanes and A. Shleifer, 'The Economic Consequences of Legal Origins' (2008) 46 *Journal of Economic Literature* 285.

5   See Chapter 1, nn. 29–43 and associated text.

securing particular patterns of employment relations and work systems, although labour law scholars have recently begun to explore how law as a social system may produce national differences in labour management styles.[6] Moreover there has also been some attempt to examine how certain forms of corporate law might broadly align with certain approaches to labour regulation, creating legal and institutional complementarities between the two.[7]

The following discussion presents an overview of the historical development of corporate law and labour law regulation since the British colonisation of Australia. Our account in this chapter of the development over time of the regulatory framework is designed to allow us to draw a meaningful characterisation of the Australian regulatory style, and, hence, to place it within this emerging international scholarship.

2.2 Corporate Law and Regulation

The Early Legislative Framework

In contrast, as we shall see, to the case of labour law, Australian corporate law has tended to adhere closely to the British pattern of legal development in respect of core legislation and concepts. Prior to the mid-nineteenth century, companies owed their existence to special permission in the form of a Crown or parliamentary charter which bestowed legal status on associations as entities in their own right. This corporate form was largely limited in Britain initially to trading companies and later to banks, insurance companies, water companies and canals. A more common business form was the unincorporated 'deed of settlement' company, based in trust and partnership law. This amounted to a private contractual arrangement utilising the concept of the trust settlement whereby the property of the company was put into the hands of a small number of trustees to hold on behalf of all the 'partners'. Many of the standard form clauses developed by lawyers for these associations were later crystallised in the early Companies Acts, including in the model set of

---

6   See S. Deakin and F. Wilkinson, *The Law of the Labour Market*, Oxford University Press, Oxford, 2005, using the work of N. Luhmann, *Social Systems*, Stanford University Press, Stanford, 1995 (trans.); and G. Teubner, *Law as an Autopoietic System*, Blackwell, Oxford, 1993.

7   See Ahlering and Deakin, above n. 2. The authors (at p. 879) note that the varieties of capitalism approach identifies a number of mechanisms that are legal in nature; that it identifies aspects of corporate and securities laws, and laws governing worker representation and rights as especially important, and that it goes on to argue that these mechanisms have a functional relationship with patterns of ownership and control. As the authors also note, however, this doesn't necessarily indicate that law or the legal system has had an independent causal influence on the emergence of particular systems of corporate governance or labour management, rather than, say, the legal system expressing the effects of norms and conventions whose origins lie elsewhere.

articles of association provided by the legislation.[8] Australian colonial corporate activity in the first half of the nineteenth century was thus dominated by deed of settlement companies or companies incorporated by act of the British parliament.[9]

In a series of Acts in 1844, 1855 and 1856, and consolidated in the *Companies Act 1862*, the British parliament routinised the incorporation process and secured limited liability for shareholders. The 1862 Act included a set of default, replaceable articles of association. There was little in these statutes which upset the basic understanding of companies as essentially private contractual arrangements between the members.[10]

Between 1863 and 1874, each of the colonial Australian legislatures (except Western Australia) enacted their first general companies statutes, based on the *Companies Act 1862* (UK).[11] Consistent with the British approach, the colonial legislation was minimalist, concerned largely with the lodgement of basic corporate and financial information with the appropriate authority. There were no audit requirements, the public registries contained little company information of use to outsiders and, compared with Britain's Board of Trade, there was no effective bureaucracy to enforce the Acts.[12] In 1896 the colony of Victoria

---

8   R. Tomasic, S. Bottomley and R. McQueen, *Corporations Law in Australia*, Federation Press, Sydney, 2nd edn, 2002, p. 13. For example, it was common to make provision for the alteration of the deed of settlement by special majority rather than by the unanimity required within partnerships. Similarly, corporate law doctrines such as the director's duty of care were adapted from the trustee's prudential duty of care: M. Whincop, *An Economic and Jurisprudential Genealogy of Corporate Law*, Ashgate, London, 2001, pp. 71–73.

9   NSW Governor Macquarie granted a charter to allow the Bank of NSW to operate as a joint stock company in 1817, however there were doubts as to the validity of the charter and the bank adopted a deed of settlement in 1828. Other early Australian companies, such as the Australian Agricultural Company (formed in 1824) and the Van Diemen's Land Company (formed in 1825) were incorporated by royal charter, largely to serve English capital.

10   The 1844 Act required each shareholder to execute a deed of settlement that was contractually binding. The 1856 Act introduced the notion of the company 'articles' and declared that the articles were contractually binding, a provision re-enacted in the 1862 Act.

11   Tomasic et al., above n. 8, p. 17.

12   For more detailed analyses of the early history of company law statutes in the Australian colonies and states, see R. McQueen, *A Social History of Company Law: Great Britain and the Australian Colonies 1854–1920*, Ashgate, Farnham, 2009; R. McQueen, 'Company Law as Imperialism' (1995) 5 *Australian Journal of Corporate Law* 1; R. McQueen, 'An Examination of Australian Corporate Law and Regulation 1901–1961' (1992) 15 *University of New South Wales Law Journal* 1; R. McQueen, 'Limited Liability Company Legislation – The Australian Experience' (1991) 1 *Australian Journal of Corporate Law* 22; J. Waugh, 'Company Law and the Crash of the 1890s in Victoria' (1992) 15 *University of New South Wales Law Journal* 356; P. Lipton, 'A History of Company Law in Colonial Australia: Legal Evolution and Economic Development' (2007) 31 *Melbourne University Law Review* 805.

pioneered compulsory auditing and financial information provisions for public companies, but also provided for the incorporation of private or 'proprietary' companies. These were companies which made no public offerings and restricted the transfer of their shares in return for lower disclosure requirements.[13]

Britain – and Australia – began with an essentially unitary company law. That is, private and public companies were recognised as different versions of the single company form, and the bulk of company law developed on the basis of an 'archetypical' medium to large company where 'the involvement of shareholders was limited to their investment'.[14] A contrast could be made with jurisdictions such as Germany, for example, which in the late nineteenth century created a distinct limited liability business form whereby smaller, less capital intensive firms organised under a different law from companies.[15] Having made that point, however, it is worthwhile to note that the development of stock exchanges and their listing rules meant that listed companies, from an early stage, were subject to an additional and more onerous regulatory regime than that found in the corporate law statutes more generally. As we shall see, the practical bifurcation of corporate regulation – as between listed and unlisted companies – takes on a further dimension with increased attempts to regulate the securities market, this latter development necessarily being directed towards listed companies.

As McQueen has argued, prior to Federation in Australia (which brought together the separate self-governing Australian colonies) at least, the relatively undeveloped size and nature of the Australian economy and individual businesses meant that there was little demand for the company form other than in the major industries of mining and banking. Although registrations of companies increased substantially from about the 1880s, this was from a very low base, and many of

---

13 *Companies Act 1896* (Vic). The accounting and auditing requirements (s 24) were a response to company failures associated with the colony's 'land boom': see Waugh, above n. 12. Prior to this, most colonies' original Companies Acts relegated auditing and accounting provisions to the optional articles in the schedule to the Act, which could be modified or largely avoided by companies adopting alternative terms in their articles. Britain made statutory provision for private companies with its *Companies Act 1907* (UK). Victoria's lead in legislating for a minimum level of compulsory disclosure at the end of the nineteenth century was followed in most other Australian States by the 1930s: see *Companies Act 1920* (Tas); *Companies Act 1931* (Qld); *Companies Act 1934* (SA); *Companies Act 1936* (NSW). As with the Victorian Act, these subsequent Acts copied the device of exempting private or 'proprietary companies' from the new accounting and auditing provisions.

14 R. Grantham, 'The Doctrinal Basis of the Rights of Company Shareholders' (1998) 57 *Cambridge Law Journal* 554, pp. 556–557. See also M. Siems, *Convergence in Shareholder Law*, Cambridge University Press, Cambridge, 2008, pp. 10–11.

15 T. Guinane, R. Harris, N. Lamoraeux and J. Rosenthal, *Ownership and Control in the Entrepreneurial Firm: An International History of Private Limited Companies*, Discussion Paper 959, Economic Growth Centre, Yale University, 2007.

these companies were wiped out in the 1890s depression.[16] McQueen's research indicates that in NSW in 1903 there were over 9,000 registrations of partnerships as compared with 157 company registrations.[17] The reality is that at this point of time underlying core legal concepts, whilst important notionally, had yet to reach the level of substantial practical significance which came only with the development of large scale enterprises.[18]

Regulating Governance

The first Company Acts, in both Britain and the Australian colonies, represented at one level a dramatic statutory intervention, especially by way of a grant of general limited liability, but they did little by way of setting rules as regards the governance structure of companies. However, this does not mean that the governance of companies took place in a regulatory vacuum.

First, early companies legislation provided for meetings of shareholders and the appointment of directors by shareholder majority, thus setting up two decision-making bodies within the company: the shareholder meeting and the board of directors.[19] The actual division of powers between these two decision-making bodies was a matter for the company's articles or constitution. Despite the passage of companies legislation, for much of the nineteenth century incorporated companies were still seen as a form of partnership, with shareholders the collective owners of the enterprise who had the right to control the business.[20] Directors tended to be regarded as agents of the shareholders, holding 'delegated' powers which the shareholders by majority vote could withdraw or modify at any time, a view apparent in the model set of rules contained in legislation at the time.[21] By the second half of the nineteenth century there was, however, an emerging understanding that, by virtue of the articles of association, shareholders in effect handed over certain powers to the directors to use exclusively, a view embodied in the standard form of articles of association contained in the *Companies Act 1862* (UK). By the beginning of the twentieth century, British and Australian law recognised a principle of day-to-day autonomy for the board: where the board

---

16   For example, the number of listed companies in Victoria declined from 231 to 130 during the 1890s: see A. Hall, *The Stock Exchange of Melbourne and the Victorian Economy 1852–1900*, Australian National University Press, Canberra, 1968, p. 230.

17   McQueen, 'Company Law as Imperialism' above n. 12, p. 199.

18   This is true also of the UK: see P. Ireland, 'The Rise of the Limited Liability Company' (1984) 12 *International Journal of the Sociology of Law* 239, pp. 244–245.

19   See, e.g., *Companies Act 1890* (Vic), Table A.

20   P. Ireland, 'Capitalism Without the Capitalist: The Joint Stock Company Share and the Emergence of the Doctrine of Separate Corporate Personality' (1996) 17 *Journal of Legal History* 41; Grantham, above n. 14.

21   *Companies Clauses Consolidation Act 1845* (UK), s 90, applicable to public utility companies created by statute. See also *Isle of Wight Railway Co v Talhourdin* (1883) 25 ChD 320.

was granted exclusive powers of management, neither the general meeting nor individual shareholders could intervene in or dictate the exercise of those powers.[22]

The general meeting of shareholders retained the right to make decisions only in certain – limited – key areas, such as altering the constitution, altering of share capital, winding up, or approving (retrospectively or prospectively) certain directors' transactions where there was a conflict of interest or where directors' acts were in abuse or excess of their powers. Shareholder meetings operated on the principle of majority rule,[23] leaving minority shareholders exposed to majority opportunism. The principle of majority rule also presented a challenge to the view of company articles as representing an essentially 'contractual' arrangement amongst company members, in that an entrenched special majority could amend the 'contract' without the agreement, and to the detriment, of minority shareholders. Courts were reluctant to intervene in corporate decision-making except where there appeared to be particularly egregious abuses of power on the part of controllers.[24]

---

22   *Automatic Self-Cleansing Filter Syndicate Co Ltd v Cunninghame* [1906] 2 Ch 34. That the model articles of the 1862 Act altered the position as it stood under the 1844 Act was not a view that immediately found favour, and the notion that directors were agents exercising delegated power persisted for some time, including in one of the few early Australian authorities on this point: *Dowse v Marks* (1913) 13 SR(NSW) 332. Cf. the view of Isaacs J in *Melbourne Trust Ltd v Commissioner of Taxes* (Vic) (1912) 15 CLR 274. See generally the discussion in K. Aickin, 'Division of Power Between Directors and General Meeting as a Matter of Law, and as a Matter of Fact and Policy' (1967) 5 *Melbourne University Law Review* 448.

23   Company law did require a 'supermajority' vote on particular issues, such as changes to the constitution, or decisions to wind-up a company or change the company form. The expanded majority required meant more attention had to be paid to the views of non-controlling shareholders, but any majority requirement short of unanimity still had the potential to leave some minority shareholders exposed to majority opportunism: P. Davies, *Introduction to Company Law*, Clarendon Press, Oxford, 2002, pp. 222–223. Pistor et al. note that the form of voting was a contentious issue in many jurisdictions in the nineteenth century, with Britain experimenting with regressive voting systems and a number of US states introducing mandatory cumulative voting in the first half of the twentieth century: K. Pistor, Y. Keinan, J. Kleinheisterkamp and M.J. West, 'The Evolution of Corporate Law: A Cross-Country Comparison' (2002) 23 *University of Pennsylvania Journal of International Economic Law* 791, p. 819; J. Gordon, 'Institutions as Relational Investors: A New Look at Cumulative Voting' (1994) 94 *Columbia Law Review* 124. See also the mandatory vote capping rules in the Sydney Stock Exchange Listing Rules as at 1932, cited in R.K. Yorstin, *The Australian Company Director*, Law Book Company of Australasia, Sydney, 1932, p. 49. The ability to be 'present' at the shareholder meeting by proxy also obviously enhanced a minority shareholder's position, which is why La Porta, Lopez-de-Silanes, Shleifer and Vishny (see the citations to their work in footnote 31 of Chapter 1) include the availability of proxy voting in their 'anti-director rights' index.

24   These instances were generally justified as 'exceptions' to the general rule regarding non-interference in internal management, and based on equitable principles,

In return for the attenuation of their direct control rights over directors, shareholders retained some protection by way of the duties imposed on directors which had grown out of the mixture of partnership and trust principles that had governed the early deed of settlement companies. These duties fell into two broad categories: a fiduciary duty that directors be loyal to the company, and a duty that they exercise due care. However, these duties were largely subjective in nature and were owed to the company, not to shareholders, with the consequence that individual shareholders lacked standing to sue directors for breach. Accordingly, the duties were of little practical impact, and courts had limited scope to review the substantive merits of directors' decisions.

In summary, by the early decades of the twentieth century, the British and Australian regulation of companies was based upon general incorporation statutes, which conferred limited liability and which were recognised as creating an association with separate legal personality. This amounted to a fairly non-interventionist statutory framework, supplemented by a small number of equitable and common law obligations impacting upon the company, its directors and its majority shareholders. Directors had a relatively free hand in forming the strategic direction of the company's business with shareholder recourse to judicial review restricted. As has been observed of the British system of corporate regulation in the first half of the twentieth century, 'neither companies legislation nor common law principles afforded much explicit protection to minority shareholders'.[25]

It also appears that well into the twentieth century such a model did not coincide with the emergence in Australia of 'liberal market' patterns of corporate control characterised by dispersed share ownership. In the early 1950s, a study of the largest public companies in Australia, including financial institutions and subsidiaries of foreign companies, indicated that founding families were in a position to control the majority of those companies through their positions on boards and through shareholdings, and only a third of domestic companies could be identified as 'management-controlled' (that is, with ownership of shares so dispersed that no single shareholding accounted for more than 5 per cent of voting shares).[26]

---

although discerning a consistent set of equitable principles from the decided cases is difficult. Early company legislation contained the provision that courts could compulsorily wind up the company if the court thought it 'just and equitable' to do so, with considerations of justice and equity encompassing oppression of the minority: e.g., *Companies Act 1893* (WA) s 107. In the 1930s, self-interested actions by directors, or unfairness to shareholders, were made specific grounds for winding up in NSW and Victoria: *Companies Act 1936* (NSW) s 208(2); *Companies Act 1938* (Vic) s 166(2). Current provisions as to winding up where it is 'just and equitable' to do so, where there is oppressive conduct, or where directors have acted in their own interests rather than in the interests of the shareholders as a whole are found in *Corporations Act* (Cth), s 461(1)(e),(f), (g) and (k).

25   Cheffins, 'Does Law Matter?' above n. 3, p. 469.

26   E. Wheelwright, *Ownership and Control of Australian Companies*, Law Book Company, Sydney, 1957.

Similarly, Australia's domestic capital market across much of this period was underdeveloped compared with those in Britain or the US. Only a relatively small number of companies sought a stock exchange listing. The capital market's prime activity before the 1890s was trading in speculative mining stock and new issues for industrial stocks remained extremely modest until the 1920s and 1930s.[27] Finally, a robust market for corporate control, often seen as a major disciplinary device in promoting shareholder interests in liberal market economies,[28] also was slow to emerge in Australia. In the first half of the twentieth century, takeovers in Australia were few, and the law allowed directors wide discretion as to what information they made available to shareholders regarding takeover offers. Managers could easily reject bids outright or defeat or modify the bid by insisting on terms to protect the interests of management or employees, or entering into transactions that made the target company unattractive to the bidder.[29] Mergers and acquisitions throughout the 1950s and 1960s were mostly friendly affairs where shareholders were invited to rubber-stamp a decision previously negotiated between the two boards of directors.[30]

The Trajectory of Corporate Law and Regulation

In the past half century or so, the statutory regulation of corporate governance has become increasingly elaborate compared with its rather minimalist nineteenth-century beginnings. The broad trajectory has been to grant greater power and/or protection to shareholders. This has been achieved partly through modifications to directors' duties and increasing the power of the shareholder meeting. But at the same time, a major new direction in corporate law and regulation can be seen in the response to the economic downturn of the early 1960s, and more critically in the aftermath of the share market boom and crash of the late 1960s and early 1970s. These events exposed several weaknesses in the regulatory framework governing

---

27   S. Ville and D. Merrett, 'The Development of Large Scale Enterprise in Australia, 1910–64' (2000) 42 *Business History* 13.

28   H. Manne, 'Mergers and the Market for Corporate Control' (1965) 73 *Journal of Political Economy* 110.

29   D. Merrett and K. Houghton, 'Takeovers and Corporate Governance: Whose Interests Do Directors Serve?' (1999) 35 *Abacus* 223. Australian courts generally took the view that as long as it was not the primary purpose of the transaction to defeat the takeover, such actions by directors were not a breach of duty: see *Pine Vale Investments Ltd v McDonnell and East Ltd* (1983) 8 ACLR 199; *Winthrop Investments Ltd v Winns Ltd* (1979) 4 ACLR 1; *Harlowe's Nominees Pty Ltd v Woodside(Lakes Entrance) Oil Co NL* (1968) 121 CLR 483.

30   D. Merrett, *Corporate Governance, Incentives and the Internationalization of Australian Business*, paper presented at the Business History Conference, Hagley Museum and Library, Wilmington, Delaware, 19–21 April 2002.

the securities market and share trading in particular.[31] Subsequent developments shifted the main focus of attention away from the regulation of companies and their shareholders to the regulation of the share market as a mechanism for the protection of shareholders of listed companies. Prior to this, the securities industry, and takeover regulation, were treated as secondary (and relatively neglected) concerns rather than as a principal focus of corporate law activity. The emerging approach to shareholder protection in Australian corporate law was one not merely centred on shareholder 'voice' within the company but extended more broadly to the integrity of the capital market itself, boardroom composition, managerial remuneration, takeovers and the regulation of disclosure.

Entwined with these developments was the gradual emergence of a truly national regime of corporate regulation as the States, over time, reluctantly agreed to vest more power in a national regulator – again, typically prompted by a series of major corporate collapses and corporate scandals. The history of corporate regulation runs parallel to the moves to have one national corporate law rather than State Companies Acts that were administered in an uneven manner by the various state corporate regulators. The Interstate Corporate Affairs Commission which existed from 1974 to 1979 was more of a co-ordinator of some of the activities of the State commissions than a national regulator. It was followed by the National Companies and Securities Commission in the 1980s which shared corporate regulation with the State regulators. In 1989 the first truly national regulator was created: the Australian Securities Commission.[32] A new 'National Scheme' of corporate regulation became operational in 1991.

It was the revised Victorian *Companies Act 1958* which provided the model for the first attempt at a pan-Australian model for State legislation, the 1961 draft Uniform Companies Bill. The 1958 Victorian Act increased direct shareholder control over the composition of the board, allowing directors to be removed at any time by simple majority vote; set out the first statutory formulation of the general law duties of directors; and pioneered a separate statutory oppression remedy which applied to the conduct both of directors and majority shareholders, giving scope to individual shareholders to bring an action.

Further corporate collapses in the 1980s and 1990s led to a reappraisal of directors' duties, with a move to strengthen directors' duty of care towards a more stringent, objective standard: in both common law[33] and legislation.[34] That

---

31   See, e.g., S. Salsbury and K. Sweeney, *The Bull, the Bear and the Kangaroo: A History of the Sydney Stock Exchange*, Allen & Unwin, Sydney, 1988; T. Sykes, *The Bold Riders: Behind Australia's Corporate Collapses*, Allen & Unwin, Sydney, 1994.

32   For additional discussion, see B. Mees and I. Ramsay, 'Corporate Regulators in Australia (1961–2000): From Companies' Registrars to ASIC' (2008) 22 *Australian Journal of Corporate Law* 212.

33   *Commonwealth Bank of Australia v Friedrich* (1991) 5 ACSR 111; *Daniels v Anderson* (1995) 16 ACSR 607.

34   *Corporations Act 2001* (Cth), s 180(1).

is, courts and parliament became more prescriptive about how directors needed to conduct themselves. In presuming the amount and quality of information and knowledge directors are to have as they conduct company affairs, the statutory provisions now 'steer directors toward appropriate patterns of conduct, rather than simply imposing sanctions for failure to meet legal standards'.[35]

Direct shareholder decision rights have also been enhanced in recent decades. We saw that from late in the nineteenth century, corporate law limited the kinds of decisions for which shareholder votes were required. Australian corporate law has evolved to give greater participatory rights to shareholders, with increased shareholder participation a particularly dominant theme in the regulatory developments following the corporate collapses of the 1980s and the more recent corporate scandals.[36] Legislative amendments allowed shareholders with at least 5 per cent of votes in the company or, alternatively, 100 shareholders, the right to request directors to call a meeting of shareholders.[37] It is now more common for legislation to require shareholder votes on an increasing range of certain important decisions: for example, in the case of companies adopting the *Corporations Act*'s replaceable rules as their constitution and setting the directors' remuneration. For a listed company, the effect of the Australian Securities Exchange (ASX) Listing Rules is that there are a number of transactions which under the constitution of a listed company can only be entered into if approved by shareholders in general meeting.[38]

Courts have also been active in enhancing the rights of shareholders. Perhaps the most prominent, and controversial, example is the decision of the High Court

---

35 A. Corbett and S. Bottomley, 'Regulating Corporate Governance' in C. Parker, C. Scott, N. Lacey and J. Braithwaite (eds), *Regulating Law*, Oxford University Press, Oxford, 2004, p. 75.

36 An example is Chapter 2E of the *Corporations Act 2001* (Cth) which regulates financial benefits between public companies and their related parties (including directors). Financial benefits that are not exempt need to be approved by shareholders. This chapter of the *Corporations Act* was a response to some of the corporate collapses of the 1980s that were caused by insiders of public companies transferring corporate funds to themselves. It can be seen that Chapter 2E is an example of a regulatory approach to governance problems that sees empowering shareholders as the solution. For a more recent example, see the Explanatory Memorandum to the *Corporate Law Economic Reform Program (Audit Reform and Corporate Disclosure) Bill 2004* (Cth) which contains numerous references to the desirability of improving shareholder participation, increasing shareholder activism, and enabling shareholders to 'influence the direction of the companies in which they invest'; and Parliamentary Joint Committee on Corporations and Financial Services, *Better Shareholders – Better Company: Shareholder Participation and Engagement in Australia* (2008).

37 *Corporations Act,* s 249D(1). Shareholders cannot call a meeting to pass resolutions relating to matters within the powers of the board: R.P. Austin and I.M. Ramsay, *Ford's Principles of Corporations Law*, LexisNexis Butterworths, Sydney, 14th edn, 2010, ch. 7.

38 Austin and Ramsay, ibid., ch. 7.

of Australia in *Gambotto v WCP Ltd*,[39] where the High Court struck down as invalid an amendment to a company's constitution where the amendment enabled the majority shareholder to expropriate the shares of the minority. The court stated that it was not a sufficient justification that an expropriation would advance the interests of the company, or secure some commercial advantage. An expropriation would be valid only if its purpose was to secure the company from detriment or harm. The decision is a powerful endorsement of the proprietary interests of shareholders, favouring these over commercial transactions that benefit the company where such transactions involve the expropriation of shares in the manner undertaken by WCP Ltd.[40]

However, as noted, we can also discern an increased emphasis on the role of market mechanisms in compelling directors and management to deliver 'shareholder value'.[41] In contrast to many of the established statutory and judge-made doctrines of corporate law which have broad application, such mechanisms mostly impact on listed companies with publicly-traded shares. Favoured strategies have included the regulation of disclosure obligations; linking managerial pay to company performance; using boards of independent directors to monitor managerial action; and allowing a market for corporate control to sanction managers who fail to promote shareholder value.

Prior to the enactment of uniform companies legislation by the Australian States in 1961, directors enjoyed wide discretion as to what information they disclosed to the market apart from the annual balance sheet and profit and loss account. Up until the late 1960s, company affairs in Australia were still often inaccurately and misleadingly reported and company failures due to fraud not uncommon, and so investors remained cautious and tended to stay with market leaders.[42] Stock exchange listing rules tended to impose greater disclosure obligations than existing companies legislation. Unsurprisingly, then, 'corporate governance' reform has increasingly focussed on an array of regulation intended to bolster investor confidence and so facilitate a liquid securities market, focussing on issues

39   *Gambotto v WCP Ltd* (1995) 182 CLR 432; 127 ALR 417; 16 ACSR 1; 13 ACLC 342.

40   For further discussion of *Gambotto v WCP Ltd*, see I. Ramsay (ed.), *Gambotto v WCP Ltd: Its Implications for Corporate Regulation*, Centre for Corporate Law and Securities Regulation, University of Melbourne, 1996.

41   On the notion of shareholder value as a corporate goal, see J. Froud, C. Haslam, S. Johal and K. Williams, 'Shareholder Value and Financialisation: Consultancy Promises, Management Moves' (2000) 29 *Economy and Society* 80.

42   G. de Q Walker, *Australian Monopoly Law*, Cheshire, Melbourne, 1967. Fleming et al. make a similar point about the difficulty faced by non-market leaders in raising equity finance for much of the twentieth century owing to low investor confidence: G. Fleming, D. Merrett and S. Ville, *The Big End of Town: Big Business and Corporate Leadership in Twentieth-Century Australia*, Cambridge University Press, Melbourne, 2004.

of disclosure,[43] and the role of 'gate keepers' (those reputational intermediaries, such as auditors and securities analysts, who provide information verification services to those participating in the share market).[44]

Adjusting the remuneration packages of senior management has also been seen as a way to produce optimal incentives for management to pursue shareholder wealth maximisation. This is done through outcome-based contracts for management pay, based on outcomes such as share price and profitability. Empirical data indicates dramatic changes in the composition of the remuneration packages of chief executive officers (CEOs), with stock options and share plans becoming an increasingly common feature of executive remuneration in Australian businesses.[45] Payments to executives, and directors, of large companies have risen significantly faster than average earnings over the past 15 years. Disquiet over the rising level of executive remuneration due to outcome-based contracts for management pay has led to a further focus on the proceduralisation of remuneration-setting mechanisms – the use of non-executive directors on remuneration committees, disclosure, adequate audit to ensure accounting-based performance measures are not subject to manipulation and so on – rather than a retreat from the general principle of performance-based pay. Since 1998 listed companies have been required to include in their annual reports a 'Remuneration Report' detailing the remuneration of all directors and the top five remunerated executives and the board's policy for determining remuneration. Since July 2004, shareholders of listed companies must now collectively express their opinion on the remuneration paid to directors and senior managers and on the board's remuneration policy through a non-binding resolution to adopt the remuneration report.[46]

There has also been strong encouragement, through the promulgation of various national and transnational 'codes' of good corporate governance, towards the appointment of board members independent of management to provide for

---

43   See, especially, the rules relating to 'continuous disclosure': ASX Listing Rule 3.1 and *Corporations Act 2001* (Cth), Ch. 6CA.

44   On recent audit and financial reporting reforms see the *Corporate Law Economic Reform Program (Audit Reform and Corporate Disclosure) Act 2004* (Cth), which is based to some degree on the recommendations contained in I. Ramsay, *Independence of Australian Company Auditors: Review of Current Australian Requirements and Proposals for Reform*, Report to the Minister for Financial Services and Regulation, 2001.

45   Surveys of Australia's largest companies show fixed pay as a percentage of the average CEO remuneration package declined from 90 to 43 per cent between 1987 and 2002, whereas short-term incentive payments increase to 23 per cent and long-term incentive payments to 34 per cent: G. Stapledon, 'The Pay For Performance Dilemma' (2004) 13 *Griffith Law Review* 57. See also G. O'Neill and M. Iob, 'Determinants of Executive Remuneration in Australian Organisations: An Exploratory Study' (1999) 37 *Asia Pacific Journal of Human Resources* 65.

46   *Corporations Act 2001* (Cth) s. 250R and s. 300A; *Corporate Law Economic Reform Program (Audit Reform and Corporate Disclosure) Act 2004* (Cth).

more effective general oversight and monitoring of company strategy. Theory suggests that independent directors can play an important role in situations involving conflicts of interest between management and shareholders, and some US empirical studies (for example, examining independent directors and takeovers) find support for this theory.[47] An emerging focus on audit and accounting practices and the requirement that companies have independent audit committees also requires companies to increase the number of independent directors.[48]

As regards the market for corporate control, in the late 1960s the federal government-appointed Eggleston Committee developed a 'takeover code', which was eventually incorporated into legislation and provided much greater transparency and protection for shareholders in the takeover process. With the advent of the Eggleston code, shareholders were required to be informed of the identity of a bidder, the terms of the bid and shareholders were to be given reasonable time to make a decision. Each shareholder was to have an equal opportunity to participate in the benefits offered by the bid to ensure that any control premium was shared equally between majority and minority shareholders. Recent adjudications of the Takeovers Panel have further eroded the board's autonomy. Management is now required to be largely passive in the face of a takeover and, for practical purposes, the interests of the company, as far as directors are concerned, is conflated with the decision the current body of shareholders wishes to take.[49] Thus, while not modifying the directors' fiduciary duties per se, the practical effect of the new position is that, for the duration of the bid, shareholders are placed in the 'driving seat', mandating greater managerial passivity in the face of takeovers and prioritising short-term shareholder wealth maximisation for current shareholders over the interests of other stakeholders.

Broadly speaking, then, Australian law has evolved to strengthen the rights of shareholders. It is clear that the pace and extent of statutory reform has accelerated in the past couple of decades in particular. Over this period there has been put in

---

47   See the literature survey in G. Stapledon and J. Lawrence, 'Board Composition, Structure and Independence in Australia's Largest Listed Companies' (1997) 21 *Melbourne University Law Review* 150.

48   A recent study of 300 Australian listed public companies indicates company boards have, on average, seven directors. Seventy four per cent of directors are non-executive directors and 26 per cent executive directors (the study did not examine the independence of directors). For the largest 50 companies, 80 per cent of the directors are non-executive directors: Korn/Ferry International, *2008 Board of Directors Study*. Another noteworthy change is that in the postwar period the board chairman of many major companies was often the CEO or had held executive positions with the company previously, but by 2000 most boards of major companies were chaired by non-executive directors: Fleming et al., above n. 42.

49   E. Armson, 'The Frustrating Action Policy: Shifting Power in the Takeover Context' (2003) 21 *Company and Securities Law Journal* 487. For further discussion of the role of the Takeovers Panel and its history, see I. Ramsay (ed.), *The Takeovers Panel and Takeovers Regulation in Australia*, Melbourne University Press, Melbourne, 2010.

place a bundle of practices which collectively aim to provide greater shareholder protection. Shareholders generally have gained greater participatory rights, greater information rights, greater rights to judicial recourse, and directors now owe a stricter duty of care. Outside of these key areas of corporate law, some of which apply to both listed and private companies, attempts to bolster the position of shareholders in listed companies have meant a growing reliance on market discipline through laws facilitating takeovers and strong disclosure requirements to support deep equity markets. Overall, such a package of protections would seem to place Australia in the liberal market model of regulation.

Whether minority shareholder protection correlates to 'shareholder primacy' is another matter. As noted in Chapter 1, minority shareholder protections serve different purposes depending upon whether one is talking about public companies with dispersed shareholdings or other companies, private or public, with concentrated block-holdings. In the former case, minority shareholders require protections against management; in the latter they require protection against abuse by the majority of shareholders. Some general corporate law sanctions for misconduct and self-dealing apply in both situations, but as we have pointed out, many of the more recent measures promoted to 'protect' shareholders are restricted in their application to the situation where dispersed shareholders of a public company appear at risk from a self-interested management. From our brief survey, it is clear that in these latter instances management must prioritise shareholder claims over those of other stakeholders when a company is subject to takeover. However, when a company becomes insolvent or approaches insolvency directors are required to give consideration to the interests of creditors.[50] Nevertheless, it remains the case that the Australian corporate law does not explicitly deal with shareholder primacy and the interests of stakeholders to the extent of section 172 of the UK *Companies Act 2006*. This section introduces the concept of 'enlightened shareholder value' into the law, together with a non-exhaustive list of factors that directors must take into account when making decisions, including the interests of employees, suppliers, customers and the environment.[51] The section

---

50   There has not been imposed a direct fiduciary duty to act in the best interests of creditors but, rather, an understanding that fulfilling the fiduciary duty to 'the company' can mean, in the case of insolvency or near-insolvency, giving priority to the interests of the creditors over those of the shareholders: *Walker v Wimborne* (1976) 137 CLR 1, per Mason J. For further discussion, see Austin and Ramsay, above n. 37, ch. 8. Outside of this development of the common law duties of directors, a more powerful development is to be found within the insolvent trading provisions under Pt 5.7B Div 3 and 4 of the *Corporations Act*. This imposes personal liability on directors who incur a debt on behalf of the company when, at the time, there were reasonable grounds for suspecting the company's insolvency. On the policy background to these provisions and an evaluation of their effects, see P. James, I. Ramsay and P. Siva, 'Insolvent Trading: An Empirical Study' (2004) 12 *Insolvency Law Journal* 210.

51   On the role of employee interests in UK corporate law, see also J. Armour, S. Deakin and S. Konzelmann, 'Shareholder Primacy and the Trajectory of UK Corporate

requires directors to act to promote the success of the company for the benefit of its shareholders and, in doing so, directors must have regard to the interests of the stakeholders mentioned in the section. The actual extent of shareholder primacy or 'saliency' in a range of Australian companies, both public and private, is explored in further detail in Chapter 4.

Several qualifications are worth making as regards our broad characterisation of the recent trajectory of Australian corporate law. First, the claim that the law has evolved to offer greater shareholder protection is a relative one. As we saw, early corporate law worked to largely shift control rights from shareholders to centralised management or boards. The more recent counter-movement towards shareholder rights and protections must be seen in this context, with the aim being to ensure that directors retain the exclusive right to manage or direct the day-to-day activities of the company rather than being beholden to shareholders, whilst assuring shareholders that management power is not unlimited.[52] Notably, however, whereas governance of the nineteenth-century company was largely left to its articles of association, this counter-movement has been effected by a trend towards increasingly mandatory law – although this trend has itself been offset by less onerous rules for proprietary or private companies.[53] This trend is somewhat at odds with the view posited by some legal origin theorists who characterise common law countries as marked by private ordering with few overriding mandatory rules as to the content of agreements.

Second, it is worthwhile being alert to differences as amongst liberal market economies and to the specific path that Australian corporate law and regulation has taken. As noted, Australia's foundational legislative interventions in this area were closely modelled on British company law.[54] Some have suggested that the more recent flurry of activity since the mid-1990s represents an 'Americanisation' of corporate law.[55] There may be a convergence on some specific matters, yet there are still key areas where Australia tracks more closely a distinctly British model. The institutional role of the Takeovers Panel and its predecessor, the Corporations and Securities Panel, for example, represents a transplant of key elements of Britain's City Code on Takeovers, which also prohibits directors, in the absence of shareholder approval, from taking action that may frustrate a

---

Governance' (2003) 41 *British Journal of Industrial Relations* 531.

52   K. Pistor et al., above n. 23. That is, corporate law tries to effect a balance 'between shareholder protection and entrepreneurial discretion in decision-making': Siems, above n. 14, p. 193.

53   See Siems, above n. 14, pp. 48–51; I. Ramsay, 'Models of Corporate Regulation: The Mandatory/Enabling Debate' in R. Grantham and C. Rickett (eds), *Corporate Personality in the Twentieth Century*, Hart Publishing, Oxford, 1998.

54   McQueen, 'Company Law as Imperialism', above n. 12, goes so far as to describe a process whereby a British model of company law was exported to the colonies despite there being little or no demand amongst business operators for the corporate form.

55   P. von Nessen, 'The Americanization of Corporate Law' (1999) 26 *Syracuse Journal of International Law and Commerce* 239.

takeover offer or that denies shareholders the opportunity to decide whether to evaluate an offer on its merits,[56] whereas in many US jurisdictions directors of a target company still have the capacity to thwart hostile takeover bids. Similarly, whereas the US response to corporate scandals early in the twenty-first century was to shift towards a 'legislative rules-based approach to corporate governance, with a higher level of mandatory standards',[57] Australia has adopted a more non-prescriptive approach, again mirroring that of the UK, whereby listed companies must comply with, or explain their divergence from, the principles set out in the ASX's corporate governance guidelines.[58]

A final example is the divergence between recognition of shareholder interests through market mechanisms (e.g. disclosure requirements) and enhanced decision-making or participatory rights for shareholders. In more recent post-scandal regulatory reforms Australia and Britain have favoured the latter path, whilst the US has tended towards the former.[59] However, not all recent US corporate law reforms can be classified in this way. For example, a shareholder advisory vote in relation to executive remuneration is now a requirement for some US companies. In 2010, the US Congress enacted the *Dodd-Frank Wall Street Reform and Consumer Protection Act*, which added section 14A to the US *Securities and Exchange Act 1934*. This section requires public companies subject to the US federal proxy rules to provide their shareholders with an advisory vote on executive remuneration, generally known in the US as 'say-on-pay' votes and provide their shareholders with an advisory vote on the desired frequency of say-on-pay votes.

Third, legal origin theorists suggest that basic minority shareholder protections will correlate with deep or liquid share markets. That is, the absence of such protections will mean block-holdings will persist as potential buyers have little incentive to take a non-controlling stake in companies. As we pointed out earlier, Australia tended to display fairly concentrated ownership patterns up until the

---

56 A. Dignam, 'Transplanting UK Takeover Culture: The EU Takeovers Directive and the Australian Experience' (2007) 4 *International Journal of Disclosure* 148; E. Armson, 'Models for Takeover Dispute Resolution: Australia and the UK' (2005) 5 *Journal of Corporate Law Studies* 401.

57 J. Hill, 'Regulatory Responses to Corporate Governance Scandals' (2005) 23 *Wisconsin International Law Journal* 367, p. 382.

58 ASX Corporate Governance Council, *Principles of Good Corporate Governance and Best Practice Recommendations*, 1st edn, 2003; ASX Corporate Governance Council, *Corporate Governance Principles and Recommendations*, 2nd edn, 2007. These principles address board role and structure, integrity of financial reporting and disclosure of company information.

59 J. Hill, *The Shifting Balance of Power Between Shareholders and the Board: News Corp's Exodus to Delaware and Other Antipodean Tales*, Sydney Law School Legal Studies Research Paper No. 08/20, 2008, and see n. 36 above. We also noted that this theme of shareholder participation underpinned Australian reforms in the area of executive remuneration: above n. 46.

middle of the twentieth century. This pattern persisted through the 1960s[60] and into the 1970s,[61] and despite the apparently enhanced shareholder protections that have been put in place in the intervening decades, and outlined above, there is little evidence that Australia has evolved to a truly dispersed pattern of share ownership. As a threshold issue, and in common with many continental European countries, the stock exchange-listed corporate sector remains a relatively small part of the Australian economy.[62] Further, even within the listed company sector, concentrated ownership patterns appear to be very common.[63] In 1996, approximately 45 per cent of the companies that made up Australia's ASX All Ordinaries Index had a shareholder other than an institutional investor that owned 20 per cent or more of the shares. In contrast, in the UK just over 20 per cent of the companies listed on the London Stock Exchange were in the same position.[64] By 1997 Australian institutional investors owned around 35 per cent of the Australian listed share market, and overseas institutional investors a further 10–15 per cent, but these institutional ownership patterns were smaller than those prevailing in the US and UK.[65] Thus, while there had been a growth in institutional investors, and a decline in individual shareholding as a percentage of the market, non-institutional block-holders continued to play an important role in the structure of share ownership. A more recent study of a sample of 240 Australian listed companies found that 72 per cent had a 10 per cent or larger non-institutional investor block-holder, 52 per cent had a 20 per cent or larger non-institutional investor block-holder and 16 per cent had an absolute controlling shareholder holding more than 50 per cent of the shares – again, significantly higher concentrations of ownership than are present in the UK or US.[66]

The evidence on whether an effective market for corporate control is emerging is more mixed. On the basis of their concentrated ownership patterns, as at 1995, 40–50 per cent of Australian listed companies were immune from hostile

---

60   E.L. Wheelwright and J. Miskelly, *Anatomy of Australian Manufacturing Industry*, Law Book Company, Sydney, 1967.

61   M. Lawriwsky, *Ownership and Control of Australian Corporations*, Occasional Paper No. 1, Transnational Corporations Research Project, University of Sydney, 1978.

62   R. La Porta, F. Lopez-de-Silanes, A. Shleifer and R. Vishny, 'Law and Finance' (1998) 106 *Journal of Political Economy* 1113. Only about a third of Australia's largest companies are listed on its stock exchange compared with two-thirds of the UK's largest companies and nearly all the largest US companies: G. Stapledon, 'Australian Sharemarket Ownership' in G. Walker, B. Fisse and I. Ramsay (eds), *Securities Regulation in Australia and New Zealand*, LBC Information Services, Sydney, 2nd edn, 1998.

63   Stapledon, ibid.; R. La Porta, F. Lopez-de-Silanes and A. Shleifer, 'Corporate Ownership Around the World' (1999) 54 *Journal of Finance* 471; A. Lamba and G. Stapledon, *The Determinants of Corporate Ownership Structure: Australian Evidence*, University of Melbourne, Public Law and Legal Theory Working Paper Number 20, 2001.

64   Stapledon, above n. 62.

65   Ibid.

66   Lamba and Stapledon, above n. 63.

takeover.[67] One survey indicated only 7 per cent of all merger and acquisition activity from 1992–2004 comprised successful hostile bids, compared with around 20 per cent in the US and UK across similar periods.[68] Yet there remains a difficulty in identifying successful 'hostile' bids, as a hostile target board can recommend acceptance late in the bid period once it becomes obvious that effective control has passed or will pass under the takeover offer. A survey of 136 takeovers for the period 1990–1998 suggests around 20 per cent fall into this category of 'reject, then accept' and so can therefore arguably be classed as hostile, and 75 per cent of bids in this category were successful.[69] Similarly, a study of successful hostile bids as a percentage of all takeover attempts places Australia higher than the US and slightly lower than the UK.[70]

Some of this empirical data – at least that concerning concentrated ownership structures and corporate control, if not that on takeovers – complicates the stylised division between liberal market and co-ordinated market economies set out in Table 1.1 of Chapter 1, raising questions about how Australia should be characterised within different groups of economies, the direction of development in the corporate governance system (i.e. that it has been evolving from an insider (co-ordinated) system to an 'outsider' system) and particularly the relevance of law in producing effectively functioning 'outsider' systems of corporate governance.

2.3 Labour Law and Labour Market Regulation

The Classification of Australian Labour Law – Origin and Evolution

In addressing the origin and evolution of Australian labour law and labour market regulation, particular attention must be directed to the system of industrial conciliation and arbitration introduced at the beginning of the twentieth century. However, before turning to a discussion of conciliation and arbitration it is necessary to note briefly the very uncertain and disordered state of labour regulation prior to the modern systems introduced in most industrialised countries during the 1900s.

As has been noted about the evolution of labour law in other common law countries, there was no straightforward, inevitable, development of labour law institutions associated with the rise and consolidation of the market economy

---

67 G. Stapledon, 'The Structure of Share Ownership and Control: The Potential for Institutional Investor Activism' (1995) 18 *University of New South Wales Law Journal* 250.

68 A. Dignam, 'The Globalisation of General Principle 7: Transforming the Market for Corporate Control in Australia and Europe?' (2008) 28 *Legal Studies* 96, pp. 107–110.

69 J. Farrar, *Acquiring Control of Australian Companies: Takeover or Scheme of Arrangement?* Master of Laws Thesis, University of Melbourne, 2000.

70 L. Nottage, *Corporate Governance and M&A in Australia: An Overview for Assessing Japan and the 'Americanisation' Thesis*, Sydney Law School Legal Studies Research Paper No. 08/28, 2008.

in Australia.[71] Deakin and Njoya have observed that the regulation of labour in Britain, through the Elizabethan Statute of Artificers and other legislation, and through the general regimes of the various Masters and Servants Acts, co-existed with economies at different stages of development.[72] Of particular importance is the fact that in the transition from medieval regulation based on notions of status, and guild controls over production and distribution, to an economy based on competitive labour and product markets, there was no simple and direct shift from servant status to an employment form based on free contract.[73]

Correspondingly, towards the end of the nineteenth century Australian labour law was made up of a 'hotch potch' of master and servant law, contract principles, factory legislation and other statutory provisions applying to unions, exhibiting little coherence in its outlook and approach to labour problems. Much of this was inherited from British law, but importantly, from about the 1820s onwards there was a pattern of specific legislative interventions in the Australian colonies to deal with local conditions and circumstances.[74] As was the case elsewhere, the idea of the contract of employment as a common concept legally defining the relation between employer and worker was slow to develop.[75] Masters and servants legislation, which along with forced labour through penal servitude formed the basis of labour regulation for most of the nineteenth century,[76] remained on the

---

71   See Ahlering and Deakin, above n. 2; S. Deakin and W. Njoya, 'The Legal Framework of Employment Relations', Working Paper No. 349, Centre for Business Research, University of Cambridge, 2007. For a detailed study of the legal evolution of British labour law, see Deakin and Wilkinson, above n. 6.

72   Deakin and Njoya, ibid.

73   For more detailed argument on this point see J. Howe and R. Mitchell, 'The Evolution of the Contract of Employment in Australia: A Discussion' (1999) 12 *Australian Journal of Labour Law* 113; S. Deakin, 'The Evolution of the Contract of Employment, 1900–1950' in N. Whiteside and R. Salais (eds), *Governance, Industry and Labour Markets in Britain and France*, Routledge, London, 1998, p. 212. It is often assumed that the transition from servant status to employment by contract was a fairly automatic functional response to the rise of capitalism and a factory economy: see O. Kahn-Freund, 'Blackstone's Neglected Child: The Contract of Employment' (1977) 93 *Law Quarterly Review* 113. Kahn-Freund's view generally formed the starting point for most historical accounts of labour law: see J. Macken, P. O'Grady and C. Sappideen, *The Law of Employment*, 4th edn, LBC Information Services, Sydney, 1997, pp. 3–8; R. McCallum and M. Pittard, *Australian Labour Law: Cases and Materials*, 3rd edn, Butterworths, Sydney, 1995, pp. 48–50.

74   See B. Creighton and A. Stewart, *Labour Law*, The Federation Press, Sydney, 4th edn, 2005, ch. 2.

75   See Howe and Mitchell, above n. 73.

76   See M. Quinlan, 'Pre-arbitral Labour Legislation in Australia and its Implications for the Introduction of Compulsory Arbitration' in S. Macintyre and R. Mitchell (eds), *Foundations of Arbitration: The Origins and Effects of State Compulsory Arbitration 1890–1914*, Oxford University Press, Melbourne, 1989, 25; M. Quinlan, 'Australia, 1788–1902: A Workman's Paradise?' in D. Hay and P. Craven (eds), *Masters, Servants, and Magistrates in Britain and the Empire, 1562–1955*, The University of North Carolina Press, Chapel

statute books in many States of the Australian Commonwealth long after it had been repealed in Britain,[77] and applied to a much broader cohort of workers than was the case in the comparable British laws. However, neither masters and servants law, nor the 'contract' of employment emerged as the principal regulatory institution in twentieth-century Australian labour markets. The idea of the contract of employment continued to evolve (as it did in Britain) as a common device explaining the legal connection between employer and worker, but played little direct role in regulating working conditions for the great majority of workers in the great majority of workplaces. Masters and servants law, like some other bodies of law regulating workplace relations and employment,[78] remained in force but was, like the contract of employment, basically marginalised in its regulatory functions within the Australian labour market.

For an understanding of the key institutions of labour market regulation in Australia, therefore, it is necessary to turn to the role and functions of the industrial tribunals, and the processes of compulsory conciliation and arbitration which they exercised. These systems of dispute resolution were legislated into all Australian States, and also at national level, by about 1915, and although there were some links in legal ideas between these statutes and earlier British and colonial legislation, the system fundamentally represented an innovative departure in labour law along the same lines as that taken in New Zealand during the 1890s.[79]

The introduction of the compulsory arbitration system was something of a social settlement engineered by liberal social reformers between capital, labour and the state.[80] Coupled with laws protecting Australian workers against

---

Hill and London, 2004, 219; A. Merritt, 'The Historical Role of Law in the Regulation of Employment – Abstentionist or Interventionist?' (1982) 1 *Australian Journal of Law and Society* 56.

77   Masters and servants legislation remained on the statute books in some States as late as the 1970s: see Quinlan in Hay and Craven, ibid.

78   An example would include the law of torts which applied to many forms of industrial action, effectively making such action unlawful in different respects: see Creighton and Stewart, above n. 74, pp. 561–576.

79   See generally, R. Mitchell, 'State Systems of Conciliation and Arbitration: The Legal Origins of the Australasian Model', and R. Mitchell and E. Stern, 'The Compulsory Model of Industrial Dispute Settlement: An Outline of Legal Developments', both in Macintyre and Mitchell, above n. 76, pp. 74 and 104 respectively; C. Fisher, 'The English Origins of Australian Federal Arbitration: To 1824', Industrial Relations Papers, Research School of Social Sciences, Australian National University, 1986; R. Mitchell, 'Solving the Great Social Problem of the Age: A Comparison of the Development of State Systems of Conciliation and Arbitration in Australia and Canada' in G. Kealey and G. Patmore (eds), *Canadian and Australian Labour History: Towards a Comparative Perspective*, Australian-Canadian Studies, Kensington, Australia and St. Johns, Canada, 1990, p. 47.

80   For argument generally on this issue see S. Macintyre, 'Labour, Capital and Arbitration, 1890–1920' in B. Head (ed.), *State and Economy in Australia*, Oxford University Press, Melbourne, 1983, p. 98; S. Macintyre, 'Neither Capital Nor Labour: The

foreign labour, and laws guaranteeing domestic industry tariff protection against international competition in return for 'fair' wages, the Australian compulsory arbitration system, at least from the second decade of the twentieth century onwards, developed into a thorough-going system of workplace regulation with important implications for employers, workers and unions. The system also formed the basis of the state's approach to employment and wages policy generally.[81]

At one level the system could be seen and analysed as a variant of the collective bargaining systems which characterised other 'liberal market' economies, and which ranged in orientation from those which were largely voluntarist to systems, such as the US system, which had some elements of compulsion.[82] In Australia, however, the compulsory aspects in particular, rendered the system far reaching both in operational scope and regulatory content, and thus, superficially at least, distinguishable from the systems of its most obvious comparators, the US and Britain.[83]

Broadly stated, the key elements of Australian labour law as encapsulated in the compulsory arbitration system were as follows: (1) the establishment of permanent state bodies for the settlement of industrial disputes; (2) the existence of compulsion at both phases of the dispute settling process (i.e. submission of the dispute to the process, and the enforcement of the outcomes of that process); (3) the registration and regulation of trade unions for the purposes of implementing and enforcing the arbitration process; and (4) the abolition or restriction of rights of direct action.[84]

Politics of the Establishment of Arbitration' in Macintyre and Mitchell, above n. 76, p. 178; G. Patmore, *Australian Labour History*, Longman Cheshire, Melbourne, 1991, ch. 5; J. Rickard, *Class and Politics*, Australian National University Press, Canberra, 1976, pp. 204–222.

81   All of this detailed regulation is studied in the works of Orwell de R. Foenander over several decades. This body of work includes *Towards Industrial Peace in Australia*, Melbourne University Press, Melbourne, 1937; *Solving Labour Problems in Australia*, Melbourne University Press, Melbourne, 1941; *Industrial Regulation in Australia*, Melbourne University Press, Melbourne, 1947; *Studies in Australian Labour Law and Relations*, Melbourne University Press, Melbourne, 1952; *Better Employment Relations and Other Essays in Labour*, Law Book Company of Australasia, Sydney, 1954; and *Industrial Conciliation and Arbitration in Australia*, Law Book Company of Australasia, Sydney, 1959.

82   See, for example, H. Clegg, *Trade Unionism Under Collective Bargaining: A Theory Based on Comparisons of Six Countries*, Basil Blackwell, Oxford, 1976.

83   There is debate on the accuracy of these supposed differences in character, both in terms of labour law form and substance: see K. Ewing, 'Australian and British Labour Law: Differences of Form or Substance?' (1998) 11 *Australian Journal of Labour Law* 44; R. Mitchell, 'The Deregulation of Industrial Relations Systems and the Rise of the Non-Union Option' in P. Ronfeldt and R. McCallum (eds), *A New Province for Legalism: Legal Issues and the Deregulation of Industrial Relations*, Monograph No. 9, Australian Centre for Industrial Relations and Teaching, The University of Sydney, 1993, p. 132.

84   See W. Creighton, W. Ford and R. Mitchell, *Labour Law: Text and Materials*, Law Book Co., Sydney, 2nd edn, 1993, pp. 11–13; Creighton and Stewart, above n.74, pp. 19–22.

Whilst important in their legal form, not all of these elements operated effectively to produce the desired public policy outcome, which was ostensibly to reduce industrial conflict by taking wages and other conditions out of competition.[85] As it turned out, over time the laws against strikes and other forms of industrial action were not particularly effective. But in two key respects, the compulsion inherent in the Australian system, at least superficially, appeared to characterise Australian labour market regulation and employment systems profoundly.

First, the processes of compulsory conciliation and arbitration, along with the compulsory application to industry and workers of awarded work conditions, meant that there was often little point in employers declining to deal with unions or resisting their organisational activities, although it seems to have been the case that the level of union representation was very centralised in Australia, and therefore not very localised to the plant or factory level.[86] At the same time, trade unions were institutionally supported by industrial legislation, their members often 'preferred' in employment over non-unionists (thus encouraging the formation of closed shops), and union officials allowed 'rights of entry' onto work sites and industrial premises. Especially in much of the earlier period, trade unions were effectively responsible for 'policing' the system.

What all of this meant was that unions occupied a statutorily supported and privileged role in representing workers, far more so than unions in comparable systems such as operated in Britain and the US where recognition often had to be fought for through industrial campaigns. There is, moreover, an obvious correspondence between the introduction of compulsory arbitration and union growth. In the very early 1900s, union density was recorded at around 6 per cent. On one set of figures[87] this had increased to more than 53 per cent as early as 1920. Thereafter, trade union density levels remained around the 50 to 60 per cent mark for most of the twentieth century. Whether there was a straightforward causal connection between arbitration and union density levels in Australia is open to debate,[88] but it appears that trade union density levels in Australia continued

---

85   H.B. Higgins, 'A New Province for Law and Order' (1915) 29 *Harvard Law Review* 13.

86   See for example, Clegg, above n. 82, pp. 65–67. For a critical view of the role of unions in the context of the arbitration system see P. Scherer, 'The Nature of the Australian Industrial Relations System: A Form of State Syndicalism?' in G. Ford, J. Hearn and R. Lansbury (eds), *Australian Labour Relations Readings*, Macmillan, Melbourne, 4th edn, 1987, p. 81. Some other scholars saw unions as being disadvantaged organisationally by compulsory arbitration, the system rendering them as little more than instruments of the state: see W. Howard, 'Australian Trade Unions in the Context of Union Theory' (1977) 19 *Journal of Industrial Relations* 255.

87   Australian Bureau of Statistics, *Labour Reports*, and *Trade Union Statistics: Australia* (Catalogue No. 6323.0). These statistics are unreliable and possibly overstate the level of union membership to a degree.

88   See Creighton et al., above n. 84, p. 891.

to compare favourably with those of many other similar countries over the post-Second World War period.[89]

The second important contribution of the compulsory arbitration system was the widespread coverage of employment conditions which it engendered across the labour market generally.[90] As noted, the prescribed conditions (awards) of the industrial tribunals had compulsory application to the parties to industrial disputes. These could be added to, or substituted for, agreements made under the auspices of the tribunals, or otherwise. In some jurisdictions, decisions of industrial tribunals took effect as common rules, in others employers (and hence their employees) could be added to awards by a fairly simple and straightforward administrative process. The result was a very high level of application of prescribed employment conditions: compared with some other similar countries, such as the US and Canada, Australian employers found it difficult to escape the regulatory net.[91] A further dimension of this regulation concerned the depth of detail in awards: these were not short simple documents in the shape of many British collective agreements. Rather, they were fully fledged sets of regulations governing everything from wages, annual and sick leave, overtime and penalty rates, to procedures for the recognition of unions and the settlement of disputes between the parties. Whilst they rarely went so far as to specify work procedure, they embodied an understanding of job content and fixed the use of labour temporally and administratively, thus impacting considerably on the organisation of the labour process.[92] As late as 1985, 85 per cent of Australian workers were covered by awards, and this figure remained at 80 per cent into the 1990s.

In certain respects then, when situated within the heavily abstracted comparative table in Chapter 1 (Table 1.1), there is some basis in argument to suggest that Australian labour market regulation, at least for a significant period of its history, and perhaps even until relatively recently, was more 'like' a 'co-ordinated' market system[93] than a 'liberal' market system of capitalist economy.

---

89   For a comparison of an earlier period see Clegg, above n. 82, ch. 2. The comparison is with the US and some other countries rather than the UK. In the UK, density levels seem to have roughly been on a par with Australia especially since the 1970s, and in the long decline of trade unions since the 1980s UK membership appears to have held up somewhat better than in Australia.

90   Described by Sykes as 'a system of industrial regulation ... to obtain *general legislative determinations of future rights and relationships*', E. Sykes, 'Industrial Conciliation, Arbitration and Regulation' (1957) 31 *Australian Law Journal* 574.

91   Whether, and if so to what extent this could also be said to have characterised British collective bargaining comparatively speaking is open to question: see above n. 83 and associated discussion.

92   See R. Mitchell and M. Rimmer, 'Labour Law, Deregulation and Flexibility in Australian Industrial Relations' (1990) 12 *Comparative Labor Law Journal* 1; R. Mitchell and R. Naughton, 'Australian Compulsory Arbitration: Will it Survive into the 21st Century?' (1994) *Osgoode Hall Law Journal* 265.

93   Perhaps even a 'state socialist' system: see R. Ward (trans.), *Metin: Socialism Without Doctrine*, Alternative Publishing Co-operative Ltd., Chippendale, 1977. See also

In short, employee representation at the workplace seems to have been more compulsory than voluntary, and the regulation of the labour market appears to have been more universalist than partial. These are, of course, only questions of degree within various categories of organisation – but if the argument were to hold water, Australia might appear to be an exception to the 'legal origins' hypothesis: an example of a common law based country which, in terms of labour market regulation, fitted the co-ordinated model.

Nevertheless, having set out this general historical characterisation of Australian labour law, we suggest for two reasons that there are important underlying similarities between the Australian system and those of other common law based countries. The first of these is drawn from a deeper, more focussed, analysis of historical sources, and sets out important ways in which the core values of the Australian model, particularly in terms of worker representation and involvement, are significantly removed from those of the co-ordinated systems. The second focuses on the trajectory of the Australian system and its apparent 'convergence' on a stylised Anglo-American liberal market model over recent decades, which is dealt with in the following sub-section of this chapter.

Notwithstanding the apparent comprehensiveness of labour regulation in Australia, recent argument based on secondary sources and empirical studies indicates underlying similarities between the Australian system and those of other common law countries across several sets of indicators.[94] One example is the issue of job security. Comparatively speaking employment protection laws were introduced relatively late in Australia, and over recent years they have been to some extent stripped back in terms of their coverage and effectiveness.[95] The Australian laws have been consistently ranked in the least effective group of OECD nations in terms of employment protection, roughly on a par with Britain, the US and Canada.[96] These rankings are generally borne out in terms of average job tenure, where Australian figures relate more closely to those of the US rather than to the co-ordinated systems of Germany and Japan.[97]

In the area of wages, we have noted the effectiveness of the award system in securing widespread attainment of minimum pay and conditions across the

R. Mitchell and P. Scherer, 'Australia: The Search for Fair Employment Contracts through Tribunals' in J. Hartog and J. Theeuwes (eds), *Labour Market Contracts and Institutions*, Elsevier Science Publishers, Amsterdam, 1993, p. 80.

94   See M. Jones and R. Mitchell, 'Legal Origin, Legal Families and the Regulation of Labour in Australia' in Marshall et al., *Varieties of Capitalism, Corporate Governance and Employees*, above n. 1, p. 60. The indicators (work relations, employment relations and industrial relations) are drawn from Gospel and Pendleton's study of the connections between corporate governance and labour management systems: see H. Gospel and A. Pendleton (eds), *Corporate Governance and Labour Management: An International Study*, Oxford University Press, Oxford, 2005, ch. 1.

95   For a brief history see Creighton and Stewart, above n. 74, pp. 450–455.

96   *OECD Employment Outlook*, OECD, Paris, 2004, ch. 2.

97   See Jones and Mitchell, above n. 94, pp. 73–74.

labour market. Historically this was also associated with less pay flexibility at the enterprise level, and more compressed income differentials between groups. It is also important to note, however, that historically there was scope within the system for market-based wage variations, and performance-based pay systems, and that these have continued to expand as the centralised award system has declined in favour of an enterprise-based bargaining system.[98]

Comparing functional flexibility within work systems is also instructive. Labour practices in the co-ordinated market systems (relational/insider) is associated with flexible employment and greater employee involvement/empowerment in the production process. As noted earlier, the Australian award system, historically, came to be deeply associated with work rigidities and restrictive practices rather than flexibility.[99] The arrival of the job-redesign movement in the 1970s was followed by a series of ideas focussed on workplace culture and production systems, including the 'post-Fordist' and 'best practice' concepts.[100] Principal impetus for work system change of this order came through new principles adopted by the Australian industrial tribunals which began to extend wage increases on the condition of increased flexibility in the work process and a broadening of job definitions and employee skills.[101]

The research covering the early period of these developments seems to suggest that not very much came of the job-redesign movement. Few firms adopted these initiatives, and those that did tended to embrace only a select few elements rather than embark upon a complete redesign programme.[102] Evidence from the Australian Workplace Industrial Relations Surveys (1990 and 1995) suggests that there was an upsurge of work restructuring measures in about one-third of workplaces in the period from the late 1980s through to the first half of the 1990s involving such practices as job-redesign, quality circles, team work, semi-autonomous work groups and so on. In a general sense these various practices appeared to exhibit greater employee involvement in the design and operation of work systems.[103] There is, however, considerable reservation in the literature over how systematic and extensive these changes have been in the Australian workplace environment. Importantly much of the research casts doubt on the extent to which job-redesign engaged with employee empowerment. Rather it suggests that the process has tended to broaden job descriptions and the scope of employment tasks, but at

---

98   Ibid., pp. 75–79.

99   See Mitchell and Rimmer, above n. 92, pp. 13–15.

100   A leading exponent in Australia is John Mathews: see *Tools of Change: New Technology and the Democratisation of Work*, Pluto Press, Sydney, 1989; *Catching the Wave: Workplace Reform in Australia*, Allen & Unwin, Sydney, 1994.

101   The 'Structural Efficiency Principle': see Creighton et al., above n. 84, pp. 718–728.

102   See C. Wright, *The Management of Labour. A History of Australian Employers*, Oxford University Press, Melbourne, 1995, pp. 154–182.

103   Jones and Mitchell, above n. 94, p. 80.

the same time to redistribute power away from employees towards employers, in fact strengthening managerial prerogative over work systems.[104] This trend is antithetical to the supposed role of worker involvement in the co-ordinated market economies.

But perhaps the most important feature distinguishing Australian labour market regulation from most 'insider' or 'co-ordinated' market systems is found in the nature of employer–union relations and the influence of formalised employee voice within enterprises. Historically Australian labour law and its institutions were organised around the idea of fundamental conflict between employers and workers.[105] As we have noted in earlier discussion there are aspects of this system which may have taken on the appearance of an 'insider' system. For example, widespread recognition of trade unions enabled them, although under tribunal supervision and in a centralised way, to act as co-regulators of industry with employers.

But these powers were perhaps not as far reaching as they might seem. They did not empower unions and employees with much influence over managerial prerogatives, nor did the system develop into a kind of 'corporatist' co-operative-style of capital/labour relations that has characterised many European systems.[106] The fact that the compulsory arbitration system required unions to manufacture an industrial dispute in order to improve or vary employment conditions, and that this often occurred on a national, occupational or regional basis, tended to exacerbate what was already an adversarial conflict-based system and at the same time to detract from an enterprise-based focus in workplace regulation.

Finally, when it comes to the issue of 'institutionalised' employee voice, the Australian system has offered little in the way of devices which are highly characteristic of the 'insider' co-ordinated market systems. As we have noted, whilst unions were highly integrated within the system overall, arbitration in operation narrowed the scope of collective bargaining to a legalistic interpretation

---

104   See Jones and Mitchell, above n. 94, pp. 80–81; M. Rimmer and J. Zappala, 'Labour Market Flexibility and the Second Tier' (1988) 14 *Australian Bulletin of Labour* 564; B. Harley, 'Post-Fordist Theory, Labour Process and Flexibility and Autonomy in Australian Workplaces' (1994) 6 *Labour and Industry* 107; A. Roan, T. Bramble and G. Lafferty, 'Australian Workplace Agreements in Practice: The "Hard" and "Soft" Dimensions' (2001) 43 *Journal of Industrial Relations* 387; R. Mitchell and J. Fetter, 'Human Resource Management and Individualisation in Australian Labour Law' (2003) 45 *Journal of Industrial Relations* 292; C. Allan, M. O'Donnell and D. Peetz, 'More Tasks, Less Secure, Working Harder: Three Dimensions of Labour Utilisation' (1999) 41 *Journal of Industrial Relations* 519.

105   See Macintyre and Mitchell, above n. 76; K. Walker, *Australian Industrial Relations Systems*, Harvard University Press, Cambridge, MA, 1970, pp. 8–11.

106   See Wright, above n. 102, p. 109; A. McIvor and C. Wright, 'Managing Labour: UK and Australian Employers in Comparative Perspective, 1900–1950' (2005) 88 *Labour History* 45; G. Palmer, 'Corporatism and Australian Arbitration' in Macintyre and Mitchell, above n. 76, 313.

of 'industrial matters' which effectively excluded employee voice from many aspects of managerial decision-making. In the period following the Second World War there was a growth in employee voice mechanisms under various influences including US-style management theories and the industrial democracy push in the 1970s. Very little seems to have resulted from these initiatives. Nor did the period of award restructuring in the late 1980s and early 1990s have much impact. Data drawn from the Australian Workplace Industrial Workplace Surveys in 1990 and 1995 indicate that while there was some growth in formal representative institutions in enterprises, less than one-third of private sector workplaces had such arrangements, and only 4 per cent indicated the presence of employee representation on the company's board of management.[107]

Whether or not the process of enterprise bargaining has done much to develop institutions of employee voice at the workplace over the past decade is questionable. There is evidence that there has been a proliferation of joint committees and work council-styled bodies in Australian workplaces.[108] However, most researchers see these institutions as predominantly creations of management in terms of structure and powers, rather than as genuine power-sharing arrangements, and this situation has been compounded by a series of legislative interventions which have stripped back most consultative arrangements from the award system.[109]

Generally, then, what we can say is that the Australian system of labour market regulation historically shaped markets and imbued employment systems within companies with some characteristics which might rank the model more closely

---

107   See Wright, above n. 102, pp. 58, 127, 142–143, 202; R. Callus, A. Morehead, M. Steele, M. Cully and J. Buchanan, *Industrial Relations at Work*, Australian Government Publishing Service, Canberra, 1991, pp. 124–128; A. Morehead, M. Steele, M. Alexander, K. Stephen and L. Duffin, *Changes at Work: 1995 Australian Industrial Relations Survey*, Longman, Melbourne, 1997, pp. 188–190; Australian Centre for Industrial Relations Research and Teaching, *Australia at Work: Just Managing?*, Prentice Hall, Sydney, 1999, p. 24.

108   See A. Forsyth, S. Korman and S. Marshall, 'Joint Consultative Committees in Australia: An Empirical Update' (2008) 16 *International Journal of Employment Studies* 99.

109   R. Markey, 'The State of Representative Participation in Australia: Where to Next?' (2004) 20 *International Journal of Comparative Labour Law and Industrial Relations* 533; R. Mitchell, R. Naughton and R. Sorensen, 'The Law and Employee Participation: Evidence from the Federal Enterprise Agreements Process' (1997) 39 *Journal of Industrial Relations* 196; Forsyth et al., ibid.; Mitchell and Fetter, above n. 104; S. Marshall and R. Mitchell, 'Enterprise Bargaining, Managerial Prerogative and the Protection of Worker's Rights: An Argument on the Role of Law and Regulatory Strategy in Australia Under the *Workplace Relations Act 1996* (Cth.)' (2006) 22 *International Journal of Comparative Labour Law and Industrial Relations* 299; P. Gahan, R. Mitchell, K. Creighton, T. Josev, J. Fetter and D. Buttigieg, 'Regulating for Performance? Certified Agreements and the Diffusion of High Performance Work Practices', paper presented to the 2nd Australian Labour Law Association National Conference, University of Sydney, September 2004.

with the 'co-ordinated' rather than the 'liberal market' economies. A more centrally regulated pay system,[110] less pay dispersion among classes of workers and greater workforce coverage than was the norm in 'liberal market' economies are obvious examples. On the other hand there are very important characteristics which are more clearly associated with the market economies of the UK, the US and Canada. These would include, most obviously, the absence of any appreciable systematised power sharing and collaboration in labour market regulation at the social level and in work and employment systems within enterprises.

The Trajectory of Australian Labour Law

Over the past three decades or so, neo-liberalism, with its emphasis on deregulation, flexibility and decentralisation in employment relations, has come to dominate debate over industrial regulation in Australia as elsewhere.[111] The consequence of this domination has been the steady evolution of Australian labour law in a deregulatory direction from about the mid-1980s onwards. Such deregulation has not brought to an end the extensive interventionist role of the state in Australian labour law. On the contrary the volume of regulatory provisions in the form of legislation, schedules, statutory regulations and forms governing the labour market has grown considerably throughout this period.[112] The present central piece of regulation, the Australian Federal Coalition government's *Workplace Relations Act 1996*, as amended by the same government's *Work Choices* legislation in 2005,[113] again by the same government's new independent contractor legislation and safety-net provisions,[114] and then amended again by the newly elected Labor government's Forward with Fairness legislation of 2008,[115] is currently comprised of over 900 sections, nine schedules (to the Act), eight chapters of regulations (to the Act), and eight schedules to the regulations consisting of various forms and so on.

---

110   See Jones and Mitchell, above n. 94, pp. 70–71.

111   See generally D. Nolan (ed.), *The Australasian Labour Law Reforms: Australia & New Zealand at the End of the Twentieth Century*, The Federation Press, Sydney, 1998; S. Deery and R. Mitchell (eds), *Employment Relations: Individualisation and Union Exclusion*, The Federation Press, Sydney, 1999; J. Isaac and R. Lansbury (eds), *Labour Market Deregulation: Rewriting the Rules*, The Federation Press, Sydney, 2005. For an account of the similar process in the UK see Deakin and Wilkinson, above n. 6.

112   See A. Stewart, 'A Simple Plan for Reform? The Problem of Complexity in Workplace Regulation' (2005) 31 *Australian Bulletin of Labour* 210.

113   *Workplace Relations Amendment (Work Choices) Act 2005*.

114   *Workplace Relations Legislation Amendment (Independent Contractors) Act 2006*; *Workplace Relations Amendment (A Stronger Safety Net) Act 2007*. On the latter see C. Sutherland, 'All Stitched Up? The 2007 Amendments to the Safety Net' (2007) 20 *Australian Journal of Labour Law* 245.

115   *Workplace Relations Amendment (Transition to Forward with Fairness) Act 2008*. For analysis see A. Forsyth, B. Creighton, V. Gostencnik and T. Sharard, *Transition to Forward with Fairness: Labor's Reform Agenda*, Thompson Lawbook Co., Sydney, 2008.

'Deregulation' thus has not meant less law or less regulation, nor has it meant less complexity in regulation. If there is consensus over anything associated with the legislation of the past two decades it is that it is forbiddingly complex.[116] What 'deregulation' has meant is a different style of regulation, one which has as its principal purpose the object of easing the regulatory burden imposed upon companies and other businesses to allow for more flexibility. Deregulation is thus taken to mean more flexibility as against greater rigidity in regulation (not less regulation per se), and in turn more flexibility is taken to signify the prospect of greater efficiency in the operation of labour markets and employment systems.

There have been two main themes in this 'flexibilisation'-through-deregulation process. One has been the 'de-collectivisation' of employment relations. In this strategy Australian labour law in large part has mirrored the policies of other liberalising states, such as the UK and the US,[117] with the substantial diminution of the role of trade unions as co-regulators in the industrial relations process.[118] Equally importantly, in Australia the de-collectivisation process has also involved the wholesale reduction in influence of the compulsory arbitration tribunals which, as we noted, have historically characterised the Australian system of labour regulation.[119] The weakening of these two sets of collective institutions, at least prior to 2008, brought about a revolution in employment standard setting, shifting the process from a centralised one based on externally mandated reasonably uniform national, industry- or occupational-wide standards to market-based, self-regulated standards particular to single enterprises or individual persons.[120]

The second, obviously related, theme was the substantial reduction in the absolute number of state-mandated employment standards, principally through the

---

116   See A. Stewart, 'Work Choices in Overview: Big Bang or Slow Burn?' (2006) 16 *Economic and Labour Relations Review* 25, pp. 26–27.

117   See, for example, L. Bennett, 'The American Model of Labour Law in Australia' (1992) 5 *Australian Journal of Labour Law* 135; R. McCallum, 'Plunder Downunder: Transplanting the Anglo-American Labor Law Model to Australia' (2005) 26 *Comparative Labor Law and Policy Journal* 381.

118   See R. McCallum, 'Trade Union Recognition and Australia's Neo-Liberal Voluntary Bargaining Laws' (2002) 57 *Relations Industrielles* 225; A. Forsyth and C. Sutherland, 'From "Uncharted Seas" to "Stormy Waters": How Will Trade Unions Fare Under the Work Choices Legislation?' (2006) 16 *Economics and Labour Relations Review* 215.

119   See A. Forsyth, 'Arbitration Extinguished: The Impact of the Work Choices Legislation on the Australian Industrial Relations Commission' (2006) 32 *Australian Business Law Review* 27.

120   See A. Forsyth, 'Decentralisation and "Deregulation" of Labour Relations Through "Ultra-Regulation": Australia's 2005 Labour Law Reforms' in S. Ouchi and T. Araki (eds), *Decentralising Industrial Relations: The Role of Labour Unions and Employee Representatives*, Kluwer Law International, Deventer, 2007; P. Waring and J. Burgess, 'WorkChoices: The Privileging of Individualism in Australian Industrial Relations' (2006) 14 *International Journal of Employment Studies* 61.

elimination of award terms and some statutory rights. Whereas in previous eras Australian employees were protected by a raft of minimum standards of employment, substantive and procedural, such was the withdrawal by the state from this process that the great majority of employees were now absolutely guaranteed five minimum conditions only, in the form of the *Workplace Relations Act*'s 'Australian Fair Pay and Conditions Standard'(s),[121] (new legislation has now partly rectified this position).

Thus, the idea that liberalised 'free' labour markets are more efficient than regulated ones (and particularly more efficient than those as heavily regulated as the Australian labour market) has helped propel a revision in Australian labour law so as to permit (or even compel) labour market participants (employers, employees and other workers) to regulate themselves according to the operation of the market pressures upon them. Whether labour markets are able to operate effectively and efficiently without legal and institutional support for employees is a source of great controversy.[122] However it is not necessary for us to deal with this issue here, perhaps other than to note that it does not appear that many of the new Australian labour laws were put in place to correct 'market failures' so much as to remove regulatory impediments to managerial- or market-based regulation.[123]

More importantly for our purposes here, it is necessary to isolate what this experience with 'deregulation' has meant for the relationships between Australian employers, shareholders, employees and other classes of workers. We suggest that the type of labour law change embodied in the 'deregulation' concept has brought about two significant changes to labour market ordering and workplace governance. These are related to each other and, in turn, have obvious implications for the corporate governance/workplace partnerships issue.[124]

First, 'deregulation' in labour law has effected a wholesale shift in labour market and workplace power from labour to management in the form of enhanced managerial authority and prerogative.[125] Second, the same process of 'deregulation'

---

121   See C. Fenwick, 'How Low Can You Go? Minimum Working Conditions Under Australia's New Labour Laws' (2006) 16 *Economic and Labour Relations Review* 85; S. Cooney, J. Howe and J. Murray, 'Time and Money Under WorkChoices: Understanding the New Workplace Relations Act as a Scheme of Regulation' (2006) 29 *University of New South Wales Law Journal* 215.

122   See Deakin and Wilkinson, above n. 6, pp. 278–294; H. Collins, 'Justifications and Techniques of Legal Regulation of the Employment Relation' in H. Collins, P. Davies and R. Rideout (eds), *Legal Regulation of the Employment Relation*, Kluwer Law International, London, 2000, p. 3.

123   Compare the arguments about the UK: Deakin and Wilkinson, above n. 6, p. 276; Collins et al., ibid., pp. 3–27; H. Collins, *Employment Law*, Oxford University Press, Oxford, 2003, ch. 2.

124   For a preliminary assessment see R. Mitchell, A. O'Donnell and I. Ramsay, 'Shareholder Value and Employee Interests: Intersections Between Corporate Governance, Corporate Law and Labor Law' (2005) 23 *Wisconsin International Law Journal* 417.

125   See I. Campbell, 'Labour Market Flexibility in Australia: Enhanced Managerial Prerogative' (1993) 5 *Labour and Industry* 11; M. Bray and P. Waring, 'The Rise of

has enabled management to engage in various cost-cutting strategies as a form of business competition. The key outcome of the deregulatory strategy in Australian labour law in cost terms is that it enables the reduction of the price of labour, either through the lowering of pay and conditions, or the shifting of risk from employer to worker through one or other forms of restructuring of work relationships.[126]

Of course, the labour law changes referred to do not necessitate a cost reduction strategy; employers have been free to compete on the basis of an innovative, high cost, high quality programme. However, the diminution of the protective shield, and particularly the pecuniary level at which it is to be maintained (for example, safety-net rather than market-guided minimum rates),[127] coupled with the various organisational arrangements through which labour is now permitted to be engaged (performance-based, contracted, short-term, casual, franchised or outsourced labour, rather than salaried, full time, permanent labour)[128] has enabled, perhaps encouraged, such an approach. Whilst the extent to which these strategies are being employed in Australia is unclear, there is plenty of evidence to suggest that cost minimisation is a preferred strategy in some industries and businesses,[129] and that both co-operative/innovative strategies and cost reduction strategies can exist within industries and even within the same business organisation.[130]

One further element should be taken account of in understanding the recent trajectory of Australian labour law. This concerns the important ideological shift in state-based regulation away from systemically-legitimised adversarialism between two opposed parties in industry towards a systemically-encouraged co-operation between employers and labour.[131]

Managerial Prerogative Under the Howard Government' (2006) 32 *Australian Bulletin of Labour* 45; Mitchell and Fetter, above n. 104.

126   On these various restructuring strategies see M. Quinlan, 'Contextual Factors Shaping the Purpose of Labour Law'; M. Rawling, 'A Generic Model of Regulating Supply Chain Outsourcing'; S. Marshall, 'An Exploration of Control in the Context of Vertical Disintegration'; and J. Riley, 'Regulating Unequal Work Relationships for Fairness and Efficiency: A Study of Business Format Franchising', all in C. Arup, P. Gahan, J. Howe, R. Johnstone, R. Mitchell and A. O'Donnell (eds), *Labour Law and Labour Market Regulation*, The Federation Press, Sydney, 2006, pp. 21, 520, 542 and 561 respectively.

127   See Fenwick, above n. 121.

128   On contracting arrangements and the reach of labour law see A. Forsyth, 'The 2006 Independent Contractors Legislation: An Opportunity Missed' (2007) 35 *Federal Law Review* 329.

129   Roan et al., above n. 104; C. Briggs and R. Cooper, 'Between Individualism and Collectivism? Why Employers Choose Non-Union Collective Agreements' (2006) 17 *Labour and Industry* 1.

130   See, for example, M. Jones, S. Marshall and R. Mitchell, 'Corporate Social Responsibility and the Management of Labour in Two Australian Mining Industry Companies' (2007) 15 *Corporate Governance: An International Review* 57.

131   For discussion see R. Mitchell and A. O'Donnell, 'What is Labour Law Doing About "Partnership at Work"? British and Australian Developments Compared' in Marshall

The decline of the protective model   In our earlier discussion of the character of Australian labour law we noted that historically the system was concerned with two core functions: the imposition of protective standards for workers, and the support for collective governance structures in industry. Minimum standards of employment, the recognition of trade unions, and regulation through industrial tribunals were the institutional features of a system designed to stabilise industry and to effect what was perceived to be a desirable level of redistribution from capital to labour in line with periodic notions of the public interest.

This system has been under a process of reform since about the mid-1980s. Although the factors which gave rise to this pressure for reform have remained fairly constant (for example, the need to re-open the Australian economy to the global market, with corresponding pressures to revise employment relations to enhance competitive capacity), the approach to reform may be seen as falling into two different periods. In the period from the mid-1980s to the mid-1990s change under the (then) Labor government was important, perhaps revolutionary, in some respects.[132] However, there was no attempt to alter the core values of the system – protective standards and collective regulation remained paramount. Importantly there was little attempt fundamentally to revoke the statutory framework of the compulsory arbitration system, with much of the reform taking place through the award (sub-legislative) level of regulation.[133] The slow, hesitant, progress of reform at this stage is extensively documented in the labour law literature.[134]

The second period of reform, which takes in the labour law policies of the Liberal-National Party Coalition government from the *Workplace Relations Act 1996* through to the *Workplace Relations (Work Choices) Act 2005*, was qualitatively different in purpose. This period of reform was associated with a major revision by the Australian government of the core objectives of the system, the withdrawal of support for the system's traditional institutions, and a major recasting of the system's legislative framework. It is thus with respect to these two pieces of legislation, and the consequent shifting and reordering of employment practices in the period between them, to which we must turn in making an assessment of what an 'effective rationale'[135] might be for comprehending the modern function

---

et al., *Varieties of Capitalism, Corporate Governance and Employees*, above n. 1, p. 95.

132   Particularly in the promotion of enterprise bargaining, including bargaining without the necessary involvement of trade unions, in the provisions of the *Industrial Relations Reform Act 1993*: see generally Creighton and Stewart, above n. 74, pp. 56–57.

133   See Mitchell and Rimmer, above n. 92.

134   R. Mitchell, 'Labour Law Under Labor: The Industrial Relations Bill 1988 and Labour Market Reform' (1988) 1 *Labour and Industry* 486; Mitchell and Rimmer, above n. 92; Mitchell and Naughton, above n. 92; R. Naughton, 'The New Bargaining Regime Under the Industrial Relations Reform Act' (1994) 7 *Australian Journal of Labour Law* 147; J. Ludeke, 'The Structural Features of the New System' (1994) 7 *Australian Journal of Labour Law* 132; G. McCarry, 'Sanctions and Industrial Action: The Impact of the Industrial Relations Reform Act' (1994) 7 *Australian Journal of Labour Law* 198.

135   See Deakin and Wilkinson, above n. 6, p. 274.

of Australian labour law, and what implications this has for corporate shareholder and employee relations.[136]

We can commence with the notion of co-operation. The trajectory of labour law in Australia clearly reflects the rejection by the state of the structured adversarialism which was the hallmark of the labour law systems of Australia and the other Anglo-American capitalist states for most of the twentieth century. In its place has emerged the idea that Australian workplaces would be more innovative, more productive and more efficient if relations between employers and workers were co-operative rather than conflictual in nature.[137]

The most obvious direct manifestation of this ideological restatement of purpose is found in the objects of the *Workplace Relations Act 1996*, where the Act's principal object was stated to provide 'a framework for cooperative workplace relations'.[138] A subsequent object of the Act was to support 'harmonious and productive workplace relations by providing flexible mechanisms for the voluntary settlement of disputes'.[139] It has been noted, however, that beyond these largely rhetorical devices, the legislative base of Australian labour law contains little if any explicit requirement or encouragement for the support of co-operative practices though, again, this has been partly rectified through new legislation.[140]

Outside of direct legislative promotion, however, there are other ways in which the traditional adversarial industrial relations system has been dismantled through labour law change. These include the abolition of automatic access to dispute settlement through compulsory conciliation and arbitration, which means that there is no longer scope for the systematised adversarialism organised around union logs of claims, tribunal hearings and the award decision process which historically characterised Australian industrial relations. At the same time union power has been severely weakened by the removal of legislative supports,

---

136   It must be acknowledged that there has been something of a retreat from some aspects of the *Work Choices* legislation, both by the Coalition government towards the end of its period in office (*Workplace Relations Amendment (A Stronger Safety Net) Act 2007*) and then by the Labor government (*Workplace Relations Amendment (Transition to Forward with Fairness) Act 2008; Fair Work Act 2009*).

137   Characterised in the UK in the 'Partnerships at Work' agenda, and in the US by the 'mutual gains' idea: see generally Mitchell and O'Donnell, above n. 131.

138   Section 3 of the Act. For background on the development of these policy concepts see Business Council of Australia, Industrial Relations Study Commission, *Enterprise-Based Bargaining Units: A Better Way of Working*, Business Council of Australia, Melbourne, 1989; and *Working Relations; A Fresh Start for Australian Enterprises*, Business Council of Australia, Melbourne, 1992.

139   Section 3 (h).

140   *Fair Work Act 2009*, sections 3, 171, 205. See Mitchell and Fetter, above n. 104, pp. 299–301; Mitchell and O'Donnell, above n. 131. In this respect the Australian position is somewhat distinguishable from the position in the UK where the policy of promoting 'Partnership at Work' has received some statutory support: see Mitchell and O'Donnell, above n. 131.

including severe restrictions on the right to strike, earlier extended to unions as recognised agents in the bargaining process, and as a consequence their capacity to act as oppositional organisations has been substantially curtailed.[141] Where unions retained extraordinary power in particular industries, such as building, these too were attacked through industry-specific legislation.[142]

In the absence of serious regulatory support for co-operative practices at work,[143] the quality of co-operative enterprise relations in Australia seems largely to be a matter of managerial making. The Australian evidence seems to indicate overwhelmingly that whilst the language of 'co-operation' between the parties has important rhetorical value in business enterprises (particularly in enterprise agreements), it is not effective in the construction of workplace partnerships which would reconstitute the idea and purpose of corporate governance.[144] This understanding of partnership bears strong similarity with Deakin and Wilkinson's

---

141   See Mitchell and O'Donnell, above n. 131, pp. 112–113; A. Stewart and A. Forsyth, 'Introduction' in A. Forsyth, J. Howe and A. Stewart, *Australian Labour Law: From 'Work Choices' to 'Fair Work'*, The Federation Press, Sydney, 2009; A. Forsyth and C. Sutherland, 'Collective Labour Relations Under Siege: The Work Choices Legislation and Collective Bargaining' (2006) 19 *Australian Journal of Labour Law* 183; S. McCrystal, 'Smothering the Right to Strike: Work Choices and Industrial Action' (2006) 19 *Australian Journal of Labour Law* 198.

142   *Building and Construction Industry Improvement Act 2005*. For background and discussion see T. Cole, *Final Report of the Royal Commission into the Building and Construction Industry*, Commonwealth of Australia, Canberra, 2003; A. Forsyth, V. Gostencnik, I. Ross and T. Sharard, *Workplace Relations in the Building and Construction Industry*, LexisNexis Butterworths, Sydney, 2007; J. Howe, '"Deregulation" of Labour Relations in Australia: Towards a More "Centred" Command and Control Model' in Arup et al., above n. 126, 147.

143   For discussion of different types of non-legislative programmes designed to develop co-operative workplace cultures see J. Howe, 'The Role of "Light Touch" Labour Regulation in Advancing Employee Participation in Corporate Governance: The Case of "Partners at Work"' in Marshall et al., *Varieties of Capitalism, Corporate Governance and Employees*, above n. 1, p. 277; A. Forsyth and J. Howe, 'Current Initiatives to Encourage Fair and Cooperative Workplace Practices: An International Survey', Report for the Victorian Office of the Workplace Rights Advocate, Workplace and Corporate Law Research Group, Monash University/Centre for Employment and Labour Relations Law, University of Melbourne, Melbourne, 2008.

144   See Mitchell and Fetter, above n. 104; Roan et al., above n. 104; Marshall and Mitchell, above n. 109; Gahan et al., above n. 109; Jones and Mitchell, above n. 94; P. Gahan, 'Employer Greenfield Agreements in Victoria', Research Report prepared for the Victorian Office of the Workplace Rights Advocate, Work and Employment Rights Research Centre, Monash University, Melbourne, 2007; P. Gahan, 'Employer Greenfields Agreements in Queensland', Research Report prepared for the Queensland Department of Employment and Industrial Relations, Work and Employment Rights Research Centre, Monash University, Melbourne, 2007.

interpretation of Stephen Wood's view of the British approach:[145] 'the strong emphasis is on the need for workers to make far-reaching commitments to their employer's business interests and objectives, and to mould themselves to its needs'.[146]

As we noted earlier in this discussion, scope for managerial direction of workplace governance has been considerably enhanced by the strengthening of managerial prerogative in Australian workplaces through changing labour law regulation. That is to say, that much of the decision-making internal to the business enterprise which managers previously shared with unions and workers has now been reassigned by law to managers alone. This has been an important shift,[147] for while labour law never radically realigned corporate decision-making structures and processes in the Anglo-American styled business organisation, it did place limitations on the ability of managers to exploit cheap labour and various labour hire options, thus placing some barriers against the alignment of the business with unconstrained shareholder interests.

The impact of the *Workplace Relations Act 1996* on managerial prerogative was most immediately apparent in the award simplification process embodied in section 89A of the Act[148] which has been described as 'a legislative reaffirmation of managerial prerogative, and ... an explicit repudiation of any notion that the award system could provide a vehicle for the democratisation of work'.[149] Most clauses in awards which limited the ability of managers to hire, or contract with, particular forms of labour were removed in this process, as were award provisions requiring union involvement in various decisions at the enterprise level. At the same time the weakening of the power of trade unions[150] and employees relative to employers, meant that there was little or no redistribution of power away from employers to labour in the terms of industrial agreements. As we noted earlier, the evidence suggests that essential managerial prerogatives were largely uncompromised in the process of negotiating agreements and recent judicial determination did cast some doubt on the legal capacity of agreement making under the Act to do otherwise even if labour's industrial power were much greater.[151] The *Work Choices* legislation of 2005 took this restoration of managerial prerogative even further. In this set of

---

145   See S. Wood, 'From Voluntarism to Partnership: A Third Way Overview of the Public Policy Debate in British Industrial Relations' in Collins et al., above n. 122, p. 111.

146   Deakin and Wilkinson, above n. 6, p. 327.

147   See Mitchell et al., above n. 124, p. 459.

148   For an early exploration of the implications of the provision see M. Pittard, 'Collective Employment Relationships: Reforms to Arbitrated Awards and Certified Agreements' (1997) 10 *Australian Journal of Labour Law* 62.

149   See Creighton and Stewart, above n. 74, p. 176.

150   Bray and Waring, above n. 125, p. 53.

151   *Electrolux Home Products Pty Ltd v Australian Workers' Union* (2004) 209 ALR 116: see further M. Pittard, 'Agreements Straying Beyond Employment Matters: The Impact of the Agreement Validation Matters Legislation' (2005) 18 *Australian Journal of Labour Law* 71.

changes the capacity for employers to set wages and working hours unilaterally was greatly increased, and some groups of employers were given much greater powers to dismiss employees without cause or justification.[152] *Work Choices* also specifically proscribed certain matters of workplace governance from inclusion in industrial agreements even in instances where employers wished to have such matters included.[153]

One final point in the decline of the protective model concerns the reduction of employment standards. It would seem that one of the core rationales in the 'deregulation' of employment systems is to permit business enterprises to increase or reduce labour standards according to market pressures.[154] There are still minimum levels of pay and conditions, but these are fewer in number than was the case under the old award system,[155] and they are now set at safety-net levels rather than at de facto market levels. With the introduction of *Work Choices* in 2005 the stripping back of minimum standards was particularly accelerated, especially in non-union forms of agreements.[156] This statutory labour law policy was matched by human resource policies within business enterprises which one could see in work agreements of all types and which increasingly made pay levels contingent rather than guaranteed, including performance-based pay, bonus schemes and share-ownership schemes for core employees, and standby/no guaranteed work/ income for other forms of labour.[157]

Co-operation, partnership and governance in business enterprises If labour law is retreating from its historically established 'protective' function, is it, at the same time, constructing a framework for the development of labour management systems which depart from hierarchical 'top-down' systems of management to flatter structures incorporating higher degrees of employee collaboration and involvement in workplace decision-making? Intuitively it might be expected that the legal restoration of substantial numbers of workplace matters to managerial

---

152   See Bray and Waring, above n. 125; Fenwick, above n. 121; Cooney et al., above n. 121.

153   See Stewart, above n. 116, p. 35; S. Cooney, 'Command and Control in the Workplace: Agreement Making Under Work Choices' (2006) 16 *Economic and Labour Relations Review* 147, p. 155.

154   Fenwick, above n. 121.

155   However, there has been some reversal of this policy under the Labor government: see CCH, *Understanding Forward With Fairness: A Practical Guide to the New Workplace Relations System*, Sydney, 2008, pp. 19–27.

156   See D. Peetz, 'Assessing the Impact of "Workchoices" – One Year On', Report to the Department of Innovation, Industry and Regional Development, Victoria, 2007. However, the Liberal/National Coalition government of the day was forced to backtrack a little from this extreme position by re-introducing a form of 'no-disadvantage' test in the *Workplace Relations Amendment (A Stronger Safety Net) Act 2007*: for discussion see Sutherland, above n. 114.

157   See, for example, the works cited in n. 129.

prerogative would tend to rule out this possibility, but there is no categorical reason why strong management would not move to the adoption of high performance workplace systems, or high involvement workplace systems, in line with more progressive human resource policies.[158] As we have noted, there has been nothing introduced in labour law to compel or induce enterprises to reform managerial structures and processes or work systems to adapt to more co-operative workplace relations.[159] Nor do internationally-based ideas like corporate social responsibility appear necessarily to make much difference in practice.[160] Indicatively, the trend in Australian labour law on this issue seems to be heading in the opposite direction even to the very mild initiatives of the British Labour government's statutory union recognition policy.[161]

On the other hand, there is scope for the development of progressive systems where management deems it valuable to pursue such policies. However the evidence on this is uncertain, and suggests that generally speaking the evolution of new or innovative workplace cultures based on co-operation is very limited. There is little case study evidence on the extent to which businesses have adopted 'high performance' or 'high involvement' work practices which is anything other than equivocal in terms of outcomes.[162]

At a formal level, the evidence also suggests that power sharing through employee involvement in decision-making is relatively confined in terms of its

---

158   See on these systems, A. Kalleberg and J. Moody, 'Human Resource Management and Organisational Performance' (1994) 37 *American Behavioural Scientist* 948; K. Whitfield and M. Poole, 'Organising Employment for High Performance: Theories, Evidence, and Policy' (1997) 18 *Organization Studies* 745; P. Edwards and M. Wright, 'High Involvement Work Systems and Performance Outcomes: The Strength of Variable, Contingent and Context-Bound Relationships' (2001) 12 *International Journal of Human Resource Management* 568.

159   Some new provisions in corporate law impose additional duties upon the controllers of companies in respect of some employee entitlements. These do not effect any change in the structure of corporate governance: see S. Bottomley and A. Forsyth, 'The New Corporate Law: Corporate Social Responsibility and Employees' Interests' in D. McBarnet, A. Voiculesco and T. Campbell (eds), *The New Corporate Accountability: Corporate Social Responsibility and the Law*, Cambridge University Press, Cambridge, 2007, p. 307.

160   See, for example, M. Jones, S. Marshall and R. Mitchell, 'Corporate Social Responsibility and the Management of Labour in Two Australian Mining Industry Companies' (2007) 15 *Corporate Governance: An International Review* 57.

161   Described by two British scholars as 'a relatively weak influence on the development of cooperative work relations when set against the context of wider constraints on partnership at work': Deakin and Wilkinson, above n. 6, p. 336.

162   Some examples include D. Rosser, P. Todd and R. Fells, 'Implementation of the Employment Relations Aspects of the Best Practice Programme: A Case Study Approach', and R. Lansbury and G. Bamber, 'Making Cars in Australia: New Models of Work and Production?' both in L. Sonder (ed.), *Current Research in Industrial Relations*, Proceedings of the 9th AIRAANZ Conference, Melbourne, 1995.

scope and extent. After 1996 a considerable amount of legislative change occurred to limit the possibility of forms of power sharing at the workplace. For example, the *Workplace Relations Act 1996* removed the legislative requirement for parties to an enterprise agreement to consult with each other over changes to the organisation or performance of work.[163] The 1996 Act also replaced 1993 provisions aimed at promoting the growth of consultative practices in the enterprise bargaining process with minimal requirements for informing employees about the terms of proposed agreements under negotiation.

As we noted earlier in this discussion the process of award 'simplification', which was legislatively introduced into the terms of the 1996 Act, had considerable negative implications for the protection of workers and unions. One of the important effects of the operation of section 89A of the Act was that workplace consultation in general became a 'non-allowable award matter', with the consequence that virtually all award provisions requiring consultation over technological change and redundancies, along with award provisions for information sharing and the establishment and operation of consultative committees, were required to be removed from awards.[164]

The expansion of labour-management co-operation through enterprise bargaining, we have seen, still remains open for exploration by the parties, but most research suggests that whilst the incidence of consultative mechanisms has undoubtedly expanded considerably over the past two decades, this has resulted in very little genuine expansion of power and information sharing between management and labour as compared with managerially controlled employment systems, processes and institutions.[165]

2.4 Conclusion

Our focus here has been upon the law relating to companies and financial markets, and the law regulating labour markets and employment systems. In our view the discussion raises interesting points for exploration in an Australian context. Although the 'legal origin' discourse has seemingly made few inroads into discussion about the Australian legal system, some scholars have already noted

---

163 Again, this position has been altered in subsequent legislation. We are relying here on Forsyth et al., above n. 108.

164 A similar weakening of the formal mechanisms for management-union consultation occurred in the Australian Public Service: see P. Weeks, 'Reconstituting the Employment Relationship in the Australian Public Service' in Deery and Mitchell, above n. 111, p. 69.

165 For some early studies see R. Lansbury and D. Macdonald (eds), *Workplace Industrial Relations: Australian Case Studies*, Oxford University Press, Melbourne, 1992. Recent data on Joint Consultative Committees in Australia and their operations is contained in Forsyth et al., above n. 108.

that there are aspects of corporate governance and labour market regulation which at least suggest the possibility of Australian 'exceptionalism' in certain respects.[166]

As our earlier discussion indicates, Australian corporate law has tended historically to adhere to the general pattern of regulation embodied in UK corporate law, and the recent trajectory in Australian law, as we have noted, has focussed increasingly on protections for shareholders, including minorities. Australia has instituted practices which are thought to elevate shareholder power and influence over management. However, as our discussion indicates, there is no clear empirical evidence that Australia has fully made the transition to a dispersed 'outsider system' characteristic of liberal market economies although the trend is in that direction.

For various reasons we have noted, the labour regulation system in Australia has historically exhibited features, at least superficially, which would place it more appropriately in the relational/insider rather than the market/outsider group. Factors to be considered here would include the 'compulsory' rather than voluntarist nature of bargaining and the near universal scope of award coverage in the Australian labour market. In this respect Australian labour law leaned away from the voluntarism and respect for private ordering exhibited by the US and UK and towards the comprehensive labour codes of civil law countries. At the same time, the scope of bargaining was constrained in Australia as in other liberal market countries by managerial prerogative, rather than the strong integration of employees in the governance structure of the business enterprise.

It follows that we might hesitate to include Australia unconditionally among the group of 'liberal market' economies characterised by a certain set of complementary arrangements and 'regulatory style' in corporate and labour market institutions and processes, and this might mean that viewed historically Australia was more of a hybrid model. On the other hand there are also clear signs of a more recent tendency to converge more closely with the 'liberal market' regulatory style embodied in the so-called Anglo/American model. In relation to corporate governance, we have noted the increasing tendency in law and regulation to strengthen the interests and capacities of shareholders to exert influence within the company. In labour law the direction of legal evolution is perhaps even more obvious, though even here it is necessary to be cautious in evaluating the strength of particular legal developments. Following legislative developments since 1996 at least, we have identified core features of a reconstituted labour law and labour market regulation system in Australia: the restoration of managerial prerogative, with collective bargaining becoming much more 'voluntarist' as well as enterprise based. As late as 2006, an extensive award-based net of conditions remained, representing at one level a comprehensive labour 'code' with extensive market coverage, but such standards were often minimal, whereas market and productivity based standards were limited to collective agreements whose coverage was uneven and partial. The modern Australian labour law system thus makes it possible for managers to pursue almost

---

166   See A. Dignam and M. Galanis, 'Australia Inside-Out: The Corporate Governance System of the Australian Listed Market' (2004) 28 *Melbourne University Law Review* 623.

any strategy along the 'high road/low road' continuum, and following the *Work Choices* legislation[167] there were strong signs that many Australian businesses were moving to radically reduce pay and conditions. Whilst this shift has been modified to some degree with the election of a Labor government and the introduction of new labour laws in 2009[168] it remains unclear to what extent this will impact on the general evolution of the law. At the same time, it is necessary to note that a recent empirical study of Australian labour law over a 40-year period has raised important questions concerning the decline in strength of the law's protective capacity over this period.[169]

As noted above these labour law developments have coincided with shifts in corporate governance which have tended to consolidate the primacy of shareholder value, and increased shareholder power and influence over management.[170] Recent reviews of corporate law seem lukewarm at best about any substantial change to directors' duties to stakeholders generally.[171] From a corporate governance perspective, all of this has left labour increasingly with little alternative but to pursue weaker options of 'voice' or 'influence' over corporate affairs through occasional 'union-shareholder activism',[172] and campaigns built around corporate social responsibility and best practice.[173]

---

167 According to one expert, under the *Work Choices* scheme Australia had the least regulated 'working time' model of any Western country: see J. Murray, '"Protected by Law": Labour Standards Under *Workchoices*', paper presented at the 15th Annual Labour Law Conference, Workplace Research Centre, The University of Sydney, 2006.

168 See A. Forsyth and A. Stewart (eds), *Fairwork: The New Workplace Laws and the Work Choices Legacy*, Federation Press, Sydney, 2009.

169 R. Mitchell, P. Gahan, A. Stewart, S. Cooney and S. Marshall, 'The Evolution of Labour Law in Australia: Measuring the Change' (2010) 23 *Australian Journal of Labour Law* 61.

170 See also Mitchell et al., above n. 124. We are noting this as a broad proposition only. It is clear that 'shareholder primacy' cannot be reduced to the simple proposition that directors generally hold the view that companies should be run in the sole, and short-term, interests of shareholders: see Chapter 4 of this book.

171 See, for example, Corporations and Markets Advisory Committee, *The Social Responsibility of Corporations,* 2006; Parliamentary Joint Committee on Corporations and Financial Services, *Corporate Responsibility: Managing Risk and Creating Value*, 2006.

172 See K. Anderson and I. Ramsay, 'From the Picketline to the Boardroom: Union Shareholder Activism in Australia' (2006) 24 *Company and Securities Law Journal* 279.

173 See Jones et al., above n. 130; J. Lewer, J. Burgess and P. Waring, 'Does Socially Responsible Investment Influence Employment Relations?', and K. Anderson, S. Marshall and I. Ramsay, 'Do Australian Institutional Investors Aim to Influence the Human Resource Practices of Investee Companies?', both in Marshall et al., *Varieties of Capitalism, Corporate Governance and Employees*, above n. 1, pp. 221 and 245 respectively.

Chapter 3
Corporate Governance and the Management of Labour: Contemporary Business Practices in Ten Australian Companies

3.1 Introduction

The 1990s and 2000s were an important era for business organisations in Australia. Many decades of relative economic decline, and the introduction of new policies exposing the Australian economy to much greater global competition, had given rise to increasing pressures for economic reform. As we have noted, the relative success of national economies is associated in the literature with the relations between distinctive or particular attributes[1] or institutional arrangements which characterise national economic approaches. Two of the most important attributes or institutions are the systems of corporate governance and the types of employment systems utilised within business enterprises. These are the core subjects of the present study.

Serious questioning about the nature of the employment model in Australia began in the early 1980s, but legislative reform emerged most strongly from about 1993 onwards. As noted in Chapter 2, these reforms gradually shifted the premise of labour market regulation away from a class conflict model towards a greater emphasis on growth and efficiency. Traditional labour institutions were weakened and labour was subjected to greater risk. These developments were accompanied by changes in human resource management thinking which emphasised the decentralised management of labour resources and individualisation in employment relations in order to increase the flexible use of labour.[2]

Revised ideas about the 'core business' of the state,[3] and a similar reappraisal within private companies, resulted in major economic restructuring from the 1980s onwards. Central to this revised view was the notion that organisations should only engage in business activities in which they are most competent, and in which they are able to compete to the greatest advantage. As a consequence of the

---

1 See S. Richardson, 'Regulation of the Labour Market' in S. Richardson (ed.), *Reshaping the Labour Market: Regulation, Efficiency and Equality in Australia*, Cambridge University Press, Cambridge, 1999, p. 17.

2 See R. Mitchell and J. Fetter, 'Human Resource Management and Individualisation in Australian Labour Law' (2003) 45 *Journal of Industrial Relations* 292.

3 See P. Self, *Government by the Market*, Macmillan, Basingstoke, 1993.

political dominance of these ideas, privatisation of a large number of Australian federally- and state-owned enterprises occurred. Many large Australian privately-owned companies also shed or outsourced those functions which they believed they could more efficiently access in the market. At the same time, reforms in the corporate law field allowed for a greater alignment of management and shareholder interests, giving rise to the perception of the ascendancy of a 'shareholder value'-oriented form of capitalism.[4]

To obtain a close understanding of business practices linking corporate ownership structure, corporate governance and employment systems for this project we undertook a study of 10 organisations. These were varied in type and size, ranging from small family held companies to large international companies with highly diffused shareholdings. They covered a range of industries including mining, financial services and manufacturing.

In each of these studies we carried out background research on the business history of the company, examining any major changes in ownership structure, and the nature of managerial/shareholder relations against a background of corporate law reform. Most of our companies had undergone various forms of capital restructuring during the 1990s through into the mid-2000s. We were also able to observe how the organisations utilised or adjusted to the changing labour market regulations of the time. As noted in Chapter 1 (see section 1.5), material for the study of the contemporary practices of the organisations was obtained through interviews with leading figures within the organisations themselves, including human resource managers, company secretaries and other managers. In relevant cases union officials were also interviewed.[5]

Analysis of the data presented in this chapter along thematic lines takes place in section 3.3 and this is followed through with further discussion in Chapter 5, following the presentation of the results of our survey data in Chapter 4. However, at the outset we think that it is worth noting that the case studies presented here to a degree present a blurred picture of the relationship between corporate ownership structure, corporate governance and the management of labour within Australian business organisations. If it can be said to be the case that there is a discernible national 'regulatory style' which characterises Australian business practices consistently with the varieties of capitalism model for example, and this is a big

---

4   See generally, S. Deakin, *Renewing Labour Market Institutions*, International Institute for Labour Studies, Central European University, Budapest, 2004, ch. 1 and 2; R. Mitchell, A. O'Donnell and I. Ramsay, 'Shareholder Value and Employee Interests: Intersections Between Corporate Governance, Corporate Law and Labor Law' (2005) 23 *Wisconsin International Law Journal* 23; S. Jacoby, *The Embedded Corporation*, Princeton University Press, Princeton and Oxford, 2005, ch. 1.

5   A more detailed version of the case studies presented in this chapter is available from the authors.

'if',[6] it nevertheless remains difficult, on close examination, to identify conformity with such style with a high degree of consistency.[7] What emerges, probably not surprisingly, is a considerable diversity in business practices between different enterprises, and, at times, within them. That does not mean, of course, that the idea of various types of capitalism has no cogency, but it does mean that it is necessary to approach such characterisations with appropriate caution.

3.2 The Case Studies

ResourceCo 1

ResourceCo 1 is a very large, international, resources-based business. Worldwide the company employed, at the time the study was conducted, nearly 38,000 persons, and engaged more than 65,000 contractors. About 40 per cent of the company's workforce was in Australia and Asia. Throughout the 1990s the company had been in difficulties following a series of poor investment decisions. Declining profits and a poor share price had resulted in considerable turnover at senior management level. However, by the late 1990s, the company had recovered its position somewhat. It had written off nearly $14 billion in failed investments globally, and had begun to implement a highly controversial industrial relations policy in parts of its Australian holdings. By 2000 the company had returned to profitability, helped by strong oil prices and a cleansed balance sheet.

In 2001 the company underwent a merger with a British diversified resource company using a dual listed structure (DLS). The legal arrangements of this structure effectively combined the operations of the two companies whilst preserving separate identities and shareholder registries. Under the arrangement the two companies retained their separate assets, but aligned their operations and shared the cash flows under the control of two boards composed of the same directors. The companies paid equal dividends to their shareholders, and shareholders had equivalent votes at shareholder meetings in line with the relative 'weightings' of the two companies established at the time of the dual listing merger. In the event that one company had insufficient earnings to pay the agreed dividend to its shareholders, there were arrangements for an equalisation payment from the other company.

The DLS was seen to offer a number of tax and cost advantages to the Australian company which it would not have obtained had the company utilised a takeover

---

6   See N. Wailes, J. Kitay and R. Lansbury, 'Varieties of Capitalism, Corporate Governance and Employment Relations Under Globalisation' in S. Marshall, R. Mitchell and I. Ramsay (eds), *Varieties of Capitalism, Corporate Governance and Employees*, Melbourne University Press, Melbourne, 2008.

7   This point has been made also by Sanford Jacoby in his informative detailed analysis of Japanese and American companies: see Jacoby, above n. 4, pp. 41 and 101.

or conventional merger option. Importantly, management was of the view that the Australian company in its merged form would have improved access to capital markets if it maintained listings in both the Australian and UK stock markets since local investors were already familiar with the respective 'pre-merger' companies, and the companies could thus continue to enjoy their 'reputational brands' in those markets. At the same time, the dual listing for the Australian company gained it access to a large overseas market, increased attention from research analysts, and potentially greater investment from institutional investors.

Ownership and corporate governance   One concern had been over the potential impact that the merger might have on the relationship between management and shareholders. Prior to the merger, a coalition of community groups, trade unions and small shareholders had expressed concerns over a range of ethical and social issues, including the potential loss of influence by Australian shareholders over the merged company's management. One perception was that the dual-listed company structure might entrench the position of the board and management by vastly increasing the assets they controlled, whilst at the same time halving the accountability they had to either set of shareholders. However, whilst it seemed to be the case that compared with some of our other company studies shareholder influence did not seem to weigh particularly heavily with the management of ResourceCo 1, it did not appear to be the case that any major change had occurred in the nature of management/shareholder relations as a result of the merger. If there has been a dilution of shareholder pressure since the merger, it is difficult to identify the DLS as the cause. The dilution of shareholder pressure may, as we shall see, have more to do with the size of the two companies prior to their merger rather than the merged companies' legal structure per se.

Prior to the merger the company largely corresponded with what has been identified in the literature as an 'outsider' model of corporate governance based on a market for corporate control. All 20 principal investors in the pre-merged company were institutional investors, with no individual group among them holding more than 15 per cent of the total shareholdings. These were supplemented by thousands of smaller investors. Since the merger, the picture has remained substantially the same. The 20 largest stockholders in the company on the Australian and UK stock exchanges are institutional investors, with the largest shareholding being around 16 per cent in Australia and 26 per cent in Britain.

It may be the case that the size and global scope of the company acts as a buffer for managers against pressure from shareholders and national media and investor scrutiny. Against this, as noted, the company's main clientele are large international organisations, indicating that at least a degree of responsiveness by management to its constituents is necessary. It is also notable that since the merger ResourceCo 1 has moved quickly to comply with corporate governance standards and adopt leading corporate social responsibility (CSR) practices. For example the company has complied with the Australian Securities Exchange Corporate Governance Council's 'Corporate Governance Principles and Recommendations' and it has also supported various international guidelines such as the United Nations Declaration on Human Rights, and the United Nations Global Compact. It also appears to be the case that since the merger British institutional investors have been far more proactive than their Australian counterparts hitherto had been in pursuing the company's conformity with CSR and sustainability standards. There is some sense within the company's hierarchy that its adoption of responsible corporate governance practices, which meet a variety of international standards (for example those set down in the New York Stock Exchange Corporate Governance Requirements pursuant to section 303A of the foreign listing Rules), takes it well beyond existing Australian standards such as those found in the *Corporate Law Economic Reform (Audit Reform and Corporate Disclosure) Act 2004*. Neither the recent changes to Australian corporate law, nor the principles adopted by the Australian Securities Exchange, were regarded by the company as particularly onerous. Nor were they seen to have greatly influenced the nature of the capital restructuring of the company.

Labour relations   Prior to the 1990s the company's labour policies were based upon a stable relationship with trade unions which involved high union coverage and the collective determination of employment conditions pursuant to union-based collective agreements or awards. However, during the 1990s the company introduced various strategies which were designed to restore its profitability after a period of downturn. Part of this strategy involved job shedding, and the introduction of a controversial industrial relations policy to 'individualise' relations with employees at some of the company's operations. This strategy brought ResourceCo 1 into severe conflict with the union movement.

Individual contracts with employees were introduced primarily into the company's Western Australian subsidiary in the late 1990s following upon similar policies adopted earlier in the decade by its competitors. The stated purpose of the policy was to bring about reforms in workplace practices for reasons of efficiency and competitiveness, reforms which the company felt unable to bring about through union agreement. Employees were offered a significant pay increase as an incentive to move on to individual agreements. Despite the apparent negative implications for unions, during the protracted court-based and public relations dispute that ensued the company denied at the time, and continued to deny thereafter, that its policy was anti-union by design.

The adoption of individual contracts between the company and its employees, and the consequent lessening in influence of collective regulatory instruments, was made possible at this time by changes to the State of Western Australia's labour laws, notably the *Workplace Agreements Act 1993* and subsequent amendments, although according to one manager, the company might just as easily have achieved the same outcome (as did some of its competitors) through the use of common law contracts. Union attempts to overturn the adoption of the policy through legal action, or to attempt to force the company to bargain collectively, were unsuccessful. By January 2000 between 40 per cent and 50 per cent of the company's award-based employees had entered into individual agreements with the company, effectively resiling from the regulation of their employment according to the award standards. Many employees who entered into individual agreements, including current union delegates and former officials and activists, formally resigned from the union. Others simply ceased to participate in union affairs. Approximately 60 per cent of ResourceCo 1's employees in its Western Australian subsidiary were on individual agreements at the time this study was completed.

However, the company's individualising employment practices were not reproduced at all of its operations. Only at one New South Wales site had the company introduced individual agreements for its blue collar workforce. This site was previously closed for some years, and re-opened as a greenfield operation. The site was subject to high security, and unions were not permitted access. With this exception, at the remainder of its New South Wales operations, including both regular and greenfield sites, ResourceCo 1 adhered to collective relations with unions, and regulated employment conditions of its blue collar workers through collective agreements.

The most significant difference between these two geographical areas of operation is the type of product mined. In Western Australia the product is iron ore which is mined for international markets (primarily China) whereas in New South Wales the product is coal which is mined for domestic use. In addition, in New South Wales there was a long-term contract in place for the supply of coal and this may have reduced pressure on company management to introduce individual agreements for its workforce. In contrast, iron ore prices have been particularly volatile, taking a downturn in the 1990s, whilst coal prices have remained buoyant in the domestic market. A further difference in practices between the two areas concerns union coverage. In Western Australia mining sites are covered by several unions who are often in conflict with each other over membership coverage and similar matters. The sites in New South Wales on the other hand are generally covered by a single, and militant, union. The union enjoys high union density and does not have any major union rivals. This strength is bolstered by its strong relationship with local communities.

Employment systems, high performance work practices and workplace partnerships   The statutory individualised agreements used by the company partly to regulate its operations at its Western Australian sites at the time of this study contained only six compulsory clauses. However, these were supplemented by individual so-called 'Staff Contracts of Employment', which, in turn, were linked by reference to ResourceCo 1's Staff Handbook, which could be varied by managerial discretion and which provided most of the specific detail about the employment duties and work systems for the company's Western Australian employees. The 'Staff Contracts', apart from covering basic duties, hours of work, leave entitlements and so on, also contained several elements of supposed 'high performance workplace systems' including various dimensions of flexible work practices. For example they typically included requirements that employees work 'outside of their normal working hours' without additional remuneration to ensure that the 'full requirements' of their job were completed, and that employees undertake duties as directed by management provided that they were commensurate with their skills. The contracts also provided for adjustment of salaries at the company's discretion including bonuses, and the right of the company to transfer its employees to other positions, operations and locations subject to reasonable notice being given. Although these agreements placed great store in the efficacy of a 'direct relationship' between the company and the employee, there was little content to indicate the importance of employee empowerment to the operation of the work system.

These agreements may be contrasted with those utilised by the company in its New South Wales operations. Apart from the particular greenfield site noted earlier, ResourceCo 1's New South Wales sites were regulated by collective agreements which exhibited, over the period from 2000 to 2005, a fairly high degree of uniformity. Generally speaking they provided trade unions with strong consultation and recognition rights, though no formal consultative committee or planning committee type arrangements formed part of the agreements. Consultation with unions was assured over aspects of 'budget setting', 'business type changes that may affect employee's earnings', 'numbers or rosters', 'mine planning' and 'safety, environment and training initiatives'. Other similar clauses in the agreements provided for unions and employees jointly to determine shift changes and redundancies among other things. Again speaking generally, whilst these collective agreements manifested some elements of the high performance workplace, on the whole functional and numerical flexibility was far more constrained than in the individual agreements, and performance incentives were collectively rather than individually based.

However, distinguishing between the individualised and collectivised natures of the company's various operations does not fully capture the degree of diversity exhibited among ResourceCo 1's employment systems. In its New South Wales unionised greenfield sites, for example, the company's agreements provided far greater levels of functional and numerical flexibility, and less consultation with the union over various aspects of work practices. Recognition of the union in these agreements tended to be more constrained. Performance incentive schemes were retained at managerial discretion, rather than forming part of the agreement. Overall the collective agreements at the company's greenfield sites appeared more oriented to aligning the interests of the company and its employees through employee development and incentives. In these respects, ResourceCo 1's collective agreements at most of its greenfield sites contained important content closely aligning the employment systems with those of its individualised Western Australian operations.

Whilst this diversity in labour management practices is driven by the different competitive regional and product market pressures on the company, it was also fostered and facilitated through a decentralised management structure which allowed regional and site managers considerable autonomy in determining the type of agreements negotiated with employees and the style of labour management. Regional and site managers sought approval for their labour strategies within the company's central management hierarchy based on business principles. A senior manager explained:

> If an (operational manager) were to come to me and say 'we're doing individual contracts', as long as you think they've got sound HR and business reasons for doing that, you don't have a particular view one way or the other ... any more than if they decided they were going to work in partnership with the union and have a collective agreement. What they have to do is have an effective and competitive workforce ... The reality is that statistics, everywhere, tell us that if you move to individual contracts you'll have a much more effective and competitive workforce, and a happy one too. So if (a manager) said to me, in one of the reviews, 'we're going to collective bargaining, we're going to get rid of our individual contracts' I would question it but I wouldn't stop it, if they could present (a good business case) ... I'd be amazed ... there might be some strange business where that would work ... I don't know where that is, but I would be very open minded about it.

At one level the study of ResourceCo 1 tells a reasonably straightforward story. In a period of poor corporate performance measured in economic terms, economic recovery and the restoration of investor confidence occurred to some extent at the expense of employment losses, job insecurity and very different working arrangements. Much of this was assisted by important systemic changes in labour laws throughout the 1990s and into the 2000s (see Chapter 2).

However what we also see in the study of ResourceCo 1 is a complex mix of different pressures upon the company, not all of which are harmonious with the governance of the business for 'shareholder value' narrowly defined, and a variety of different employment systems utilised, not all of which can be described categorically as antithetical to co-operative or 'partnership-style' relations with employees and their representative institutions. It seems safer to speculate though that notwithstanding the strong influence of corporate social responsibility-type policies, partnership relations are less likely to be fostered with trade unions than they are with employees directly.

Inevitably these findings require us to look more closely at other issues to do with the presence of autonomy among business sites within enterprises, the relevance of regionalisation and its significance for trade union power, and the importance of product market conditions in particular. We return to these issues in section 3.3.

ServiceCo

ServiceCo is a large business servicing both domestic and international markets. At the time of the study, the company employed something in the order of 38,000 workers, including a reasonably high proportion of casuals and contractors. Our account of the company focuses upon its transition from an Australian government owned and controlled enterprise to a wholly privatised business.

The period of the 1980s and the 1990s was one in which Australian governments 'initiated a process of disengaging the state from the organisation, ownership and control of government businesses'[8] with a view to capturing perceived benefits from the greater 'marketisation' and reduction of government debt which 'privatisation' would engender. The 'oil shock' of the early 1970s had ended the period of sustained profitability for the company, and throughout the 1970s and the 1980s the company's levels of debt had continued to rise. Poor performance was also contributed to by a history of turbulent industrial relations between the company, its employees and trade unions. ServiceCo was historically (and remains) a highly unionised company, both in terms of density levels, and in terms of the number of trade unions involved in employee organisation. For example in 1989 ServiceCo's workers were represented by 26 separate unions (the figure is now between 10 and 15).

During the 1980s various factors exacerbated the industrial relations environment within the organisation. The Labor Party's Accord with the trade union movement from 1983 onwards acted as a brake upon wage increases. However, at the same time, a period of international expansion in the industry meant that the wages paid by ServiceCo were perceived as well below market rates, reducing the company's ability to attract new senior staff in particular and stimulating greater militancy among engineers and maintenance workers also. Further employment problems arose from two decisions taken in 1982, one of which was to reduce apprenticeship levels, and the other of which was to cut the company's commercial cadet programme. These decisions led to a serious problem of managerial succession by the late 1980s.

Between 1978 and 1989 it is estimated that there were nearly 70 separate industrial stoppages within the company, severely disrupting its business operations. Although various reviews of the company's operations had been carried out in the 1980s, resulting in some rationalisation and productivity improvements, by the late 1980s government attitudes had hardened, supporting management against perceived union intransigence in breaking a lengthy dispute in 1989.

Although the government had progressively provided the company's management with greater autonomy and operational freedom throughout the 1980s, the decision was taken in 1989 to abandon government control over financial target

---

8   P. Fairbrother, M. Paddon and J. Teicher, 'Introduction: Corporatisation and Privatisation in Australia' in P. Fairbrother, M. Paddon and J. Teicher (eds), *Privatisation, Globalisation & Labour: Studies from Australia*, Federation Press, Sydney, 2002, p. 2.

setting and corporate governance, and to undertake a partial privatisation of the company by selling off 49 per cent of its value. A record profit in the financial year to June 1989 was followed in 1990 and 1991 by substantial losses in a period of economic downturn. In 1992 the Australian government announced that ServiceCo would purchase a domestic service company to enable it to better compete in the domestic market. Following this merger more than 1,800 workers were retrenched voluntarily or redeployed. Full privatisation of ServiceCo occurred with the sale of a 25 per cent stake to a British company in 1993 and a public float of the remaining stake on the open share market in 1995. Foreign ownership was limited to 49 per cent of the company's shares.

The experience of ServiceCo is one of re-regulation rather than deregulation or marketisation. Prior to the privatisation of the company it was acting commercially in what was always a price sensitive, highly competitive market. In that commercial sense it was largely indistinguishable from its private competitors, apart, perhaps, from serving a form of public job creation mechanism in its earlier years. As a consequence whilst ServiceCo's privatisation was a very important event in Australia's industrial history, this event did not significantly alter the company's day-to-day modus operandi.

Ownership and corporate governance   Before its privatisation, ServiceCo's corporate governance and capital structure generally conformed to an insider/ relational form of company identified in the literature. However, since privatisation ServiceCo appears to have corresponded more to the liberal market/outsider form. At the time the study was undertaken, ownership of the company was very diffused: about 30 per cent of shareholders owned small parcels of shares and with the sale of a major interest purchased by a British company in 1993, the largest shareholders held up to about 6 per cent of the company's total shares in each individual case. Exactly what impact this diffusion of ownership had is difficult to say. Managers characterised time-lines for strategic planning and corporate reporting as both short-term and long-term in nature. On one hand there was considerable pressure for short-term profits and increases in share price. In part this pressure arose from the volatility of the market in which the company operated, and the accompanying unpredictability in earnings and profits. Profits were also subject to erratic prices in the cost of core service components. As a consequence of these factors, investors in this industry tended to be short-term in orientation, trading according to rises and falls in the share market cycle. Coinciding with these pressures was the relative novelty of the company's appearance on the stock market.

On the other hand, managers were also compelled to plan long-term in this industry because of the high cost of the operational assets owned by the company and the complexity of the regulatory environment. Operational assets had to be ordered sometimes months, and often several years, in advance. New business opportunities, for example new markets to exploit, were, at the same time, highly dependent upon government support and bilateral negotiations with comparable foreign companies and their respective governments.

Notwithstanding ServiceCo's wholly privatised character, the company continued to operate in a highly regulated environment, arising from both explicit and implicit government expectations, some of which may have been linked with the company's earlier status as a public body. One such regulatory limitation which was in operation at the time our study was undertaken was the requirement that there be a 49 per cent limitation on foreign ownership in ServiceCo. There was also an important perception within the organisation that to some extent it was required to show national leadership in what was a signal industry. Community and government expectations set some limits on employment policies and systems, impacting upon industrial relations and human resources policies. Consultation with government was not required on a day-to-day operational basis, but was required on major issues.

Labour relations and workplace partnerships   The relationship between the company and its large workforce was heavily mediated by trade unions. More than 90 per cent of the company's 38,000 or so employees were members of at least 13 different unions, and union presence within the company has been quite proactive. Collective negotiations with unions, and regulation of ServiceCo's employment systems through enterprise agreements with unions occurred throughout the business, including its more peripheral activities. Importantly, management–union relations were monitored very seriously at board level, including monthly reporting on the state of industrial relations within the organisation and the progress of any current bargaining taking place. This level of supervision was unusual amongst the rest of the companies in our case study sample.

Despite the fact that management perceived that its industrial relations strategies were to some extent compromised by public expectation and by union pressure, the privatisation of ServiceCo clearly impacted upon labour in terms of strategies introduced by the company to reduce costs. In 1997 the company announced its intention to reduce personnel costs by 20 per cent over a four- to five-year period. Job cutting and efficiency gains were a recurring theme over the next several years. In 2001 some 1,500 positions were cut over a period of six months owing to competitive pressures. Further competitive crises in the industry led to further restructuring, resulting in a 3.5 per cent reduction in full-time employment positions in 2004.

In May 2004 ServiceCo announced the launch of a new lower-cost arm of its operations, based on reduced labour and supply costs. This was partly based on specific agreements with unions and suppliers, but also included reductions in the numbers of full-time 'core' employees by increasing the use of casual, part-time and third-party labour hire workers which managers perceived would not have been possible in its standard operations. As one manager put it:

> By using third party labour hire, third party part-timers, a casual pool, we've to start to chip away at the rate issues around the core workforce. So now we have this peripheral workforce and we've got a smaller expensive core if you like. And that pretty much has been the strategy over the last five or six years because we simply cannot maintain that cost base and make a buck.

Whereas the increased utilisation of marginal labour might also be expected to impact negatively upon union influence within the organisation, it does not appear to be the case that this was part of management's design. Lower labour costs in this new service were negotiated with unions rather than through the types of union avoidance strategies that have been utilised in other industries. The principal motivation seems to have been cost driven; reduction of the core workforce better enabling the company flexibly to match labour resources with assets.

Flexibility and high performance work practices   Generally speaking, as noted, ServiceCo introduced several initiatives designed to improve the flexibility of its workforce. Enterprise agreements made since the company's privatisation increasingly provided management with the power to employ workers on a part-time, or fixed-term, basis, and to contract out the performance of jobs through labour hire and competitive tendering. At the time of this study, management estimated its flexible labour as constituting 16 per cent of its total workforce. Its aim was to increase this to 25 per cent of total labour. Nevertheless, for most employees length of tenure in the company is high and employment security for core workers remains stable. The company undertakes specialist and apprenticeship training, in what is a relatively tight internal market for labour.

Employment systems and standards vary within ServiceCo between the company's core and non-core activities. Major forms of temporal flexibility for core workers were not evident in many of the enterprise agreements and other policy documents examined for this study, but were present in some agreements covering the company's more peripheral workforce. For example, the agreements covering core workers provided that the company could vary the length of work shifts following adequate consultation and negotiation with the relevant union. In comparison, management appeared to have greater discretion to alter the normal roster cycle 'to meet business needs' in the case of union agreements covering the company's peripheral services. In other areas, for example functional flexibility, the company's employment agreements appeared to have little scope or influence. Job classifications appeared quite rigid, and agreements frequently restricted the use of labour in 'higher duties'.

Various other employment practices were introduced to unify or harmonise the interests of the company and its employees At the outset of the company in its privatised form, ServiceCo's 1994–1995 Enterprise Agreements introduced an employee share ownership plan which entitled all employees to a certain number of free shares, and a certain further allotment of free shares 'subject to the company reaching a performance target based upon an acceptable return on shareholders' funds'. This scheme was being pared back at the time the study was undertaken, having failed, in the eyes of management, to achieve its objectives. There are other performance objectives offered by the company, but overall individual pay flexibility is quite limited apart from at the executive level.

Apart from representation through unions the company also used a range of minor methods for direct communication with employees. These included attitude surveys, direct meetings with employees through which financial results and corporate strategies were presented, and subjected to question and discussion from the floor, and an email service through which complaints and concerns could be expressed. There was no formal employee representation committee or other similar structure.

As was the case with ResourceCo 1, the picture presented in our study of ServiceCo exhibits considerable complexity. Despite its privatisation and consequent exposure to market forces, and the 'outsider' nature of its finance and governance, it would be wrong to suppose that labour–management relations in the company were completely antithetical to the presence or maintenance of 'partnership relations' with employees or unions.

On one hand it was clear, and acknowledged by management and unions alike, that there was a reasonably high level of conflict; an understanding that the interests of the company and its employees were to some extent opposed. In this context the company's relationship with its resident unions varied according to the different levels of militancy among them. Some management also attested to a sense of an 'us and them' attitude on the part of the company's employees and expressed frustration at being unable to deal more directly with employees as 'part of the company'.

On the other hand, however, whilst relations with unions are not always harmonious or collaborative, ServiceCo appears to have been committed to an ongoing consultative and bargaining relationship with unions since privatisation, even in instances where the emphasis was on lowering labour costs and introducing more flexible labour practices. Whilst, as we noted, many economic efficiency and productivity measures were introduced, these were of the same order as in other parts of the labour market, and in certain key respects the employment systems operating at ServiceCo retained many of the key characteristics of those in place prior to the company's privatisation. Little attempt was made to adopt human resource strategies which would seek to alienate the loyalties of employees from their representative unions in favour of direct contracting with the company. Length of tenure among a substantial core workforce probably indicated a good underlying relationship between the company and most of its employees.

As with ResourceCo 1 we may find it instructive to look more widely for explanations of this continued pattern of management–labour relations at ServiceCo. Continued regulation of the particular service market in which

ServiceCo operated obviously points to one line of inquiry.[9] Issues particular to the capital market in which ServiceCo is based may point to others (see further 3.3 below).

ResourceCo 2

ResourceCo 2 is a large international resources-based company, formed as the result of the merger of a UK company and an Australian company in the mid-1990s. Historically the UK company had at various times held a very high volume of the Australian company's shares, and still retained a 49 per cent interest in the company at the time of the merger. The merger took the form of a dual listing by the company on the UK and Australian exchanges. Under the dual listed companies structure the two companies continued as separate entities, with separate shareholder registries. There was no change in the legal or beneficial ownership of the assets of either company, but contractual arrangements were put in place, and the articles of association of each company were amended to ensure, as far as possible, that the two companies operated together as a single enterprise. Gradually the two companies have developed a common corporate identity, beginning with a name change shortly after the merger took effect.

The share register of the Australian arm of ResourceCo 2 at the time of the study showed the interest of the UK company at about 38 per cent, but otherwise the company was dominated by large institutional investors, none of whom held more than 5 per cent of the company's total shares. The board was a standard outsider board, comprised of four executive and six non-executive directors.

The merger reflected a view held within the company that such resource-based companies needed to globalise and to reduce competition for limited resources worldwide. It was thought that Australian investors would benefit from exposure to global opportunities in resources and from greater power in effecting takeovers.

One of the first major reviews of the company's operations post-merger saw a focus on cost-cutting and efficiency improvements. The Australian arm of ResourceCo 2 had already signalled from the early 1990s onwards that its commitment to extending its operations in Australia depended particularly upon changes in the industrial relations climate to allow for major improvements in productivity. At this stage the company had already begun a strategy to bypass trade unions and the centralised industrial relations authorities in order to pursue direct relationships with its employees based on individual contracts.[10] These contracts

---

9   See generally S. Deakin, R. Hobbs, S. Konzelmann and F. Wilkinson, 'Working Corporations: Corporate Governance and Innovation in Labour-Management Partnerships in Britain' in M. Stuart and M. Martinez Lucio (eds), *Partnership and Modernisation in Employment Relations*, Routledge, London, 2005.

10   The role of various resource-based companies in leading the push to de-collectivise the regulation of Australian industrial relations is examined in S. Cooney, 'Exclusionary Self-Regulation: A Critical Evaluation of the AMMA's Proposal in the Mining Industry' in

introduced a thorough restructuring of the regulation of the company's workplaces at many sites. The contracts also had the effect of considerably weakening the industrial and on-site power of trade unions. They effected major changes to work systems, including the introduction of 12-hour shifts, the elimination of overtime and penalty payments, annualised salaries, the use of contract labour and multi-skilling. These changes were effected by offering increased salaries to those workers who would agree to switch from the union-award form of regulation to the individual contracts. A substantial volume of workers did so, causing a substantial decline in union membership.

Corporate social responsibility and labour relations   Following the merger the company steadily emphasised its commitment to local communities and other stakeholders as a yardstick for assessing its performance. Profit for long-term shareholders was designed to be delivered only within a framework of ethical and sustainable development practices. The adoption of this high profile 'corporate social responsibility' (CSR) stance led to increased scrutiny of the company's practices across the board. This in turn meant that whilst the company still operated through wholly or partly owned subsidiary companies or joint ventures, a relatively high degree of centralisation of control developed through which the company demonstrated how its CSR policies were implemented.

The dominance of this CSR strategy seems, at least in principle, to have had important implications for the company's labour relations and employment practices. The content of the CSR programme was set out in documents which guided the way operations were conducted across the group. The content of this was, in part, set at the international level because of the company being a signatory to the United Nations Global Compact, and a supporter of both the United Nations Universal Declaration of Human Rights and the US/UK Voluntary Principles on Security and Human Rights. In these types of regulatory instruments, the rights of individuals to associate in trade unions and to enter into collective bargaining agreements are key provisions. Other relevant sets of principles to which the company adhered included the International Labour Organisation's Declaration on Fundamental Principles and Rights at Work, and the Organisation for Economic Co-Operation and Development's Guidelines for Multinational Enterprises, which similarly contained strong support for collective workplace regulation. In fact the OECD document went beyond the mere right to representation, requiring enterprises to enter into 'constructive negotiations', to provide facilities to employee representatives as necessary to facilitate collective agreements and to provide information necessary for meaningful negotiations.

How these declared principles work out in practice is, however, another matter. As a company operating across different commodity markets and operational sites the company seemed to exhibit a high degree of diversity in industrial relations. On

C. Arup, P. Gahan, J. Howe, R. Johnstone, R. Mitchell and A. O'Donnell (eds), *Labour Law and Labour Market Regulation*, Federation Press, Sydney, 2006.

one hand the company did not re-establish collective regulation at its previously de-unionised sites, maintaining these as individualised operations through direct contracting with employees. On the other hand, many of the company's other subsidiary operations around Australia exhibited more orthodox patterns of union representation and collective bargaining. For example of 13 agreements entered into by the company and its subsidiaries between 1999 and 2005, nine were union-based collective agreements. Some operations involved the replacement of contractors by permanent employees, whilst others utilised contract labour only. Average job tenure in some subsidiary companies was high, indicating a long-term view to the development of the business.

It is important to note, though, that many of these collective arrangements reflected the type of work arrangements which ResourceCo 2 pursued at other operations through its de-collectivisation strategy. Most of the company's union-based agreements subsequently included 12-and-a-half-hour shifts, annualised salaries, company rights to contract-in (or out) labour and prohibitions on demarcations on job roles. Some of the union agreements also expressly permitted employees subject to them to opt either for 'staff' employment or to enter statutory individualised agreements. With more than 30 operations around the country, the number of union-based agreements was still low, and union officers interviewed for this study indicated that only certain limited sectors of the company could now be regarded as unionised.

Occupational health and safety, and training, were two further key aspects of the company's labour relations strategy. Significant investment in training and process development was made with a view to meeting published annual safety targets and sustainability reports. Executive bonuses were withheld where safety targets were not achieved. Considerable support was provided to employees to help develop the skills and competencies of workers through professional development programmes and self-education.

High performance work practices and workplace partnerships As noted, ResourceCo 2 had, in many of its operations, largely moved away from a collectivist form of regulation to an individualised pattern which was to some degree grounded in its CSR reporting. These reports carried overtones of a partnership-style relationship between the company and its employees. They spoke of mobilising the workforce in pursuit of common goals by involving the employees in the business; giving employees specific business information; seeking employee input on the best way to secure work objectives; and collaborating with employees on workplace change (including both production, process and cultural change).

On the other hand, however, the focus on partnership in the company's CSR programme was directed explicitly towards its relations with local communities, civil society groups and other stakeholders. Under this umbrella, the company produced a significant amount of information about its approach to these 'partnership' relations and listed the organisations with whom it worked in partnership. Nothing in these documents suggested that ResourceCo 2 identified itself as working in 'partnership' with either trade unions or employees.

As noted, the company utilises a variety of different work systems, many of which were based on individualised, non-union arrangements, and some of which were conducted under trade union collective arrangements. Under all forms of agreements the company had sought to maximise flexibility, as we have seen, in work scheduling and in work function, and in its presentations to the market ResourceCo 2 often emphasised the flexibility of its workforce. In this respect, in some of its operations the company used some high performance work practices, including lean production, so-called 'communication flows' and '360 degree feedback mechanisms' and so on, though it is difficult to determine how widespread these were.

One area where the company did appear perhaps to have altered its practice was in relation to employee consultation and job control. Generally the view taken of the company's approach to labour relations prior to the merger was that it was seeking to regain managerial 'prerogatives' lost to trade unions through the operation of labour law. In that context many of the changes introduced by the company, particularly through its individualised workplace systems, appeared to characterise a 'low road' approach which was designed to restore profitability through cost reductions, rather than higher quality performance.[11] More recently the company's practice emphasised consultation with employees. Management systems across all operations were required to address mechanisms for consultation and dialogue with employees. Where the company utilised a 'lean manufacturing' system, this was based around a certain level of job input from, and control by, employees. The company's most recent CSR reports at the time of the study described employee communication as an area of specific ongoing promotion within the organisation.

ResourceCo 2 is a typical example of a company with an 'outsider' governance structure. Its board at the time the study was undertaken was composed of four executive and six non-executive directors, and it had a highly diffused pattern of share ownership. Prior to the merger with its UK partner, the Australian company had forced through cost readjustments by using extremely radical labour relations policies. Subsequently these types of policies were sanctioned through labour law changes by both State and federal governments. Nevertheless, since the company's merger, its radical approach to its dealings with its workforce appeared to have come to an end. The company and its subsidiaries now operated under a variety of work systems, some of which involved dealings with unions and some which did not, but there was no indication of a further rolling out of the company's former de-unionisation strategy.

11   See S. Deery and J. Walsh, 'The Character of Individualised Employment Arrangements in Australia: A Model of "Hard" HRM' in S. Deery and R. Mitchell (eds), *Employment Relations: Individualisation and Union Exclusion – An International Study*, The Federation Press, Sydney, 1999.

Once again the complexity of this situation requires further examination. There is some suggestion that the break in the company's radical labour relations approach was due to pressure from its UK partner concerned about the threat to the company's reputation due to negative publicity from union-shareholder campaigns at company meetings and in the media. But there are other possible explanations. Probably the most important of these has been the revival in recent years of high profitability in the resources sector in which the company trades. A second important factor is likely to be the general weakness of trade unions, and hence their willingness to comply with managerial changes to work systems for flexibility and efficiency gains.[12]

EnergyCo

The history of EnergyCo is tied to the history of the privatisation of utilities in the Australian State of Victoria. Prior to the 1990s the generation and supply of electricity in Victoria was owned and managed by a State monopoly, the State Electricity Commission of Victoria (SECV). However, in 1992 the State government introduced the *State Owned Enterprises Act 1992* which authorised the government to restructure its various state-owned and controlled businesses through commercialisation, corporatisation and, eventually, privatisation. In 1993 the SECV was vertically separated into three segments (generation, distribution and transmission) and sold to private owners. EnergyCo emerged from this process in 1994 as a privatised business in the energy distribution industry.

Ownership structures   Since its creation in 1994, EnergyCo has undergone three changes of ownership. It was first acquired by a US company in 1995. It was subsequently sold to a Scottish company in 1999, and, finally, bought by a Hong Kong consortium in 2000. In the early 2000s EnergyCo acquired another Victorian electricity distribution company, owned by a different set of US owners. As a wholly owned subsidiary of a foreign company, EnergyCo's corporate governance and ownership structures may best be described as insider/relational according to the Gospel and Pendleton typology. Whilst at the time of the study the board had a number of independent directors, as well as those representing the owners, it was clear that the owners wielded a strong level of control. Debt finance was raised through bonds, and the view seemed to be that the financial health of the company left little room for strong influence on the part of creditors.

---

12   This position may be used to describe a partnership arising out of union acquiescence with enhanced managerial power rather than a maturing of employer and employee attitudes in the pursuit of mutual gains: see R. Mitchell and A. O'Donnell, 'What is Labour Law Doing About "Partnership at Work"? British and Australian Developments Compared' in Marshall et al., above n. 6; and J. Kelly, 'Social Partnership Agreements in Britain' in Stuart and Martinez Lucio, above n. 9.

At the same time, although the experience under previous owners had been mixed, management's view was that the present owners were long-term in orientation. They required less frequent reporting than the previous Scottish owners, but reporting on a wider range of issues such as health and safety, employee satisfaction, and community reputation. There was a focus on investment in infrastructure which was lacking for some time following the company's privatisation, and a refocus also on training apprentices which had correspondingly been allowed to slide. These renewed strategies reflected an appreciation of the likely growth in demand.

A further development, particularly since the Hong Kong-based takeover, was the establishment of the company as a known brand with a reputation for quality. According to management this outlook particularly reflected the view of the Hong Kong owners that consumers and the public were important stakeholders in the business, and this was important in a business environment in which continued operations were contingent upon the granting of licences by the relevant authority. Prior to privatisation the relationship between the company and the community was moderated by the government. Subsequently this became a matter for the business itself. It employed various strategies to this end including philanthropic activities, and the maintenance of a 'community consultation committee' which functioned as an advisory board, and included key community bodies in its membership.

The regulatory framework   It is important to note that the privatisation process was not merely a matter of selling off government assets. Strong regulatory measures were put in place to ensure appropriate levels of service provision protecting the public interest. EnergyCo's activities were primarily regulated by the Victorian Essential Services Commission (the Commission). The Commission's general regulatory powers were set out in the *Essential Services Commission Act 2001* and were applied to the electricity industry through the Victorian *Electricity Industry Act 2000*. The Victorian industry was regulated further through a National Electricity Law and National Electricity Code which operated pursuant to the *National Electricity (Victoria) Act 1997*.

The Commission's primary objective was to protect the long-term interests of Victorian consumers with regard to the price, quality and reliability of essential services including electricity. In pursuing that objective the Commission was required to promote 'competitive market behaviour', but also 'to ensure that regulatory decision making has regard to the relevant health, safety, environmental and social legislation applying to the regulated industry'.[13] Competition was thus limited in a number of important respects. First, companies were required to obtain a licence to distribute electricity, and the licensing agreements substantially regulated the behaviour of the licence-holders. Secondly, the Commission had the power to set electricity prices, following information gathering and analysis, and formal consultations with stakeholders.

---

13   Sections 8(1) and (2) of the *Essential Services Commission Act 2001*.

In this regulatory environment increased costs might not have been able to be passed on to the consumer, and this placed particular pressures upon management. In the case of EnergyCo it was recognised that the objective of management was essentially to deliver upon shareholder expectations. Accordingly it was expected that lower prices would inevitably have some impact upon employment costs rather than returns to capital. However, as a consequence of the current owner's focus on reputation and stakeholder relations, these would be expected to be met from productivity improvements, not necessarily job losses.

Employment changes following privatisation   Across the electricity industry in Victoria it is estimated that the workforce declined from about 27,000 in 1996 to about 9,000 in 2003. Most of this occurred as the privatised companies eliminated various non-core businesses and streamlined their operations to core activities, reducing employee numbers and capital overheads in the process. According to one manager:

> The major driver was cost and productivity at the time because we had a lot of remote regional operations and through the history of agreements with unions … those operations were, in some cases carrying, say, 20 line workers when you only needed eight. They were operating out of facilities where the capital investment was too high for what was actually being delivered.

Many of the non-core businesses were spun off into new companies which were provided with start-up capital (which had to be repaid over time) and other support from the core enterprises. These start-up companies were given guaranteed contracts by the core enterprises for the first few years. Thereafter they were required to re-tender for the continuation of their contracts. EnergyCo subsequently was party to more than 20 long-term contracts with firms which were originally part of the main SECV group.

It was not only non-core activities which were outsourced in the case of EnergyCo. The company also made it a practice of contracting out many of its core activities to 'stand alone' contractors who worked under the umbrella of the organisation. For example, in the networking section of the company the manager reported at the time of this study that there were approximately 700 employees and 300 contractors. Known as 'umbrella contractors' their operations were tightly supervised and controlled by the company, including supervision of the contractors' sub-agreements and accounts. At the same time EnergyCo was giving less attention to training. This created major problems for the company as a significant skilled labour shortage developed, with many workers being lured to other States by higher wages.

Overall the consequences of privatisation appear to have been beneficial for both the company and its core employees (including 'umbrella contractors'), but less so for its peripheral workers and those who lost their jobs during the staff reductions of the late 1990s. EnergyCo's enterprise agreements offered favourable terms and conditions of employment, including annualised salaries developed to suit particular categories of employees, the continued availability of overtime and so on. Union officials saw these favourable outcomes for core employees and 'umbrella contractors' alike as the result of favourable labour market conditions arising from the shortage, as noted, of skilled labour in the industry generally. Whilst line managers had reduced wage costs through outsourcing, there was a limit to which such costs could be reduced without risking labour supply.

For its part the company had benefited from the productivity improvements brought about at least partly (new technology is also a major contributor) through specialisation. In the words of the CEO:

> We're probably twice as productive now as we were ten years ago. But what is driving that? ... Certainly contracting out has been part of the reason ... We used to do 30 things, we now do 14. We don't dig holes any more so we concentrate on the 14 things we do well.

Labour relations and workplace partnerships   Prior to the company's privatisation the relevant trade unions were highly integrated into the operations of the industry generally. With the exception of senior executives virtually all employees, including divisional and sectional managers and professional staff such as engineers and accountants, were members of unions, and regularly attended union meetings. The SECV provided for something in the order of 40 of its employees to be engaged in union activities on a full-time basis. These arrangements came to an end with the company's privatisation. Unions were no longer given the previous level of support, company paid union positions were abolished and union membership declined accordingly. At the same time the company made a move to strengthen the management function within the organisation. Higher paid positions with a much greater diversity of managerial skills and experiences were introduced, considerably widening the gap between the salaries of senior employees and those at non-managerial levels.

Notwithstanding these changes the evidence gathered for this study suggests that the company still continued to operate through a 'stakeholder'-type approach with both unions and employees. One of the company's enterprise agreements of 1997 recognised that 'the interests of the Company, Employees and Unions are interdependent, and that their future prosperity in the power industry rests with a commitment from all to maintain a competitive edge'. The agreement continued on to say that the parties 'recognise the need for a consultative and participative approach into the future'. EnergyCo's Mission Statement also emphasised a commitment to what it calls its 'primary stakeholder groups', shareholders, customers and employees.

In keeping with these sentiments, the company subsequently continued to commit itself to the collective bargaining process and collaboration with trade unions. There was frequent disputation between the parties, but this was regarded as reasonably amicable rather than threatening cohesion within the organisation.

The company's agreements provided for a formal right of entry to the company's premises for accredited union officials during working hours for the purposes of consulting with union representatives, investigating grievances or complaints, posting bulletins and so on. Further agreements in 2002 and 2004 also provided for shop steward education leave, time release for shop stewards and adequate facilities in the workplace for union delegates. The 2004 agreement went so far as to encourage all employees to participate in union meetings and exercise their voting power in considering employment issues arising out of employer and employee relations. Judged by the standards of most employment agreements these were highly unusual types of provisions.

Apart from its commitment to management–union relations, the company also gauged its performance in terms of employee relations. Its annual reports detailed various objectives in relation to employees, including its aim to improve employee satisfaction, commitment and motivation, and to improve health and safety performance. Again, these were quite unusual commitments to employees measured by the standards of most Australian companies.

In terms of employee 'voice', beyond trade union representation there were other communication measures used within EnergyCo. The 1997 enterprise agreement established a joint consultative committee, the assigned role of which was to improve business performance, ensure local working conditions were adequate, develop and foster effective communication, and improve productivity. One of the major issues dealt with by the committee was the issue of 'contracting out' parts of the company's business.

As noted, a high proportion of EnergyCo's business operated through so-called 'umbrella contractors' which performed an important role in the company's strategy for flexible employment practices. All the company's enterprise agreements provided for the ongoing use of contractors, outsourcing and temporary employment through external agencies. However, apart from the use of contractors for certain functions, other use of non-regular labour, such as outsourcing 'internal functions' and using temporary employment for 'workload peaks' and short-term requirements were subject to agreement between the parties. In the pursuit of efficiency, the agreements stressed the potential for both downsizing and growth in employee numbers, and relocation of employees subject to conditions.

In addition to this type of numerical flexibility, EnergyCo's agreements also provided for some degree of flexible pay contingent upon the performance of the business itself, and also on the personal performance of the individual employee. The company's agreements also included increasingly more scope for flexible working-time arrangements. Agreements entered into in the mid-to-late 1990s permitted hours of work to be varied only following negotiations between the company, the employees affected, and the relevant union. However, later agreements entered into between the company and unions indicated a more business-oriented view (the 'span of hours [worked by employees] may be used to safely and efficiently program work to meet business and client objectives'), albeit subject to an ongoing commitment by the company to negotiate with unions regarding variation of hours and continuance of shift rosters. The company's agreements over this time also show evidence of efforts to implement family-friendly work practices, including working from home in appropriate cases.

As a privately held company, EnergyCo had all the qualities of an 'insider' organisation, and appeared to offer what might be deemed to be 'partnership'-style relations with its employees and their representative organisations. Consultation and communication were important instruments for fostering trust and co-operation between the parties whilst recognising that there were genuine conflicts of interest. There was also evidence of high performance work practices in the shape of various flexible employment forms. At the same time, however, there is some evidence that the flexible working patterns impacted less well upon those who had their work outsourced or 'contracted' rather than maintained as 'core' employees, and that all groups were working much longer hours, some of which was unpaid, as a result of the more flexible work time arrangements introduced under the company's agreements.

Perhaps these do not seem like very surprising results, but the question which must be asked is why EnergyCo did not take greater advantage of the opportunities offered through labour law changes to introduce more radical industrial relations policies than was the case at the time of our study. We return to this issue in section 3.3.

CommCo

CommCo, an Australian telecommunications company, is a wholly owned subsidiary of a Scandinavian international business organisation. Between the early 1990s and 2005 CommCo underwent a transition from a highly successful designer and manufacturer of communication devices and infrastructure to a business specialising in communications logistics and infrastructure. That change in business strategy came about as the result of major competitive pressures in the international and Australian markets (particularly the deregulation of the Australian telecommunications monopoly Telecom) causing the company to redefine its core business and to redesign the roles that its regional subsidiaries played within that business.

In 1997 CommCo was contributing 15 per cent of local turnover on research and development. It also carried out substantial manufacturing in Victoria. However in mid-1998 the company decided to close its Victorian manufacturing facility. This closure was carried out fairly smoothly from an industrial relations perspective owing to the company's ability to redeploy 250 workers elsewhere, and generous redundancy packages offered where redeployment was not possible. Further rounds of job shedding occurred in 2001 and 2002 as part of a global strategy by the international business to reduce costs. In 2002 CommCo also decided to close its Australian research and development arm, and to relocate this part of its business to Europe. This decision resulted in the loss of a further 450 jobs.

Overall, during this period the Scandinavian parent company had reduced its global workforce by some 25 per cent. The Australian workforce, over the same period of time, had declined from about 3,000 employees to about 1,400 by 2002. This transformation in the company's core business also brought about a radical change in the constitution of its workforce. What had once included a substantial number of 'blue collar' factory-based employees became a largely 'white collar' workforce with a substantial component of 'contract' workers. On the whole none of these changes, substantial as they were, appeared to have impacted particularly negatively upon CommCo's name and reputation.

Corporate governance and parent company control   Over the period in review, the ownership of CommCo and its board structure remained fairly stable. Generally speaking it conformed with the 'insider/relational' corporate governance 'type' identified in the literature. CommCo's board was comprised of three directors all appointed by the company's parent organisation. These included the managing director, the chief financial officer and a senior management representative from the parent company. In general terms the company was largely shielded from many regulatory pressures (not being listed on the Australian Securities Exchange, nor being a telecommunications carrier), and, as a wholly owned subsidiary of a foreign company, it was also largely buffered against direct pressure by shareholders and creditors. However, the form of corporate governance and capital structure of the company did not appear to result in greater 'patience' on behalf of capital. The most significant influence upon corporate strategy was thus the parent company itself which had been reacting to short competitive pressures in order to regain profitability in recent years.

In this respect the parent company's scrutiny and control extended to virtually all aspects of CommCo's business and this appeared to produce a level of frustration at local management level. There was some feeling that the company to all intents and purposes was fundamentally a representative of the international business organisation rather than a separate operation in any real sense. According to management, the parent company's influence was:

> transposed at various levels to specific directives from each of the business units in the global organisation, who indicate exactly the basis on which we (which terms we are meant to) agree to with customers, and everything from financial arrangements, payment terms ... and all those sorts of things.

There were several examples of this important role of the parent body in setting policy for CommCo. The Chief Legal Counsel of CommCo reported the level of frustration felt about the mass redundancies made globally as the international company restructured:

> it was a decline in the business globally in the early part of the decade ... it impacted upon us particularly hard. We had a research and development

operation here with 400 plus people ... one of the leading research and development operations in Australia ... and that was closed down ... which got a bad press and we lost significant skills amongst all those people. So we have had some pretty major structural changes that have had a big human resources impact and a lot of them have been directed globally.

A further instance is seen in the acquisition by the parent company of another global telecommunications business. This company also had large operations in Australia, and these consequently had to be merged within CommCo's business. There had been no consultation with CommCo by the parent company prior to the acquisition.

Employment agreements and work practices   Prior to the major restructuring of CommCo's business from the late 1990s to the early 2000s the company offered very attractive employment conditions under a regime marked by forward-thinking human resource management practices aimed at fostering 'continuous improvement' for technological change. Industrial agreements covering the significant body of CommCo's employees reflected this philosophy, including provisions for work systems and work organisation of the 'high performance' type, such as work groups and teams with important independent powers to set job functions, employment classifications and employee numbers. Job tenure was lengthy, and ancillary benefits, such as recreation facilities, in-house medical services and lengthy maternity leave were also common.

These industrial agreements also provided for some levels of temporal flexibility (hours of work to be determined by the work group within a 38-hour week framework), high levels of numerical flexibility (including levels of contract labour hire with increases to be determined by the work group), and high levels of functional flexibility with an emphasis on training. On the other hand the agreements contained little in the way of pay flexibility in the shape of individualised performance bonuses and so on.

Throughout this time unions had an important role in the workplace through their recognition in the industrial agreements, and the recognition of their role in the work groups, albeit at a very decentralised level. The structure of labour relations over this time strongly indicates 'partnership-style' relations between the parties.

However, the company's major business restructuring also induced a substantial change in the constitution of its workforce. The closing of CommCo's manufacturing arm, the consequent decline of the company's blue collar workforce, and the increase in the number of white collar professionals and contract/consultant labour (between 500 and 700 at any one stage) led to a natural decline in the unionisation rate within the company. One consequence of this was that no union-based collective agreements were introduced at CommCo after 2001 because of the small number of unionised workers, although unions from time to time continued to play a role in workplace decision-making (for example negotiating redundancies).

There have been other changes to labour relations and work practices. Wage levels appeared to be less competitive than they were during the 1990s due to the pressure of international competition on costs. Profit margins were much lower, and the workforce appears to have been under much greater strain as a consequence of this market pressure. The demand for flexibility was placing great stress upon the ability of employees to balance work with private/family life. As one manager put it:

> Are they [the workers] working longer and harder? My bet is absolutely ... you're out there talking about work/life balance and yet you're flogging people to produce [to these] time lines ... in some of the deals we make we get very little margins so there isn't the money available to give [workers] that time.

At the same time many of the very generous ancillary employment conditions extended to CommCo's employees in earlier years were discontinued.

In this high pressure environment CommCo was finding it difficult to retain employees, causing it to question the value of its high investment in training:

> We generally invest something like between $7,000 and $10,000 a head on development. Can we afford to do that ... if we're going to continually lose people? There's a challenge about what ... we should do for people's own development versus what's needed for the organisation.

Job tenure, even amongst permanent employees, is becoming increasingly shorter. Employees are now less concerned with the 'family' type security and benefits offered in former times, and are seeking more immediate and individualised rewards. All staff are now on short-term incentive plans, of between 10 and 20 per cent (and more in the case of sales staff).

CommCo was evidently subjected to serious short-term market pressures notwithstanding the absence of any direct shareholder demands from Australian shareholders. The major restructuring of its business which occurred from the late 1990s and into the early 2000s, and which was accompanied by an externally imposed drive to contain costs, led to major changes in the nature of its employment relations and work practices. Importantly these changes did not appear to have been contributed to in any major respect by the strengthening of managerial prerogative through new labour laws, but seemed to be due more to the nature of the business itself, and the more intense national and international competition induced by Australian government policies towards privatisation and globalisation.

FinanceCo 1

FinanceCo 1 had a lengthy history as a mutual organisation providing life insurance policies to members prior to the 1990s. Such organisations tended to be organised for social rather than purely commercial purposes, including the provision of financial benefits in the case of injury or death to family breadwinners. Membership was acquired through the purchase of a product (such as an insurance policy in the case of FinanceCo 1) and voting rights were usually on a membership basis rather than the level of financial commitment. Mutualised organisations were able to distribute surpluses among members, either as cash or in the form of reduced fees and premiums. They also had the capacity to re-invest surpluses, thus creating capital reserves.

In the period from 1985 through to the late 1990s conversion from a mutual organisation to a listed public company was relatively common among life insurance businesses, building societies and credit unions in the Australian financial sector. In the case of FinanceCo 1 there were several reasons lying behind the decision to convert the organisation into a listed company. Given that the business already had substantial capital reserves, the need for access to external sources of capital was not, at that stage, an overriding concern. More important was the changing environment in the finance industry generally, including the deregulation of the finance sector in Australia, globalisation, the breaking down of the traditional barriers between banking and insurance services, technological change, the growth of superannuation and so on.

In the view of the company's board of directors this new industry environment called for a completely different type of ownership structure to enable it to adjust and develop. A proposal for members to exchange their membership rights for shareholdings in a new company, listed on the Australian Securities Exchange, was accepted by a large majority in 1997, and the company was listed in the following year.

Ownership structure, corporate governance and accountability Academic literature seems to suggest that despite the fact that membership in mutual organisations offers similar governance controls to those able to be exercised by shareholders of companies, management in many mutual insurance companies is basically self-appointing and free from much supervision or control by members.[14] The view of management within FinanceCo 1 was that with demutualisation and share market listing had come a sharper business focus driven by higher levels of accountability.

The company's ownership and governance structure following conversion to a listed company was fairly typical of a large listed 'outsider' style of company. The make-up of the board current at the time this study was undertaken was a

---

14   H. Hansmann, 'The Organisation of Insurance Companies: Mutual Versus Stock' (1985) 1 *Journal of Law, Economics and Organization* 125.

standard 'outsider' type, comprised of only one executive and six non-executive directors. The company's shareholdings were diffused. The top five shareholders, all institutions, held between 3 and 13 per cent of the total shares in the business. Around 70 per cent of the company's shares were still held by retail or smaller non-institutional shareholders many of whom received their shares in exchange for membership at the time of the demutualisation. The share ownership profile was also characterised by an unusual overlap between shareholders, customers and employees as a result of employees and policy-holders being given shares as part of the demutualisation process.

The company was protected by legislation against any threat of a takeover in the first five years of its demutualised existence, and the market for corporate control was somewhat muted by the company's size, though there was a perception that the business might be open to merger moves from one of the major banks. Nevertheless, the company's very clear direction was to pursue 'shareholder value' as its key performance objective and rapidly to increase the value of investment in the business. According to the company's officers this approach reflected a cultural change within, as the company transformed itself from a mutual organisation which had 'an almost monastic culture' to one with:

> The sort of efficiency of a busy surgeon ... where you've got to get it [the job] done ... That's the sort of cultural change it feels like as you move from being a mutual where you can have long term perspectives. You haven't got the market yapping at your heels everyday.

Following this line, the company appears more explicitly than most to shape its human resources strategies to suit this 'shareholder primacy' characterisation. Asked to rank in order of priority a number of stakeholders, the company's head of human resources stated:

> I think as HR Manager, my role is to sort of optimise the output from the human resources for the good of the shareholders; so I've put the shareholders ahead of the employees.

Labour relations and employment systems   Historically the industrial relations approach of FinanceCo 1 was founded on collective bargaining and a constructive engagement with the relevant union. In the early years employees were represented by an in-house union or staff association. Relations between the association and the company were not strongly adversarial, and when the association joined a national union representing salaried and professional staff in the 1950s it withdrew within a few years because of the militancy of the larger union. Subsequently the association merged with various unions covering bank and insurance employees during the 1980s.

For much of the time prior to the company's demutualisation it had a solid reputation as a generous employer. Employment, at least for males, was secure, and the company offered the opportunity for employees to work their way through the ranks up to the highest level, with promotion linked more to length of service rather than performance. It was not until the late 1980s that a managing director was appointed who had not spent his entire working life with the company.

In terms of working conditions, the company offered generous benefits. Salaries were usually paid at above award rates, and both sick leave and long service leave compared generously with comparable sectors. The company provided study leave, medical benefits, low-cost home and personal loans and cheap meals in the staff cafeteria.

FinanceCo 1 began slowly to withdraw from this kind of employment relations culture during the 1970s, and in the 1980s and 1990s these changes began to intensify driven by a downturn in the company's performance, increased competition and a general slump in the economy. The change was facilitated in particular by the system of enterprise bargaining introduced during the first half of the 1990s. Consultants engaged to advise on ways of reducing costs recommended less generous treatment of the company's employees and substantial job shedding. In response, the company retrenched almost 2,000 employees, and began to link progression within the company to performance rather than to age and gender. The company's enterprise agreements of the early 1990s quickly revealed an intention on the part of FinanceCo 1 to modernise its employment systems based on performance-based pay, job evaluation, and employee development systems, rather than lifetime employment security.

In the years following demutualisation, a period of major financial losses for the company, its labour relations strategy also underwent a reappraisal. Whereas the company had been prepared to pursue a collective approach to enterprise regulation throughout most of the 1990s, collaborating with unions on agreements designed to improve efficiency and productivity, its relationship with unions became very different. Although relations between the company and unions still remained fairly cordial at the time of this study (there was, for example, some degree of formal consultation between the company and unions on such matters as restructuring and retrenchments), there was no longer an ongoing bargaining relationship between the parties. No new agreement was negotiated after 2000, and a major decline in union membership since the mid-1990s saw the union's power within the company considerably reduced. Whilst the company seemed content to regulate employment on an individual basis, for its part the union did not seem to regard the negotiation of a new agreement as a high priority. The attitude of both management and union seems best summed up in the statement by one union official that 'we probably don't figure on each other's radars at the moment'.

High performance work practices   As noted the company had been committed to the development of a more 'constructive culture' since the mid-1990s and continued to provide reports to the market on its progress in this respect. A key aspect of this culture was the development of a 'high performance workplace', including culture measurement and management techniques focussed on the skills of the workforce. Many of the company's work systems were based on the Six Sigma model for quality assurance, one of the most commonly used methodologies for business process improvement. This model, focussing on process improvement and customer focus, provided statistical tools and management systems designed to reduce variation in output by controlling input and reducing or eliminating errors. It also emphasised team-based approaches to work performance.[15]

As indicated, the company's enterprise agreements of the mid-to-late 1990s introduced significant changes in pay flexibility, and flexible working hours. The company also moved away from the rigid classification of work towards a form of functional flexibility which allowed movement within particular job 'families'. The company also adopted various systems of performance-based pay which rewarded high performing employees over lower performers. There was, further, a generous (in some cases personalised) employee share ownership scheme.

On the other hand there was very little in the way of formal structures for employee involvement in the management of FinanceCo 1. In the absence of strong union representation, or consultative committees, the company tended to rely on mechanisms such as feedback lines and employee surveys. Generally speaking the attitude of the company's management seemed to be that employee involvement was a 'non-issue'. According to the company's HR manager:

> If the business is going to make any great changes, then the manager who is responsible for that area is obviously going to consult with his people and drive the change through in a way that empowers the people in there. So it's all about good management really.

Partnership relations?   It follows from the foregoing discussion that FinanceCo 1 cannot be said to work in 'partnership-style' relations with either its employees or trade unions. In fact the company explicitly rejects the concept of partnership in relation to its employment systems. When asked about the extent to which the union would be consulted about major changes, the HR manager responded that the union would be told what was happening but not involved in discussions as 'there were just some things that had to be done'.

In respect of employees the same manager reported that the term 'partnership' was not an appropriate one to apply to employment:

> It's an employee relationship. They've got managers, they've got objectives to do and their managers are there to help manage them ... so there is a sort of a command and control structure even though we don't actually adopt a command and control kind of directive approach.

---

15   T. Devane, *Integrating Lean Six Sigma and High Performance Organisations*, Centre for the Study of Work Teams, Pfeiffer, 2004.

FinanceCo 1 is a good example of the ways in which corporate governance and labour management regimes within enterprises both may change markedly in response to a substantial restructuring of capital and ownership arrangements. The company's transformation from an 'insider' controlled business with highly protective conditions for employees to a market-oriented organisation with much less employee security is clear from the facts presented in the study. During the period of its re-orientation FinanceCo 1 seems to have been assisted, especially in the early and mid-1990s by the changing labour law framework. However, unlike some other companies examined in this study, the company does not seem to have required the use of more radical labour law policies introduced in the second half of the 1990s in order to shift from a collectively regulated to an essentially managerially regulated workplace. That transition seems more to have come about in circumstances of large-scale reductions in employee numbers prior to and since demutualisation, and the decline in union membership which occurred contemporaneously with those developments.

BiotechCo

BiotechCo was founded as a private company in 1995 by a group of scientists for the purposes of undertaking the commercial development of their discoveries. The company subsequently operated in partnerships with American-based businesses. It had several products in the development stage. The company had about 40 employees, most of whom were professional scientists.

In 2003 the company was listed on the Australian Securities Exchange, and in 2006 it merged with another similar company to create a full range of products between the discovery and 'market approval' stages. Prior to its stock market listing BiotechCo's dominant source of finance was venture capital. Venture capital is not merely a source of finance for fledgling companies, but its providers may also offer other support in the form of intellectual capital and know-how, and connection with other networks.[16] As a form of finance, venture capital appears more closely to resemble the kind of relational finance typically found in insider systems of corporate governance. In the US for example, venture capital organisations typically engage in detailed monitoring through board memberships and strong relations with management. Although some Australian evidence suggests that board membership by venture capitalists is rare,[17] in the case of BiotechCo, most of the capital providers were on the board, or at least had 'observer' status, before the company went public.

---

16   L. Cyr, D. Johnson and T. Welbourne, 'Human Resources in Initial Public Offering Firms: Do Venture Capitalists Make a Difference?' (2000) *Entrepreneurship Theory and Practice* 77; N. Wells, B. Coady and J. Inge, 'Spinning Off, Cashing Up and Branching Out: Commercialisation Considerations for Bio-Entrepreneurs in Australasia' (2003) 9 *Journal of Commercial Biotechnology* 209.

17   Wells et al., ibid., p. 216.

With the public listing of BiotechCo the influence of venture capital in the company's affairs correspondingly declined. At the time of the listing the proportion of shares owned by venture capital organisations was 60 per cent. This subsequently declined to about 15 per cent, and the finance and governance structure of the company accordingly then reflected a more typically 'outsider' model. The company's board was comprised of two executive directors and four non-executive directors. Four of the top five shareholders were large institutional investors. The largest shareholding by a single body was around 13 per cent, and only two shareholders held 10 per cent or more of the company's issued share capital.

On the other hand the market for corporate control in the biotechnology sector remained relatively weak. There was very little merger and takeover activity, and the volume of trading in shares in the sector was very low. The company's subsequent takeover of another listed biotechnology company was the first 'public to public' takeover in the Australian biotechnology market.

The venture capitalists were largely replaced by institutional shareholders, but these institutional shareholders were perceived by the company's management to provide stability and an understanding of the need for appropriate governance structures that would assist the company to develop. While the literature suggests that venture capital funding is more akin to relational investing, BiotechCo's experience of venture capital was that while it offered a longer time frame for investment return, it was at the same time a very rigid form of finance. Says the Chief Financial Officer:

> There seems to be a very narrow outlook and I think the fundamental issue is
> that the VCs (are) looking for an exit; they're all looking for an exit so nobody
> is saying I want to build a sustainable business.

The CFO was not of the view that BiotechCo's institutional investors were particularly driven by short-term objectives. There was, however, a short-termism built into the market that created pressures to have 'announceable milestones'. These were largely centred around the many regulatory hurdles the company was required to clear in order to get its products to market. The company was also required actively to manage shareholder expectations against short-term outcomes and did this by making it very clear to prospective investors that the company offered a sound longer term investment strategy, but also that there were no short cuts in terms of product development and commercialisation.

Human resources strategy   There appeared to be no pressure upon the company's human resources manager to shape the company's approach to human resources policies with a view to shareholder value or cost restriction. The company had no relationship with any trade union and regulated its relations with its employees through common law individualised contracts built upon the statutory minimum standards set out in the relevant labour laws. There were no collective 'voice' mechanisms in the organisation, nor was there any formal employee consultation apart from the annual performance appraisal process, although more recently the company had used external consultants to gather employee opinion on some issues.

In terms of pay, the market was an influence on the remuneration system as would be expected in an outsider company. However because the market for scientists' salaries was primarily set in the university sector, the company had adopted a system in which fixed administrative principles rather than performance were the dominant factor in determining base salary. Consequently the company adopted an incremental pay system similar to that used in the university sector. The company used adjustments to salaries in that sector and any relevant market salary surveys as a general guide to the amount by which salaries for the company's employees increased beyond incremental rises. The company did have a performance bonus tied to company rather than individual performance. The company also had an employee share ownership scheme. Generally speaking salaries at the executive and senior management level were relatively low when compared with other listed companies although this group could earn as much as 30 per cent under the company's performance bonus scheme.

Training and professional development were obviously important issues and the company used a combination of in-house and externally provided training. The company had a budget for conferences and similar professional development matters, and the extent to which the particular interests of the company's scientists could be met depended largely upon its resources at any point of time. In this respect, recruiting and motivating employees appeared to be a potential problem, when compared with the relative security and resources of the university sector for example.

During its relatively short history the company had already had one round of retrenchments for financial reasons, which resulted in the reduction of the company's workforce by about 40 per cent. This episode remained something of a concern for the remaining staff, and the company's management perceived there to be difficulties in a strategy of trying to achieve cost savings through reducing the size of its workforce on a regular basis. At the same time there was a perception that the company's workforce was 'primarily motivated by doing interesting science' and was not particularly motivated by traditional human resource management techniques. By way of example, whilst there was a view that the company's employee share ownership scheme played some role in motivating staff as well as educating them in the ways of the market, the company's HR manager noted that without evidence of a direct causal link between their individual performance and the company's performance many of the employees would have remained sceptical about the benefits of the scheme. This, in turn, would have tended to undermine the share plan's motivational impact.

Work organisation, high performance work practices and workplace partnerships   Factors such as the inability to offer job security and the relatively restricted opportunities within the company had the potential to undermine the loyalty of the employees. In recognition of these circumstances employees were not expected to devote a lifetime to the company – rather it was acknowledged that they would have legitimate interests separate from those of the company, and that these would, to some degree, be accommodated. Thus the company utilised the performance development and review process to ascertain the future aspirations of employees either within or beyond the company. Where it was clear that a particular employee felt constrained by the lack of opportunities offered by the company, attempts were made to find other roles for the person within the organisation that would keep them motivated and assist them to move on to other areas of work. This approach seems to have been underpinned by the notion of mutual gains: the company believed that it gained by having motivated employees with broad potential for further skill development even if they had aspirations beyond the company, and employees gained by the company assisting them to find positions suitable for their skills and interests.

The highly skilled nature of the work also meant that most employees had a high level of control over their own work processes. There was a work flow plan and there was management by objectives, but many of the so-called 'high performance work practices' were unsuitable for application to this type of process. Despite this, however, the company did report that it was looking towards the application of some type of 'team performance' culture based on performance outcomes in the future. Although the company did not identify itself as having a 'partnership' culture, the company's human resources goal was described by the HR manager in the following terms:

> To all work together towards the one common goal and to make sure that everyone knows that they are part of it, that all feedback is ... taken seriously and valued ... [That's] the only way we can progress.

BiotechCo presented an interesting case in which the nature of the industry and the stage of the company's development within it produced an unusual set of relationships between corporate governance, capital and labour. The company was widely exposed to market forces, but the speculative nature of this market type, and the active management of shareholders' expectations of short-term returns, reduced pressure from this source and permitted longer term relations with major shareholders. On the labour side, the company in a number of respects was unable to offer the security and professional advancement which might attract scientists to other (principally public sector) employers. Nevertheless problems of labour turnover, motivation and long-term commitment to the company appeared to be ameliorated somewhat by the fact that the company's employees prioritised a commitment to their profession over and above the commercial and financial rewards associated with it. At the same time, the company was careful to avoid actions which might have undermined the trust and security of its workforce.

To all intents and purposes then, despite its diffused capital structure BiotechCo operated in some ways as an 'insider'-type company featuring a collaboration between management and the principal shareholding institutions. In this arrangement labour worked in an individualised and non-oppositional relationship with management, and with few formal legal protections. But at the same time, the skilled nature of the workforce, its accumulated know-how and the long-term nature of capital's commitment provided a form of implicit security.

FinanceCo 2

FinanceCo 2 was founded in 1978 by three people who had developed a new specialised software system for company share registry services. The company began with one client, but grew steadily, and by the early-to-mid 1990s it had secured about 80 per cent of the particular market in which it operated. It was listed on the Australian Securities Exchange in 1994, and subsequently grew into a business with established markets in the UK, the US and Europe, and with developing markets in Asia, all based on a business strategy which combined organic growth with strategic acquisition.

At the time of the company's listing on the securities exchange it had five shareholders. The listing was primarily motivated by the need to secure further capital for future expansion generally, to return funds to the vendor shareholders, and in particular to finance a move into the UK market. The listing coincided with the introduction of a new system for facilitating the computerised settlement of share trades[18] which the company was then able to capitalise on. This contributed to the $2.6 million profit made by the company in its first six months of trading.

As noted, the company developed strongly in international markets following its public listing. By 2000 it had secured 50 per cent of the UK market, and this was followed by further acquisitions in the US and Germany. In 2004 the company acquired another US firm for just under $400 million, increasing its share of the US market to more than 25 per cent. In the 2006–2007 financial year alone the company acquired a further seven major businesses.

Ownership, governance and corporate strategy The executive directors of FinanceCo 2 held a large proportion of the company's shares (over 40 per cent) at the time of its float and subsequently reduced the extent of their interest, though only gradually. Overall the proportion of shares held by the executive directors, management and staff remained fairly stable (estimated at between 30 and 40 per cent at the time of the study). The company's annual report showed that the company's founder, who was still in a senior management position at the time of the study, held around 10 per cent of the issued shares. Taken together with the holdings of the other founders, the group held about 25 per cent of the shares in total. As part of the public listing process employees were given a substantial

---

18   The Clearing House Electronic Sub-register System (CHESS).

portion of shares and the company continues to offer shares to employees as part of its remuneration and incentive schemes. As a consequence, while the company also had a significant number of institutional shareholders, the relatively high level of internal holding somewhat differentiated FinanceCo 2 from the typical 'outsider'-type company. This also provided a level of protection against a takeover. In other respects the company resembled an 'outsider' type. The majority of the company's board, for example, was constituted by independent directors (five out of nine) in keeping with the Australian Securities Exchange Corporate Governance Council's 'Corporate Governance Principles and Recommendations'.

The company's dominant business strategy was one of growth. That is to say that whilst the pursuit of shareholder value was important, it appeared to receive a somewhat different emphasis in FinanceCo 2 from other 'outsider'-type companies. This strategy seemed to emphasise the interests of both shareholders and staff. During the years of rapid increases in both share price and profit, there were various reports of shareholder unrest about the low level of dividend paid. At the company's annual general meeting in 2000, the Chair of the company's board responded to these complaints with an argument that shareholders were better rewarded through capital growth (share price) than through dividend payouts. To a large degree this seemed to reflect the outlook of the company's founders and the fact that this group still retained a major interest in the company. According to one of the company's senior managers:

> a big chunk of the shares are owned by [names of Chief Executive Officer and other executive directors] and a few others ... [this changes] the way a business operates because at the moment that particular shareholder group would still consider the company as a private family company and they believe that their actions are the way the business should be run ... I think he (the CEO) still thinks this is my company and this is the way I'll run it.

Corporate strategy and human resources   At the time of the company's listing on the securities exchange it employed approximately 40 people. Such had been the rapidity of its expansion that at the time of this study it had a global workforce of more than 10,000 employees of whom some 1,600 were employed in Australia. As noted, 'looking after our people' (the company's employees) was a key part of the company's business strategy although the human resources strategy was very 'business driven':

> We have ... taken on a business driven HR philosophy. It's ... like the engineering group of a manufacturing company ... just trying to get that perfect circle where if you do the right thing by the people, you get the right thing out for the company and the right thing by the shareholders. But at the end of the day HR in this company works for [FinanceCo 2], it doesn't work for the staff members.

The company did not regard itself as unduly restricted by regulatory impositions. It was subject to the usual constraints of the Corporations Act, Securities Exchange listing rules and so on, but according to the company's secretary the industry itself was largely unregulated. Labour law was not listed by the company's management as a restriction apart from the difficulty of keeping abreast of the varying occupational health and safety provisions of different Australian State and federal jurisdictions.

As a relatively new business in the non-unionised growing services sector of the economy, the company was able to establish its own individualised mechanisms for regulating the employment systems of its workers free from the constraints of collective bargaining. There were some attempts by a union to engage with the company, and the acquisition of a more highly unionised company increased the number of union members employed in the business. Nonetheless, there was an absence of significant pressure from either internal sources, or the external regulatory environment of the order to shift the company from its individualised regulatory policy.

In terms of employment relations, the company appeared to use a combination of 'insider' and 'outsider' practices. It valued longer-term relationships with employees rather than seeking strategies which permitted the company to adjust the workforce to peaks and troughs in the labour market. Many of the staff who were employed at the time of the company's listing on the securities exchange were still with the company at the time the study was carried out. However, one area in which the workforce was adjusted to workflow demands was in the customer-contact call centre. Here the company preferred to draw on a pool of casuals, using labour hire centres where necessary. Even in this part of its business though, FinanceCo 2 still maintained a more protective outlook than comparable businesses. Turnover in the call centre was two to three times higher than in other parts of the company, but at the same time, according to the company's HR manager, was still lower than the industry standard for call centres. The company had also won awards for the standard of its call centre based on physical environment, staff participation, employee satisfaction, training turnover and absenteeism.

Employee-friendly policies were used by the company as tools for recruitment and retention. Benefits such as flexible working arrangements, salary packaging, a gym and a cafeteria were offered because according to one manager: 'It's treating people well. It's making people want to stay here. We don't seem to have much trouble attracting people'. The company was also careful to avoid large-scale retrenchments if possible. The company also placed a great deal of emphasis on training and professional development. It employed 10 in-house trainers and had several training, mentoring and professional development programmes, including graduate development, technical training and global assignments. Graduates were recruited from a wide range of disciplines and given the opportunity to work in a number of different parts of the business.

Wage dispersion was relatively compressed for such a large, listed public company. The company regarded itself as setting sensible and moderate remuneration structures for executives. There was, however, also a performance-based pay system tied both to individual and company outcomes, and a highly regarded employee share-ownership scheme in which 80 per cent of the workforce were participants.

High performance work practices and workplace partnerships   Management of FinanceCo 2 appeared outwardly to be sceptical of the value of any standardised approach to work organisation of the 'best practice' type. However, there were several practices and procedures based around quality control and improvement which the company utilised in its operations. The emphasis on quality suggested a 'get it right first time' approach which was consistent with a high performance workplace style of management, and the company's quality control team encouraged employee input into its work systems. Generally there appeared to be a fairly open culture in the company which also emphasised employee involvement in charting the direction of the company. This took place through some formally structured voice mechanisms, such as annual staff surveys, and 'employee forums' which were held at particular times to deal with specific issues or in order simply to check if there were any underlying concerns of the workforce which needed to be aired. However informal communication was also important within the organisation. According to one manager:

> People know [the Chief Executive Officer] for instance, and they feel they can walk up to him and talk to him and ask him a question … anywhere in the world. And [the] regional managing director, they know him … [T]hey can challenge things that are being done, they can email.

The company reported that it had made strategic acquisitions on the basis of staff suggestions. Consistent with these practices both the employee share scheme and the performance-based pay mechanism were aimed at aligning employee interests with those of the company.

Although FinanceCo 2 did not self-identify specifically as a 'partnership'-style organisation, it was nonetheless recognised by management that various aspects of the company's human resources approach, whilst not embracing joint control with unions or employees, did lend themselves to a partnership analogy. One of the principal elements in the company's business strategy was to offer the benefits of growth to employees as well as shareholders. The company, apart from in one section of its business, offered long-term employment security to employees and took care with recruitment to try to avoid the necessity of retrenchments. At the same time, as we have seen, employees tended to be actively involved in the company's strategy and organisation. The company's HR manager found the concept of 'partnership' in relation to the company's relations with its employees a little puzzling but concluded: 'If you've got people that feel like they own the company then yes, you work in partnership with them'

FinanceCo 2 had many of the characteristics which would have tended to categorise it with the 'outsider'-type corporate governance model: it was a listed public company, with quite dispersed shareholding and an independent board. Yet on the other hand, in terms of its modus operandi the company exhibited 'insider' tendencies, including strong leadership and control from the company's founders, close commitment to employees and a fairly long-term relationship with capital. The case of FinanceCo 2 thus suggests much greater complexity in the 'styles' of capitalist organisation than the 'insider/outsider' dichotomy would suggest. How one explains this complex situation, and the factors which may influence diversity within national systems are further considered in section 3.3 of this chapter.

ManuengCo

ManuengCo is a small privately owned diversified metal manufacturing and engineering company based in an Australian country town. The business originated as a blacksmith and wheelwright in the 1880s and has been owned and controlled by descendants of the original founder for its entire history. At the time of the study, the managing director (a fifth-generation member of the family) had a majority shareholding in the company. The remainder of the shares were held by other family members, and by employees through an employee share plan. The company's board was comprised of a majority of executive directors, with only one non-executive member. Senior managers were generally recruited from within the company, many having progressed through the company from the lowest levels.

The company appeared to give priority among stakeholders to customers and workers in the local community. The company's mission statement was described as being the supply of metal products, with a vision of providing 'solutions to the customer'. The company also envisioned part of its responsibility as providing employment opportunities to local workers: 'we like to think we're a very people based company ... We like to think at least part of what we're here for is the provision of employment'.

On the other hand the concept of shareholder value as a dominant management goal did not emerge from either the company's publications or the outlook of the managing director:

> The shareholders are pretty hands-off. The family member ones [family shareholders] don't actively seek information ... and the employee shareholders are really probably more concerned about the day-to-day management stuff, so they have got a fair understanding of the business ... They're not a group that you mentally have to think ... 'how do we keep the shareholders happy?'

This means that there was virtually no shareholder-based pressure for performance outcomes. The family shareholders had inherited rather than purchased their shares in the company, and the family connection provided a more compelling

intangible reason for continuing an association with the company than the pursuit
of short-term profits. For all of these reasons the company tended to operate on
longer term planning cycles, and fear of losing the family business no doubt acted
as a greater regulator of the governance of the organisation than the search for
returns to shareholders.

Human resources   ManuengCo is a very small company (about 180 employees),
and had no distinct human resources function beyond a payroll officer. The
management of workers came directly through supervision by the company's
executive directors. As noted, the company had a long-term view of its relations
with its workers. The great majority were permanent full-time employees, and
the company engaged only a minimal casual workforce in response to peaks in
demand for the company's products. Wages were negotiated individually as part
of an annual performance process. Most workers knew the wage levels of others
and that necessitated that some attention had to be paid to retaining appropriate
relativities between them.

The company invested fairly heavily in occupational health and safety training.
It also had a strong apprenticeship programme. At the time this study was carried
out, the company had almost 30 apprentices enrolled across the four years of
trade training. These apprentices constituted the most important source of new
tradespeople for the company.

The company's employee share plan was introduced by the managing director's
father to link employee expectations with the ebb and flow of the business's
fortunes. The eligible employees were those based at the site of the company's
main operations (about 140 workers) and of these about half joined the scheme.
The scheme operated by way of returning 10 per cent of the company's profits to
eligible employees in the form of a bonus with which they could purchase shares
in the company. Employees were prohibited from purchasing shares in any other
manner (i.e. with their own money). The bonus was based entirely on company
profit, and contained no elements of individual- or work unit-based performance.
These 'employee class' shares were required to be sold when an employee left
the company. The shares then went into a pool and could be purchased by other
interested employees. In the managing director's view the scheme encouraged
an interest by employees in the overall progress of the business, but also acted,
through the annual general meeting of shareholders, as an important vehicle for
the provision of information from management to the workforce.

Labour relations   ManuengCo and its employees were covered by an award,
but basically the employment relationship was regulated through common law
agreements between the company and each individual employee. The company
had never been highly unionised, nor had it had ongoing relationships with
trade unions. The company had no current enterprise agreements, and had never
engaged in enterprise bargaining. The managing director did not see the company
as anti-union, but rather one which had always dealt directly with its employees

and wished to continue that relationship without the intervention of third parties. The managing director attributed the lack of a union presence on-site as partly due to the effects of the employee share ownership scheme and its intangible effects on employee morale.

The relevant union, on the other hand, presented quite a different picture of the company's approach. An official interviewed for this study thought that the culture at ManuengCo was one in which union membership was frowned upon if not actively discouraged. Contact between the company and the union had been minimal, but visits aimed at recruiting members, facilitated under previously existing union right-of-entry provisions, were uncomfortable and fruitless from the union's point of view.

Perhaps as might be expected in a family-owned and -controlled company without a human resources structure or trade union presence, there were few formal employee consultation mechanisms at ManuengCo. The company had tried various strategies over the years, but apart from the legally mandated health and safety committees, there were no remaining formal structures in place. As noted, the most important institutionalised form of information flow between management and the workforce occurred at the company's annual general meeting, benefiting only those employees who were share owners. However, in such a small organisation problems were usually quickly identified and dealt with informally.

Work organisation and high performance work practices   Being a manufacturing company, quality played an important role in the way work was organised at ManuengCo. The company advertised itself as working to the ISO 9001 standard[19] and it was reported to us that this had had a great impact upon how the company operated when it was first introduced. The main reason for introducing the standard was customer satisfaction, given added impetus by the pressure surrounding the need to adopt the standard at the time. The prevailing view was that 'you had to have the tick [the mark of compliance with the standard] [or] you would never get any work from anyone'. Although it appears that there is now greater flexibility in the market than when the system was first introduced the standard still played an important role subsequently in the company's safety quality management system.

The company did not describe itself as working with a 'high performance work system' and the managing director of ManuengCo tended to regard such stereotypes with some scepticism. However, the use of the ISO 9001 standard, its emphasis on employee involvement, and the use of processes which facilitated quality output had similarities with the Six Sigma model (discussed briefly in the study of FinanceCo 1 above) and with 'just in time' high performance work systems.

On the other hand the company operated with what the managing director described as a 'remarkably traditional sort of working environment' without

---

19   International Organization for Standardization, *ISO 9001 – Quality Management Systems – Requirements*.

anything like the array of flexible workplace practices which are said to characterise high performance workplaces. Generally employees worked either a nine-to-five day (office staff) or a seven-to-three (workshop staff). The company appeared to operate within this framework because it suited the kind of working environment of the rest of the (local) community, and because in the absence of pressure for change from investors or the share market, managers were able to accommodate the business to that type of culture.

Workplace partnerships?   Asked whether or not he saw the company as working in partnership with its employees the managing director's response was an unequivocal 'yes'. He saw the partnership as extending throughout all levels of the company, and as being founded particularly on the familiarity made possible by the family business environment:

> We try and make it a habit of getting out and walking around the place and saying g'day to people and knowing their last names ... that family business type stuff
> ... It just means that when push comes to shove generally speaking you've got the right of reply. And generally speaking if people are [annoyed] they won't just go and resign, they'll come and say 'listen' and we'll sort something out.

There were other features of the human resource and organisational systems of ManuengCo which were a consistent fit with this broader depiction of 'partnership'. These include, for example, the implicit employment security offered to the company's workers, the company's commitment to training and the relatively advanced form of internal labour market operating within the business.

ManuengCo is typical of many small businesses. At the time of the study it was 'insider' oriented and governed, with strong commitments to both employees and customers. Several factors beyond market forces appeared to act as a regulatory constraint upon the company's strategy for growth and profit. These included the company's physical location in a small local community, and its lengthy 'family-owned and -controlled' status. The extent to which the business operated as a partnership between the family and its employees is less certain. Unions had no direct role in the regulation of the company's employment systems, and it is unclear whether the 'informal' methods of employee consultation acted as a brake upon managerial prerogative in any real sense. The general conclusion to be drawn is that management largely operated in this business without serious constraint from either capital or labour – fitting more the model of 'personal capitalism' discussed by Berle and Means[20] and others.

---

20   A. Berle and G. Means, *The Modern Corporation and Private Property*, Macmillan, New York, 1932.

ManufoodCo

ManufoodCo is a small to medium sized meat manufacturing company which was created as the result of a merger between two smaller companies (one based in Queensland and the other in country Victoria) which had each been operating since the early 1900s. The Victorian plant, which was the focus of this study, had been established by a local family and had remained in the same hands for more than 100 years. Prior to the merger, the Queensland company had converted from a co-operative to a public company in February 2002, and had then been taken over by a Singaporean company in March 2002. The merger took place in 2003, and coincided with the retirement from management of the family who had owned and controlled the Victorian business hitherto. The Singaporean investor, through this process, remained in control of the merged business. The purpose of the merger was for the business to capture control of the market for its goods across the entire Eastern seaboard of Australia.

The company produced for the small goods market and was one of the top four producers by volume and market size in the country. Only some of the company's products were branded as those of the company itself. A large proportion of the products were supplied to supermarkets and released under the supermarket's brand. The increasing market concentration amongst supermarkets has had a notable impact on the company's business. The substantial market power wielded by supermarkets meant that it was crucial for the company to maintain good relations with these clients by delivering goods of the required quality punctually. However, the supermarket sector of the economy was also volatile, being subject to mergers and acquisitions. As a consequence, the company often found itself dealing with new managements, and new buying strategies of supermarkets.

There was an increasing move towards in-house brands amongst supermarket chains. This was suitable to the company as a substantial part of its product was already unbranded and thus appropriate for supply of this nature. However, this also meant that supermarkets were tending to demand greater control over the quality of the product and the means and timing of its supply. Leaving these pressures to one side, the single most important pressure upon the company was on price: 'Pricing is the fundamental competitive issue' according to the company's HR manager. This in turn had direct flow-on effects for human resource management, as the principal human resource objective of the company was one of cost control. Shortly after the merger the company began to pursue a strategic plan which required the reduction of operating costs, and improving production efficiency. It decided to do so by entering into an enterprise bargaining agreement with the relevant union. This decision was strategically driven rather than a response to union power. In effect the company at this stage had formed the view that the best way it could bring about systemic changes to work organisation and pay structures was in association with the employees rather than through straight out managerial power.

Labour relations   In 1996 union membership in the Victorian-based enterprise was about 15 per cent of the workforce. Membership was largely confined to the company's metal workers, and at very low levels among the product workers. This mostly reflected the anti-union stance of the company and the considerable allegiance of the workers to the family owned business and to the managing director personally. Under the award system the union had been engaged in the regulation of wages and conditions in the industry generally. It had also historically engaged in making above-award agreements with other similar plants around Victoria, but it had never been able to form such arrangements with ManufoodCo due to the anti-union stance on the part of the owners, and the general level of loyalty to the company among the company's employees. According to the HR manager:

> You had the family tradition, you had a management and [the owner] who was the managing director who was very much literally into the business. You were just as likely to see him playing around with a sausage machine as sitting in his office. The feeling of loyalty to family and company in the early days was very, very strong. The union was irrelevant. The union was seen as external to the business.

One consequence of this, according to the union, was that the workforce at ManufoodCo had been earning below industry-level wages for many years.

However, union membership levels had increased markedly over the several years prior to this study, and sat at about 60 per cent (100 per cent of the company's metal workers and slightly more than 50 per cent of its product workers). This growth had been assisted by several factors, including an increase in size of the workforce overall, the increase in the numbers of employees travelling from around regional Victoria to the plant, and a concerted recruitment drive by the union in the context of the merger between the Queensland and Victorian businesses. According to the company's HR manager:

> The company was getting larger and more remote from the [owner's name] family and ... the catchment area [the source of employees] was getting increasingly broad ... and mobile ... slowly over time you were getting people ... coming in who didn't have the unquestioning old country work ethic where you simply do your job and you're grateful for a day's work ... The modus operandi of how the company has looked after its people wasn't changing in the same way ... you have an influx of people who believe they have rights and ... will look to unionism to pick that up.

Allied with the increasing union membership was a commitment by the company's HR manager that the introduction of the required new production systems could be accomplished more readily through an enterprise bargaining agreement made with the union.

The new agreement: costs and flexibilities In August 2005 the management of ManufoodCo and the union commenced negotiations on a new agreement designed to enhance the long-term viability of the business and job security for the company's employees. The agreement was to be based on a number of fundamental principles. The overarching principle was the establishment of a culture of 'common purpose' between the company and its employees as joint stakeholders in business improvement. Other principles included workforce flexibility, improvement of labour efficiencies, enhancing employee satisfaction and well-being, and a commitment that in moving to work practices designed to maximise business performance there would be no reduction in ordinary time earnings for employees.

The draft agreement subsequently presented to the union in early 2006 proposed a number of important changes to work practices. One of the most important was the introduction of a competency-based classification system and the extension of managerial control over the functions or roles to which employees could be allocated. The agreement also sought to increase temporal flexibility by rearranging shift times. For some workers these arrangements would probably have interfered with child care or family responsibilities. In addition to improving functional flexibility the competency-based 'skill specific' classification system was designed to create a career path for employees. In the words of the HR manager:

> One of our goals is to become an employer of choice ... you can actually start here working on the floor literally handling [the raw materials]; you can actually progress through to supervisory roles; you can move across into the quality stream and that will also be part of the career path structure and from there you can go through and do your ... technology and university qualifications ... My goal is that we have local youths ... hoping for the day when they can work here.

Numerical flexibility in terms of workers on the other hand was not an important objective for the company. The award had always permitted the engagement of permanent casuals, but generally speaking the company's employment of casual labour had tended to decline since the 1990s basically due to the relatively low base wage paid to permanent workers at the plant.

A further important objective of the restructuring process was for the company to establish new teamwork practices and greater consultation with employees over work methods and workplace change.

Finally, in the area of wages the draft agreement proposed to increase the base wage of employees but to decrease meal allowances in the event of overtime. This appeared to result in the potential for a reduction in take-home pay for some employees, but was agreed to in principle by the union due to its perception that the agreement was, in overall terms, beneficial for the company's employees, and also because of what was foreshadowed as a new era of closer consultation between management and labour.

New management and further business restructuring   In the second half of 2006 several events occurred which interfered with the progress of the negotiations over the new enterprise agreement. In August the Singapore-based business owners installed a new company president. This position ranked above the chief executive officer in the hierarchy of management. Around the same time several decisions were taken to restructure the company's business. One of these involved closing the processing plant belonging to the Queensland branch of the company and relocating its operations to the Victorian site. This decision was made on the basis that there would be economies of scale in consolidating production, and because the existing processing machinery at the Victorian plant was of better quality and more efficient than that of the Queensland plant. This relocation had major implications for the Victorian plant, which was consequently required to enlarge its processing capacity by adding some machinery transported from Queensland and purchased elsewhere, as well as employing extra staff to meet the changed production needs.

Two further events disrupting the negotiations involved the closure of the Victorian plant's distribution facility and the closure of its Victorian-based supply facility. Both of these were outsourced to other companies. These closures led to a substantial number of employee redundancies. Most of these employees were offered alternative positions as process workers at the enlarged Victorian plant, but very few chose to take up this option.

The company's new senior management then made some decisions which cut across and compromised the role of the HR manager and her team in negotiating the agreement. It was decided that the proposed shift changes and the cutting of meal allowances would be introduced unilaterally. This meant that about two-thirds of the workforce lost about $50 to $60 worth of tax free allowances per week, and a large proportion were inconvenienced in relation to child care arrangements. At the same time, senior management also presented an ambit claim to employees with the purpose of rationalising weekend pay rates.

As a consequence of these events negotiations between the company and the union virtually came to a halt and movement towards an enterprise agreement was postponed. Wage increases in line with the decisions of the Fair Pay Commission were passed on to the workforce, but there was no move to introduce any of the other productivity measures (including the competency-based classification process) foreshadowed in the draft agreement. The company's HR manager resigned in the wake of these developments.

Despite all of these developments there was no industrial unrest amongst the employees, many of whom either lacked readily transferable skills or still retained some loyalty to the company although labour turnover remained high as many of the company's disgruntled workers sought to move on to other employment. Relations between the company and the union also remained reasonably harmonious. Although the union was not optimistic that there would be successful negotiations leading to a completed agreement, mindful of its very weak position under the current labour laws it preferred to preserve its membership base and maintain its foothold inside the company rather than initiate industrial action.

ManufoodCo is a further example of a relatively small regionally located business enterprise, historically locked into a local community, and essentially 'insider' controlled. As the result of its merger with another business, control by a foreign company was substituted for control by a majority-owning family after 2003, and this led to a somewhat different approach to labour relations within the Victorian operation. However, this changed approach was more one of appearance than substance. The company, under its new management, continued the previous practice of holding the union at arm's length and dealing with employees directly. Its tactics according to the union are locked into what has been labelled a 'low road' to success.[21] This entails competing within markets on the basis of low wages and conditions, outdated production systems and work practices, and managerial unilateralism rather than modernised systems, performance incentives, employment security and employee involvement in workplace strategy.[22]

3.3 Outcomes and Implications

What do these studies tell us about the relationship between corporate ownership structures, corporate governance and labour management? In particular do they suggest a recent pattern of development which links changes in ownership structure with a more market-oriented, shareholder-oriented, form of corporate governance accompanied by adverse or negative outcomes for employees and workers generally?

It is useful to start here by reaffirming a point made earlier in this chapter. The closer one empirically investigates business enterprises, even within common systems, the more one becomes aware of the overwhelming complexity of business practices constituted by the heterogeneity of styles in corporate governance, labour management systems and much else besides. Not surprisingly there is an associated difficulty in drawing major conclusions linking governance and management style with the larger themes embodied in the varieties of capitalism and legal origins literature noted in Chapter 1. For that reason the case study findings should be viewed cautiously: in many important respects they tell us more about difference than uniformity, and even where certain similar orientations appear, it does not follow that these necessarily characterise Australian regulatory style and business practice as a whole.

21   C. Gill and D. Meyer, 'High and Low Road Approaches to the Management of Human Resources: An Examination of the Relationship Between Business Strategy, Human Resource Management and High Performance Work Practices' (2008) 16 *International Journal of Employment Studies* 67.
22   See, generally, Deery and Walsh, above n. 11.

In most of our studies, in the time period under review, ownership change or capital reorganisation occurred which could be said to have exposed the relevant company to greater 'market' or 'outsider' pressure. In some cases these changes merely exposed what were already classic 'outsider'-type governance models to larger capital markets. These companies (ResourceCo 1 and ResourceCo 2 for example) could be said already to have had 'shareholder-oriented' outlooks in their style of corporate governance and nothing occurred to vary that approach. But there were, on the other hand, examples among our studies where the greater exposure to market pressures had obviously resulted in a re-orientation of the corporate governance outlook away from a more 'stakeholder' inclined model towards a 'shareholder-primacy' approach. The two most outstanding examples of this are seen in the privatisation of the former government-owned ServiceCo, and the demutualisation of FinanceCo 1. In each of these instances the change in business orientation was seen to have direct negative implications for employees and trade unions in much the same way as was the case in ResourceCo 1 and ResourceCo 2, although there were also some important complexities in these arrangements as we note below.

However, not all cases favoured an 'increased market-exposure/increased shareholder orientation' interpretation. For example, in the case of both BiotechCo and FinanceCo 2 share market pressure appeared to have little relevance to corporate governance following upon the public listing of each company. In the case of BiotechCo this was in large part due to the type of industry in which it was engaged. However in the case of FinanceCo 2 the existing owners continued to manage the company with more 'insider/relational' strategies than with 'market'-oriented strategies notwithstanding the company's changed financial structure. In other instances we found that existing owners would continue to exercise governance strategies oriented towards consumer and public interest notions in addition to share market considerations even after a privatisation/listing process (EnergyCo). Shareholder primacy might also be restricted in the case of relatively small businesses operating in local communities.

What role did the regulatory framework play in these changed governance structures? Whilst it is the case that in Australia, as elsewhere, legal and regulatory measures were introduced during this period to give greater protection to investors,[23] and generally speaking while the regulatory environment may have stimulated certain orientations and approaches in corporate governance at this time, it does not appear that particular corporate behaviour towards shareholders in our studies was stimulated by any statutory or other legal obligation in any highly specific sense. Thus, while it may be the case that corporate law reforms resulted in a number of changes, it is less clear that they were the precise stimulus for the various management strategies in the cases we observed.

This does not mean to say, though, that regulation was irrelevant to the governance approaches of companies during this period of change. For example

---

23   See Mitchell et al., above n. 4.

in the case of our studies of privatised businesses, specific government regulation, and forms of self-regulation, were associated with, and in some instances survived the marketisation process, placing boundaries around the company's ability to pursue shareholder-oriented strategies by maintaining public standards and expectations deemed appropriate for leading Australian service providers. Other kinds of regulation which must at least be acknowledged as relevant are those labelled as standards of 'corporate social responsibility' or 'corporate social accountability' in the literature.[24] Some of our studies featured companies which had adopted voluntary regimes of self-regulation designed to position their corporate governance practices within a framework of ethical conduct towards non-shareholder constituents (for example, ResourceCo 1 and ResourceCo 2). However, as important as these might seem to be, the literature in this general area suggests that self-regulation of this type in Australia is embryonic and mostly concerned with the formulation of policies and processes. As a consequence it has had a modest impact on corporate decision-making in practice.[25] For these reasons we cannot assume that all forms of socially-oriented governance regulation operate equally effectively.

Marketisation or greater market exposure, then, does not always lead to simple shareholder primacy, or perhaps even heightened shareholder preference, as an objective of corporate governance, but nor, too, do socially-oriented policies, particularly of the voluntary kind, necessarily inhibit a shareholder-oriented approach. It follows that changes in ownership structure/governance type (say from an 'insider'-type to an 'outsider'-type) do not necessarily alter the nature of the relations between the company and its shareholders, and, where relations are affected, they may not change in ways that are predicted. For example in some of our studies, as we have noted, change in ownership structure barely altered the style of corporate governance in any formal sense, though the pursuit of shareholder value was more clearly pronounced than under the previous governance regimes in those companies (ResourceCo 1 and ResourceCo 2).

Other case studies indicated more of a formal shift from what we have described as 'insider'-governed to 'outsider'-governed as a result of important changes in ownership style (principally in cases of privatisation or share market listing). Sometimes when this occurred there was a noticeable accompanying change in the relationship between the company and its shareholders, whereby management indicated a greater awareness of, or reacted more readily to, shareholder pressure (FinanceCo 1, ServiceCo, EnergyCo).

Frequently these developments translated into labour shedding and associated cost reductions through the adoption of such practices as casualisation, labour

---

24   H. Anderson, 'Corporate Social Responsibility: Some Critical Questions' (2005) 24 *University of Tasmania Law Review* 143.

25   See, for example, M. Jones, S. Marshall and R. Mitchell, 'Corporate Social Responsibility and the Management of Labour in Two Australian Mining Industry Companies' (2007) 23 *Corporate Governance: An International Review* 57; Anderson, ibid.

hire under contract and so on (ResourceCo 1, ServiceCo, EnergyCo, FinanceCo 1), but this was not always the case. In the cases of BiotechCo and FinanceCo 2, other influences such as the particular type of industry in which the company operated and the particular type of growth strategy adopted by management meant that greater exposure to capital markets did not translate into higher shareholder-oriented governance. In these two companies, despite public listing, management of shareholder expectations continued to exhibit more 'insider' than 'outsider' qualities.

As noted earlier, the greater exposure of business to market pressure is perceived to have implications not merely for management–shareholder relations but consequently also for systems of labour management. One key issue in this perspective is how companies choose to improve shareholder value, assuming that such an orientation always has some influence in terms of pressures from shareholders. To some extent we have answered this question by pointing out that adjustment for shareholder value is not always an immediate or necessary response. But if it is, companies still have some choices about how to respond to this pressure, between strategies based on cutting labour costs (wherein labour is principally treated as a fixed external expense to the company), and those based on some form of high-value approach in which the company invests in labour and treats its labour force as one of its stakeholders.

Here again our case studies indicate a mixture of predicted and some unpredicted outcomes. In virtually all of our studies (the most obvious exceptions being the two small family-owned businesses) there were substantial changes made to labour management or employment systems arising from, or coinciding with, the noted changes in ownership structure and increased market exposure. This held true even of instances where there was no apparent emergence of a hard 'shareholder primacy' orientation in governance nor a major shift in company–shareholder relations as a result of the change of ownership. However the type and degree of these changes in labour arrangements varied considerably from business to business.

Some companies, including those which already resembled the typical 'outsider'-governed model, and to some degree those which were privatised and/or listed for the first time underwent important, sometimes systemic, labour adjustments which included job shedding, de-unionisation, individualised agreements with management, increased levels of casualised and contracted (as opposed to employed) labour, and the return to a high degree of unilateral (rather than joint labour–management) managerial power (ResourceCo 1, ServiceCo, ResourceCo 2, EnergyCo, CommCo, FinanceCo 1). Even in instances where management continued to deal with their workforces collectively through unions, and where some degree of collective power was still in evidence, labour concessions to managerial demands over broad aspects of the employment system were common (for example ServiceCo and EnergyCo).

It appears from this summary that in the chain of development purportedly linking changed ownership structure with a more shareholder-oriented style of corporate governance, and in turn with a changed approach to labour management, it is the less protected and secure role of labour in corporate employment systems which is the most pronounced and uniform characteristic of our case studies. Again, however, the position is not without some complexity. The degree to which de-unionisation, or weakened unions, has occurred may depend, as we noted in the case of ResourceCo 1 and ServiceCo, on a variety of factors including the particular product or service market in which the business operates, and even on geographical location. As we observed in the instances of management decentralisation which occurred in several of our companies, attitudes to types of employment systems may even vary within business organisations according to the choice of individual managers at different work sites, and differences in the strength of unions in different regions (for example, ResourceCo 1). Consequently the level of impact of a shift in corporate governance strategy upon labour may reveal strong variations between and within businesses according to all of these sorts of factors.

In our studies we attempted to examine empirically how employment systems were readjusted in each case to deal with the greater market exposure to which most of our companies were subjected. The important point to note here is that just as management in these companies did not uniformly seek a fundamental 'shareholder value' approach, nor were their responses to their labour systems uniform, even though, as we have noted, they were generally negative for labour. The change in the labour law and industrial relations environment we thought offered management a choice in how they readjusted (a choice between the so-called 'high road' and 'low road' to success)[26] and we sought to establish which of these approaches was being pursued in the cases we examined through the use of the 'partnership' metaphor.

One development that is clear is that in the large majority of our cases control of workplace organisation and systems had more or less decisively shifted away from unions and workers to management, a point commonly noted in the wider Australian literature.[27] This meant, in some cases, a shift from collective bargaining and negotiation systems between management and unions to non- or weakened-union systems (for example, ResourceCo 1, ResourceCo 2, EnergyCo, CommCo, FinanceCo 1). Generally, where unions remained important within negotiated systems they were nevertheless under pressure and forced into concessions bringing them more into line with less regulated companies. But, as noted, unions might still continue to exercise more traditional levels of power and influence in industries which were competing in less volatile markets (for example ResourceCo 1), and in some instances industries with strong union traditions were able to a degree to

---

26 See above n. 21.

27 See R. Mitchell and A. O'Donnell, 'What Is Labour Law Doing About "Partnership at Work"? British and Australian Developments Compared' in Marshall et al., above n. 6; M. Bray and P. Waring, 'The Rise of Managerial Prerogative Under the Howard Government' (2006) 32 *Australian Bulletin of Labour* 45.

maintain those for special reasons we have outlined (for example in some formerly government-owned privatised companies ServiceCo and EnergyCo).

Most of these developments we documented had overall negative consequences for labour. Generally there was downward pressure on wages and conditions, though it would appear that in some cases the shift to more flexible, less regulated, employment systems had secured appreciable financial benefits for some workers in the form of higher wages. However, this had come at the cost of much less control by workers over their working lives, and much less employment security with the shedding of jobs (ResourceCo 1, ServiceCo, FinanceCo 1, CommCo) and the 'vertical disintegration' of some industries (EnergyCo) among our set of company studies. Those made particularly vulnerable in these developments included non-core groups hired back in as contractors, casual employees or associated-businesses. These non-core groups were now much more exposed to labour market fluctuations than was the case under earlier labour laws.

On the other hand it was difficult for us to find any real or substantial indications of alternative moves to more 'partnership-style' relations among our case study companies, either between management and unions or between management and employees directly. Various forms of high performance workplace systems were in evidence in some instances (for example ServiceCo, ResourceCo 2, FinanceCo 1) but these appeared to rely more upon flexible employment and employee involvement directed through managerial prerogative, rather than genuine worker empowerment. Very few formalised employee involvement practices (such as joint committees or works councils) were found. Possible exceptions to this general picture included EnergyCo and FinanceCo 2 where there were at least some indications of meaningful joint arrangements. However, in the case of EnergyCo, these partnership relations were limited to 'core' employees. The position at ResourceCo 1 appears mixed as between its Western Australia sites and those in New South Wales. Partnership arrangements as defined for this project seemed not in evidence in the smaller family-owned businesses. Again these results appear to bear out the general findings in the academic literature, though it must be emphasised that this research work has relied on the content of formal and informal agreements and other human resource documents rather than case observation of work performance on the ground.[28]

Finally it is necessary for us to consider the role of labour regulation in influencing these outcomes. As we have noted earlier it does not appear that recent changes in the corporate regulatory framework have contributed in a highly specific sense to the generally observed shift in corporate governance practices in our case studies although there has no doubt been some influence. For example, the move to have more independent directors has been strongly influenced by this being

28   Mitchell and Fetter, above n. 2; S. Marshall and R. Mitchell, 'Enterprise Bargaining, Managerial Prerogative and the Protection of Workers' Rights: An Argument on the Role of Law and Regulatory Strategy in Australia Under the Workplace Relations Act 1996 (Cth.)' (2006) 22 *International Journal of Comparative Labour Law and Industrial Relations* 299.

a recommendation of the Australian Securities Exchange Corporate Governance Council's 'Corporate Governance Principles and Recommendations'. But has the changed labour law framework impacted decisively on the way that companies have been able to restructure their labour management, or their employment systems, and if so how? Our starting point for analysis on this point, as noted in Chapter 2, is that whilst there may be scope for argument about the character of the Australian labour law system viewed historically, generally speaking it was more consistent with a 'market/outsider'-based model of corporate governance than otherwise. Moreover the trend in labour law reform over the past decade-and-a-half overall has been more consistent with the 'outsider' model.[29]

We can characterise the impact of Australian labour law by looking at it in two stages. In the late 1980s and in the early 1990s various regulatory changes occurred which altered the role of the state authorities and introduced various legislative amendments to the core regulatory scheme. These changes heralded a new outlook from both sides of politics towards Australian labour market regulation, though this was perhaps not immediately apparent at the time, and had a long-term influence in shifting the core values of Australian labour law.[30] The new approach included a period of award restructuring,[31] a less regulated approach to irregular forms of employment, initial moves to enterprise bargaining, and restrictions on the legitimacy of trade unions. Declining union membership and changes in the social climate further undermined union industrial power. These combined events served to create a new environment which both questioned the legitimacy of regulation external to the business and also questioned the legitimacy of trade unions in regulating workplaces.

When the non-labour Liberal/National Party government regained office at a federal level in 1996, these accumulated changes had served to pave the way for far more radical reforms which legally consolidated individualised bargaining and non-unionised bargaining, weakened the role of unions in pursuing industrial action and, critically, shifted industrial power from labour to capital.[32]

---

29   See M. Jones and R. Mitchell, 'Legal Origin, Legal Families and the Regulation of Labour in Australia' in Marshall et al., above n. 6.

30   For details of this process of debate and regulatory change see R. Mitchell and M. Rimmer, 'Labour Law, Deregulation and Flexibility in Australian Industrial Relations' (1990) 12 *Comparative Labor Law and Policy Journal* 1; R. Mitchell and R. Naughton, 'Australian Compulsory Arbitration: Will it Survive into the Twenty-First Century?' (1993) 31 *Osgoode Hall Law Journal* 265.

31   For discussion see *Progress at the Workplace: Workplace Reform and Award Restructuring – Private Sector Services* and *Progress at the Workplace: Workplace Reform and Award Restructuring – Public Sector*, Reports to the Department of Industrial Relations, National Key Centre in Industrial Relations, Monash University, 1992.

32   *Workplace Relations Act 1996* (Cth). These federal laws were also matched on occasion by important legislation introduced at State government level, e.g. the *Workplace Agreements Act 1993* (WA).

The emergence of a non-union or weakened-union industrial relations climate in which managerial prerogative over employment systems has been radically reinforced appears to have been important in the adaptation of a number of our case study companies to the business environment. That is to say that whilst it is not easy to point to specific legal provisions in stimulating particular managerial initiatives among our studies, the general regulatory environment has empowered corporate management in the systemic adjustment of the employment systems under its control. In a number of our studies, the fact that unions were already in a weakened position presented opportunities for managers to pursue direct relationships with employees, without union intervention. For instance, new businesses BiotechCo and FinanceCo 2 were established in a period of union weakness and in sectors in which there was traditionally low union activity. They were thus able to bypass unions when they were established. Whilst a union had occasionally made approaches to FinanceCo 2 since its establishment, its strategies had largely been ineffectual and had not resulted in larger union coverage. In CommCo, union coverage had declined with the process of restructuring of core business activities which meant that the workforce was now mainly white collar whereas previously it had been blue collar in make-up. In FinanceCo 1, also, de-unionisation followed listing on the securities exchange, but occurred some time afterwards and without a battle with employees over this issue. In both these companies terms and conditions were now largely regulated through common law agreements, whereas in an earlier era they were likely to have been regulated through awards and/or collective agreements.

The general easing of regulatory controls over numerical and temporal flexibility in terms of employees has also had an evident impact. This has been particularly stark in the case of increases in numerical flexibility resulting in greater deployment of casual and contracted labour. In EnergyCo and CommCo, for instance, the proportion of employees to contractors had shifted considerably in the years leading up to the study. Contractors now outnumbered employees in many worksites. In EnergyCo, whilst there were clauses in the certified agreement which regulate this issue, and one of the purposes of the company's joint consultative committee was to make determinations on the increase of contract labour, the numbers of contractors nevertheless continued to increase, suggesting that the purpose and outcome of these regulations was not to stop or stem the increase but to gain union consent. In ResourceCo 1 and ResourceCo 2, even where union coverage was high, unions had agreed to terms which were not unlike those introduced through individualised agreements with regards to the introduction of more flexible work organisation and work-time.

In other instances, specific legal change had created the conditions under which some businesses had been able to move towards more radical labour management systems. Unlike ResourceCo 2, which chose effectively to de-unionise its employment arrangements through the use of common law contracts, ResourceCo 1 apparently waited until individualised agreements became available under legislation before making the same transition in its labour management strategy, even in areas where it was in direct competition with ResourceCo 2. Subsequently ResourceCo 1 also began to utilise greenfield agreements, a form first made available in the 1996 federal labour legislation, to give effect to non-union strategies elsewhere.

One of the major aims of this study was to examine and better understand the connection between corporate restructuring, ownership structure, corporate governance, and systems of labour management. In particular we have been concerned to ascertain the extent to which changes in corporate ownership structure and corporate governance have produced heightened shareholder primacy and a corresponding decline in the interests of labour. Taken as a whole our studies confirm that where companies underwent listing on the securities exchange or structural change leading to greater exposure to shareholder pressure, their governance strategies became more shareholder focussed. The extent to which the corresponding observed changes in labour management were caused by this heightened shareholder orientation is less straightforward, however. Most companies underwent increased exposure to market forces during the period of our study, and were subject to increased competitive pressure for a range of factors. The limitations of our specific focus meant that we were unable to investigate all of these factors in detail. Whilst it might be the case that increased pressures arose from concerns to retain the support of investors, it is likely to be the case also that the global integration of consumer and product markets, the entry of companies from low cost developing countries into product markets, and so on, were important variables affecting competitiveness. It is difficult to identify the extent to which any of these contributed to changes in the employment systems of affected companies.

Overall the most decisive and profound change affecting employment systems among our case study companies was the rise of relatively unchecked managerial prerogative, and the corresponding decline of union power. When we looked more closely at what types of employment relations systems might be emerging in this non- or weakened-union climate we found little to suggest the creation of new 'workplace cultures' involving workers and their representatives, at least in the content of workplace agreements and written policies. With increased managerial prerogative came widespread reduction in employee representation and consultation across the broad cross-section of enterprise regulatory instruments (awards, agreements, policies and so on). Put another way, as companies moved more towards the 'outsider' form they tended to abandon those features of their relations with employees which might be characterised as partnerships. This pattern of development fits the pattern of the Anglo-American model generally, where, the research suggests, cultural change in workplaces, incorporating various worker involvement strategies, has been both difficult to implement and difficult to sustain over time.[33]

---

33   See S. Deakin and F. Wilkinson, *The Law of the Labour Market*, Oxford University Press, Oxford, 2005, pp. 331–332.

There are broader questions remaining concerning what this evidence tells us about the role law has played in the formation and shaping of particular corporate governance and labour management approaches in Australian businesses. Is it accurate to say, for example, that change in corporate law and labour law has been responsible for the way in which companies have re-directed their governance strategies, re-aligned their relations with shareholders and readjusted their relations with employees and other workers? Or is this to put too strong an emphasis on the importance of law in regulating business practice?

Recent scholarship on the relationship between law, the process of 'legal evolution', and the adoption of particular business and social forms and practices has stressed both the highly complex nature of the relations between legal institutions and economic and social development, and also the indeterminate and open-ended nature of legal change.[34] Law is not merely a functional response to economic and social developments, nor does law determine social and economic developments. Rather, the process is one of 'mutual influence' between the two spheres, the legal and the economic.[35]

Following this line of thought, our analysis of the trajectory of corporate law and labour law in Australia over the past two decades or so suggests certain responses from regulatory systems to economic developments and certain opportunities arising from them for further economic reorganisation. However, we should be careful not to draw overly simplified conclusions from these changes. Changed business approaches to the management of labour were evident well before the dismantling of the federal arbitration model began in the early-to-mid 1990s.[36] In some instances these changes were facilitated or encouraged by legal reform at State government level, but this was not always the case. In some well known instances radical employment practices appeared both to have preceded legal change, and probably to have stimulated it.

This complex interplay of legal change and business trends appears most prominent in large companies which have the capacity to act as trend setters and to influence policy at the highest levels. For example, among our case studies both ResourceCo 1 and ResourceCo 2 had the financial resources to monitor global unionising and bargaining trends, and to develop and adopt new business practices, sometimes against considerable political and industrial opposition. Some of these practices flowed through into new legislative measures,[37] and were subsequently adopted by smaller companies. These larger internationalised companies sometimes are also observed to have adopted trends in international corporate governance well in advance of the adoption of such initiatives by

---

34   Ibid., pp. 26–35.
35   Ibid., p. 32.
36   See '10 Deals that Shook the World', *Workplace Change*, Issue 1, March 1996; M. Rimmer and C. Verevis (eds), *Award Restructuring: Progress at the Workplace*, Industrial Relations Research Centre, The University of New South Wales, 1990.
37   For example, in the provisions of the *Workplace Relations Act 1996* (Cth).

Australian regulatory agencies. For example both ResourceCo 1 and ResourceCo 2 acted to change their corporate governance structures and reporting methods prior to the introduction of some of the Australian government's corporate law reforms and the Australian Securities Exchange Corporate Governance Council's 'Corporate Governance Principles and Recommendation' by virtue of their need to meet the requirements of international exchanges on which they are listed. On the other hand, continuing 'public interest'-type regulation in the privatised industries we examined, at least initially, probably obstructed a more extreme approach to the labour management systems in those industries which might have been engendered through the more radical labour laws of the mid-1990s.

Chapter 4

Attitudes and Outlooks of Australian Company Directors to Stakeholders: The Survey Data

4.1 Introduction

As we have noted in earlier chapters there is a complex interplay between ownership structure, corporate governance and the types of employment systems utilised by companies. Among the sets of relevant problems arising from these complex relationships are those which concern the decisions made by corporate directors and how they are to be accommodated in the overall business design and strategy of the company in question. For example, do company directors balance the interests of shareholders and employees, or do they prioritise one over the other? If they do prioritise among stakeholders, why and when do they do so, and how? And if the interests of shareholders are prioritised over employees, how does that impact on the management of labour?

We also noted in Chapter 3 that over the past decade a number of Australian companies appear to have shifted towards a more shareholder-oriented approach to corporate governance, signalling a general decline in the interests of labour in those businesses. This was usually in the context of a change in the structure of ownership, and increasing market pressures imposed by changing economic conditions and globalisation. In this general process we observed a rise in managerial prerogative and a decline in trade union power as important factors also. There was an issue as to which of these various pressures were important, and the relative influence of regulation on managerial decision-making.

Another set of important issues revolved around the concept of 'partnerships at work' and what this might mean. As noted in Chapter 1 we have attempted to identify what 'partnership relations' between a company and its employees might mean objectively in observing various business practices, and their evolution over time.

In thinking about these various issues, and in developing a deeper understanding of them, it is valuable to have some appreciation of how corporate directors think about such matters. It is important, for example, to have some understanding of how directors perceive their duties to various stakeholder interests, and where they might think their primary responsibilities lie. It is also important to know whether, and if so to what extent, directors are influenced in these perceptions by changing ownership structures, by varying market conditions or by regulatory design. In examining the idea of workplace partnerships, it might also be helpful to understand what corporate decision-makers might think 'partnership' means, and how they perceive relations within their own companies when measured against this concept. In earlier work we have questioned any supposition that law provides a regulatory structure supporting the development of partnership practices within the meaning of that term as used here.[1]

In Chapter 1 we also set out an argument to the effect that law and regulation are perceived to be important factors influencing the various dimensions of the core problems set out in this book. Certainly 'legal origins' theory,[2] and the varieties of capitalism literature generally,[3] support this view. This argument suggests not only that law is important, but that it is of primary significance in the establishment and evolution of a national 'style' or 'type' of regulation, embodying certain core values, and, hence, a variety of political economy. An associated line of argument also suggests that there might be a tendency for economies to converge on one or another 'style' of regulation as part of a process of economic integration.

Accordingly, in Chapter 2 we undertook an examination of the regulatory framework provided by Australian corporate law and labour law, with particular attention to those elements which might be thought important to the core issues of concern here: corporate ownership structure, corporate governance and the management of labour systems.

The survey data presented in this chapter enables us, to a degree, to assess how directors think about these issues, and the importance they attribute to the various, perhaps competing, demands of employees and shareholders. We also obtain some insights into how directors perceive the regulatory system in which they operate, and the culture of that system. Some additional case study data presented also enables us to say something about the degree to which directors might be susceptible to pressures from institutional investors in formulating policy relating to the employment systems of their respective companies.

4.2 Responsibilities to Stakeholders

As noted, the literature suggests that there would be a tendency for directors of Australian companies to demonstrate a primary obligation to the interests of

---

1   See R. Mitchell and A. O'Donnell, 'What is Labour Law Doing About "Partnership at Work"? British and Australian Developments Compared', and M. Jones and R. Mitchell, 'Legal Origin, Legal Families and the Regulation of Labour in Australia', both in S. Marshall, R. Mitchell and I. Ramsay (eds), *Varieties of Capitalism, Corporate Governance and Employees*, Melbourne University Press, Melbourne, 2008, pp. 95 and 60 respectively.

2   See E. Glaeser and A. Shleifer, 'Legal Origins' (2002) 117 *The Quarterly Journal of Economics* 1193; J. Botero, S. Djankov, R. La Porta, F. Lopez-de-Silanes and A. Shleifer, 'The Regulation of Labour' (2004) 119 *The Quarterly Journal of Economics* 1339.

3   See P. Hall and D. Soskice (eds), *Varieties of Capitalism: The Institutional Foundations of Comparative Advantage*, Oxford University Press, Oxford, 2001.

shareholders (and perhaps even to the short-term interests of shareholders) over other stakeholders. This expectation flows principally from the fact that Australia would typically be ranked amongst countries with a 'market/outsider' style of corporate governance, as we noted in Chapter 1. However, others have noted that so-called national 'styles' can be deceptive, particularly when individual companies are viewed more closely,[4] and this suggests that the propensity for individual companies to match national type deserves closer attention.

We tested the broad assumption of 'shareholder primacy' in a number of ways. First, using a ranking exercise adapted from a study conducted by Francis[5] we asked directors to rank stakeholders in the order in which they prioritised those stakeholder's interests. In addition to this exercise we utilised a scale to assess the relative influence of key stakeholders over the decision-making of directors. Third, we asked directors about the priority they assigned to particular shareholder-oriented matters such as dividend policy and share price. These three tests enabled us to form an assessment of the shareholder orientation of the surveyed group. The exercise also added to our understanding of what directors might mean in ascribing a 'partnership' description to the relation between the company and its employees. This aspect of the findings is dealt with in section 4.4.

Our survey targeted company directors as those responsible for the corporate strategy within companies. The survey was undertaken through a self-completion mail-out form which was posted to 4,000 company directors. The survey asked a total of 52 questions, testing not only the attitudes and opinions of directors but also seeking factual information about the relevant company. The initial survey sample was obtained from Dun and Bradstreet,[6] according to various criteria, including a roughly equal distribution in company size,[7] a random mix of companies from all Australian States, and a random mix of all industries. Prior to the mail-out, the survey was piloted with six directors selected through our networks. We obtained useable completed responses from 367 directors. Whilst this is a low level of response,[8] such a rate of return is not unusual in surveys of

---

4   S. Jacoby, *The Embedded Corporation*, Princeton University Press, Princeton, 2005, p. 101.

5   I. Francis, *Future Direction: The Power of the Competitive Board*, Pitman, Melbourne, 1997.

6   Dun and Bradstreet conducted the random sampling from their database. At the time the survey was conducted the database was titled *The Business Who's Who of Australia*. It has now been retitled *Company 360* and information about the database is available at www.company360.com.au.

7   The three size groupings used were those employing between 50 and 100 employees, those employing between 101 and 250 employees, and those employing 250+ employees.

8   The results in this chapter are based on analysis of 351 responses as the final 16 completed surveys were delivered after analysis had commenced. Around 200 surveys were returned due to incomplete or incorrect mailing details, and a further 50 were returned with apologies for lack of ability or capacity to complete the survey.

senior personnel.[9] There is information about the characteristics of the companies of which the respondents were directors in section 4.6.

Table 4.1 sets out the results of the priority ranking exercise. It is evident on the one hand that shareholders constitute the interest group accorded the highest priority by the directors in our sample. Forty-four per cent of directors ranked shareholders as their highest priority, followed by 40.4 per cent who ranked the interests of the company as their number one priority. Only 6.7 per cent ranked employees as number one priority. On the other hand in the earlier Francis study 74 per cent of directors ranked shareholders as their first priority.[10] Assuming the two studies to be broadly comparable, this would suggest that over the past decade Australian directors have moved sharply away from a predominantly 'shareholder' view of the company towards a more 'stakeholder' perspective.

Table 4.1   Stakeholders in order of priority[#]

Stakeholder	Average ranking	Percentage ranked 1	Percentage included in top 3
1. Shareholders	2.23	44.0	78.2
2. The company	2.25	40.4	71.1
3. Employees	2.87	6.7	72.8
4. Customers	3.53	8.2	44.8
5. Suppliers	5.99	1.2	3.9
6. Lenders/creditors	5.83	0.6	10.6
7. The community	6.43	0.3	3.4
8. The environment	7.07	0.6	2.0
9. The country	8.41	0.3	1.1

Note: # Directors were asked to rank the list of stakeholders in order of priority between 1 and 9, with 1 being the highest priority and 9 the lowest. The smaller the average rank, the higher the priority.

However, we also sought to test the 'shareholder primacy' norm in a more nuanced way according to a scale adapted from a study conducted in the US.[11] Here we sought to move beyond the assumption that particular stakeholders have a fixed position of influence in relation to the company, and to apply a more flexible model

---

9   See S. Jacoby, E. Nason and K. Saguchi, 'The Role of the Senior HR Executive in Japan and the United States: Employment Relations, Corporate Governance and Values' (2005) 44 *Industrial Relations* 207, p. 216; B. Agle, R. Mitchell and J. Sonnenfeld, 'Who Matters to CEOs? An Investigation of Stakeholder Attributes and Salience, Corporate Performance and CEO Values' (1999) 42 *Academy of Management Journal* 507, p. 513.

10   Francis, above n. 5, p. 354.

11   See Agle et al., above n. 9.

Table 4.2   Shareholders' salience scale

Thinking about the relationship between the company and its shareholders over past year, shareholders...	% of directors agree[#]	Mean score*
Had the power to influence management	81.2	4.03
Were active in pursuing demands or wishes which they felt were important	66.5	3.61
Actively sought the attention of our management team	64.6	3.54
Urgently communicated their demands or wishes to our company	48.8	3.20
Demands or wishes were viewed by our management team as legitimate	78.7	3.88
Received a high degree of time and attention from our management team	65.0	3.61
Satisfying the demands or wishes of shareholders was important to our management team	83.3	4.02

Notes: # Includes responses 'strongly agree' and 'agree'.

* Directors were asked to rate the extent to which they agreed or disagreed with each statement on a scale of one (strongly agree) to five (strongly disagree).

of stakeholder salience (or importance) based on the idea that relative prioritisation of different interest groups will depend on the perception by directors of the relative power held by each group, and the urgency and perceived legitimacy of their claims in differing contexts.

In order to address these issues, a series of propositions were presented to the surveyed group concerning the relative influence of shareholders, employees and creditors. Directors were asked to rate the extent to which they agreed or disagreed with these propositions on a scale of one (strongly agree) to five (strongly disagree). Table 4.2 sets out both the proportion of directors who agreed with each proposition (in relation to shareholders) and the mean score for that proposition. As Table 4.2 demonstrates, both the power of shareholders and the perceived legitimacy of their interests remains a high priority among corporate directors. The items 'shareholders had the power to influence management' and 'satisfying the demands or wishes of shareholders was important to our management team' achieved the highest scores and had the largest proportion of directors who agreed. The item 'shareholders demands and wishes were viewed by our management team as legitimate' also scored highly. On the other hand these high levels of legitimacy and power do not seem to be associated with similarly high levels of activity on behalf of shareholders as measured by the items 'shareholders were active in pursuing demands or wishes', 'shareholders actively sought the attention of management' and 'shareholders urgently communicated their demands or

Table 4.3   Proportion of high and low ratings on salience scale

Stakeholder	% High 3+	% Low <3	Mean score
Shareholders	73.7	17.9	3.70
Employees – Active	71.7	19.3	3.49
Employees – Legitimate[#]	68.6	31.0	3.49

Note: # For the employees' legitimate scale, 'high' is a score of 4 or more due to very high overall scores.

wishes to our company'. This suggests that shareholder power and the legitimacy of shareholder interests for directors arise, at least in part, independently of any direct pressure exercised by shareholders over directors in terms of governance strategy. In other words, shareholders have a level of power that is independent of their specific demand activity.[12] This distinction between different types of shareholder salience, as we shall see later in this chapter, becomes more important when companies are disaggregated according to certain company characteristics.

Taken as a whole, these outcomes establish that 'shareholder primacy' is prominent in the attitudes of our respondent company directors. This is confirmed when we compare the relative importance of shareholder interests and employee interests. Table 4.3 shows the breakdown between the high and low ranges of the scale for both shareholders and employees and the mean scores for each. Shareholders have a high level of salience with 73.7 per cent of directors in the high range of the scale, and an overall average score of 3.70 (the highest of any of the stakeholders we tested). There was a slightly lower percentage (71.7 per cent) of directors in the high range of the 'employees active' scale and the overall score for employees was lower in both employee scales.[13]

---

12 For analytical purposes, then, the scale can be split into two: the group of statements which gained a higher ranking are, for the sake of simplicity, called 'shareholders legitimate' whereas the less high ranking group of statements are called 'shareholders active'.

13 The items in the scale measuring shareholder salience were all highly correlated and averaged for a scale that runs from high (average score of 3 or higher), which represents the strong influence of shareholders, to low (average score of less than 3), which represents a weak influence. For the employee salience scale all the items were not highly correlated and so the scale has been arranged as two scales: employees active and employees legitimate. The 'employees active' scale contains the items: (a) power to influence management; (b) active in pursuing demands; (c) actively sought the attention of management team and (d) employees urgently communicated their demands or wishes to our company, which were all correlated. The scale runs from high (scores 3 or over) representing strong active influence of employees to low (scores under 3) representing weak active influence of employees. The 'employees legitimate' scale contains the items: (e) demands or wishes of our employees were viewed as legitimate; (f) employees received a high degree of time and attention; and (g) satisfying the demands or wishes of employees was important. These items were all correlated. Scores are averaged and run from high (scores 4 and higher) representing strong

We can gain further insight into the extent of shareholder primacy by analysing the results of our question on the matters that are important to directors. However, we get a less distinct picture from this analysis. We had hypothesised that the matters which are relevant to the interests of shareholders (dividend policy, increasing share price, reducing costs and special dividends) would be valued by a greater proportion of directors than those matters relating to employees or other stakeholders. This hypothesis was based on the results of a previous study from which this question was drawn. In that study, a comparative study of US and Japanese management,[14] the shareholder-value model of governance in operation in the US was evident in the fact that share price was ranked most important to chief financial officers and second in importance to human resource executives. In Japan, by comparison, with a more stakeholder-oriented governance model, share price was much less important. On the assumption that Australia sits closer to the US model of governance, we predicted that Australian directors would be similarly concerned with shareholder related matters.

Table 4.4   Importance of matters to directors

Item	% of directors who rated item important[#]
Ensuring customers/clients are satisfied	97.4
Growing the business	95.4
Ensuring employees are fairly treated	94.2
Improving productivity	92.8
Improving employee morale	87.3
Reducing costs	80.1
Ensuring other stakeholders are satisfied	67.2
Safeguarding existing employee jobs	66.2
Diversifying and expanding into new markets	48.8
Creating job opportunities within the company	46.3
Increasing share price	45.0
Dividend policy	41.0
Making a contribution to society	32.1
Special dividends	6.6

Note: # where rated either most, or very, important.

---

legitimate influence of employees in the company, to low (scores under 4) representing weak legitimacy and influence of employees. In this scale only, the scores must be 4 or 5 to be classified as high because the overall scale scores were high and there were too few under a score of 3.

14   Jacoby et al., above n. 9, p. 232.

The results, however, were not as predicted. Table 4.4 indicates that 'ensuring that customers and clients are satisfied' was the item that was most important to the directors surveyed (97.4 per cent of directors). 'Growing the business' was also very important (95.4 per cent) as was 'ensuring employees were fairly treated' (94.2 per cent), with 'improving productivity' highly valued as well (92.8 per cent of directors believing it was important). 'Reducing costs' was considered to be important by 80 per cent of directors. Contrary to the shareholder primacy/ shareholder value conception of the company, the results show that some of those items relating specifically to shareholders' interests (dividend policy, increasing share price, special dividends) were rated as important only by a minority of directors.

4.3 Conceptions of Regulatory Obligations

In this section we report on our findings with regards to whether the priority accorded by directors to shareholders' interests compared with other stakeholders has a basis in perceived legal obligation.

Directors owe no legal obligation directly to shareholders in corporate law. Such legal obligations as there are to influence the overall strategic decision-making of boards of directors, are owed not to the shareholders as such, but to the company.[15] Directors are legally required to act in the best interests of the company. The interests of the company are usually regarded by courts as those of the company's shareholders.[16] However, recent Australian government inquiries have confirmed the legal competence of directors to adopt a broader set of interests in pursuing corporate strategy.[17] In other words, in the interpretation of the obligation for directors to act in the best interests of company, it is recognised that legally directors also have the power to consider the interests of a broad range of stakeholders of the company. Still the question remains whether directors perceive this to be the case, or whether they act under a degree of mistaken apprehension as to their legal duties, or whether they disregard their legal obligations to some extent due to the strength of other pressures.

---

15   Section 181(1) of the Australian *Corporations Act 2001* (Cth) requires directors and other company officers to exercise their powers and discharge their duties 'in good faith in the best interests of the corporation'. For analysis of the meaning of the 'interests of the corporation' see R. Austin, H. Ford and I. Ramsay, *Company Directors: Principles of Law and Corporate Governance*, LexisNexis Butterworths, Sydney, 2005, ch. 7.

16   Ibid. Two of the best known cases are (from the UK) *Greenhalgh v Arderne Cinemas Ltd* [1951] Ch 286 and (from the US) *Dodge v Ford Motor Co.*, 204 Mich. 459, 170 N.W. 668 (1919).

17   See Corporations and Markets Advisory Committee, *The Social Responsibility of Corporations*, December 2006, ch. 3; Parliamentary Joint Committee on Corporations and Financial Services, *Corporate Responsibility: Managing Risk and Creating Value*, June 2006.

To test this question, we pursued two lines of enquiry. First, we asked respondent directors to indicate which of a number of statements best described their understanding of their obligation to act in the 'best interests of the company' as required by law. Second, we asked them to indicate whether they believed that the current law on directors' duties was broad enough to allow them to consider the interests of stakeholders other than shareholders, or whether it required them to consider the interests of shareholders only.

Table 4.5   Directors' understanding of the scope of directors' duties

Primary obligation: I must act in the best interests of the company and this means acting in the	% yes
Short-term interests of shareholders only	0.0
Long-term interests of shareholders only	6.6
Interests of all stakeholders to achieve short-term interests of shareholders	0.3
Interests of all stakeholders to achieve long-term interests of shareholders	38.2
Balancing the interests of all stakeholders	55.0
Parameters of law on directors' duties	
I must only be concerned with shareholders' interests	5.7
Allows me to take account of interests other than shareholders	94.3

Again, working from the 'shareholder primacy' idea, we had predicted that directors might understand that their primary legal obligation was to act in the best interests of the company and that they might tend to define this as acting in the interests of shareholders in the short- or long-term.[18] However, as Table 4.5 indicates, this was not the case. None of our survey group equated the 'best interests of the company' with the short-term interests of shareholders alone, and only a very small proportion of directors (6.6 per cent) equated the 'best interests of the company' with the best interests of shareholders in the long-term. A significant proportion (38.2 per cent) equated the 'best interests of the company' with the interests of all stakeholders as a means to achieving the long-term interests of shareholders. Perhaps surprisingly, the majority of directors (55 per cent) understood acting in the 'best interests of the company' as requiring them to balance all stakeholder interests as an end in itself. An overwhelming majority (94.3 per cent) of directors believed that the law of directors' duties was broad enough to allow them to take into account the interests of stakeholders other than shareholders. The answer to our question posed at the

18   This seems to be generally consistent with the outcomes in an earlier Australian study: see R. Tomasic and S. Bottomley, *Directing the Top 500: Corporate Governance and Accountability in Australian Companies*, Allen & Unwin, Sydney, 1993, pp. 70–71.

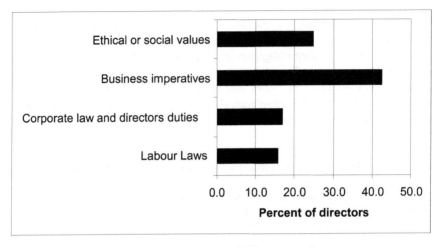

Figure 4.1   Dominant source of responsibility to employees

start of this section then is clearly in the negative. Consequently, it would seem to be the case that where the 'shareholder primacy' norm is influential, its influence does not stem from an understanding by directors that they are under a legal obligation to pursue shareholder-oriented strategies.

Our survey findings also revealed that neither labour laws,[19] nor corporate law[20] were regarded as the dominant source of obligation to employees for the majority of directors. As Figure 4.1 indicates, directors are far more likely to see either business imperatives or ethical and social responsibilities as the major source of their obligations to employees. Figure 4.1 shows that directors were most likely (42 per cent) to agree with the proposition that 'my responsibilities to employees derive primarily from their importance to ensuring the success of the business', that is, they believe that business imperatives underpin their obligation to employees. A further 25 per cent agreed with the proposition that 'I have an ethical or social responsibility to ensure the wellbeing of employees of the company'.

Generally speaking, then, our findings do not appear to provide strong evidence for law and regulation being the dominant influence in relation to directors' views of their obligations to shareholders and employees. Other influences seem to

---

19   We asked directors which of several options best described the dominant source of their responsibilities to employees. The labour laws option was worded in the survey as follows: labour laws (for example, the *Workplace Relations Act* and occupational health and safety laws). However, it was envisaged that this might also include common law employment rights and obligations.

20   This option was worded in the survey as follows: corporate laws and directors' duties (that is, considering the interests of employees is fundamental to acting in the best interests of company/shareholders). It was envisaged that this option would encompass statutory obligations and common law obligations.

have greater sway upon the views of directors, at least in a direct sense. At most, the evidence seems to point to a far more indirect, 'contextual' or 'boundary' setting role for legal influence in prioritising the interests of stakeholder groups. The implications of these findings for the 'legal origin' argument generally are discussed further in Chapter 5.

4.4 Partnerships with Employees?

A key question in this study is whether or not companies can be said to be working in 'partnership relations' with their employees, and, if so, what the nature of those partnerships might be. In our survey we have investigated directors' perceptions of the nature of the relationship between the company and its employees. We also consider how a 'shareholder primacy' perception of the company held by directors might impact upon their views about the existence of 'partnership relations' between the company and its employees.

It is argued by some authors that the rise of the 'shareholder value' norm has had harmful consequences for the employees of companies in the form of lower levels of employment security, poorer working conditions and the decline of legitimate voice or representation within the company.[21] Whilst our survey was not designed to test this proposition directly, it does provide information which to a limited degree allows us to understand how directors perceive their priorities in relation to employee interests. We explore this question first by examining the evidence on the relative positions of shareholders and employees as revealed by our analysis of the 'salience' scales, and, second, by comparing aspects of company practice, such as the human resources matters raised at board level in companies that have a high level of shareholder orientation with those that have a lower level of shareholder orientation. We also examine the intentions of directors regarding their priority actions as they affect shareholders and employees, in the event of an improvement or decline in the financial performance of the company.

The first point to note is that the idea of 'partnership' relations between companies and employees appears to have a high level of influence among directors. Seventy-seven per cent of the respondents to our survey responded positively on this point and indicated that they viewed the relationship between the company and its employees as one best described as a partnership. Further, regardless of whether or not the director's view of company–employee relations was one of partnership, the general understanding of the relationship was dominated by the perception that the interests of employees and the company are the same. We divided the respondent directors into two groups: the 77 per cent who responded

21   See J. Froud, C. Haslam, S. Johal and K. Williams, 'Restructuring for Shareholder Value and its Implications for Labour' (2000) 24 *Cambridge Journal of Economics* 771; W. Lazonick and M. O'Sullivan, 'Maximising Shareholder Value: A New Ideology for Corporate Governance' (2000) 29 *Economy and Society* 13.

affirmatively to viewing the relationship between the company and its employees as one of partnership and the 23 per cent of directors who responded negatively. Of the first group (those who perceived the company–employee relationship to be one of partnership), 71 per cent took the view that the company and its employees were parties with the same interests and with common goals. Only 29 per cent of directors who believed there was a partnership took the view that the company and its employees were parties with separate interests, working nevertheless towards common goals. Overall this indicates that directors might hold a more unified idea of the company than some literature would suggest.

Most directors who rejected the idea that the company was in partnership with its employees also took the view that the interests of the company and its employees were one and the same. Forty-three per cent of directors who rejected the idea of partnership did not conceive of the company and its employees as having separate interests. Thirty-eight per cent of directors who responded negatively to the idea of a company/employee partnership held what might be termed a 'command and control'-type concept of the company; that is they took the view that the company and its employees were parties with the same interests, and that employees were working under direction in order to further the goals of the company. To this extent 'partnership' relations could not arise because the parties were not 'separate'. In only 18.5 per cent of cases did directors rule out the possibility of 'partnership' relations between the company and its employees because the company and its employees were parties with separate and sometimes conflicting interests.

We had hypothesised that a strong corporate emphasis on the interests of shareholders would be antithetical to 'partnership'-style relations between the company and its employees, and thus we anticipated that directors in companies in which shareholder primacy was high would be less supportive of the 'partnership' perspective. This would be consistent with the argument about corporate ownership and labour management practices previously advanced by Gospel and Pendleton[22] and the notion of 'complementarity' espoused in the varieties of capitalism literature.[23] Whilst this literature is generally grounded in a national systems approach, there are some studies which also explore the link between corporate governance and labour management systems at the level of the individual company,[24] and, as we noted in Chapter 1, we have also sought to develop our analysis at that level in the present work.

22   H. Gospel and A. Pendleton, 'Finance, Corporate Governance and the Management of Labour: A Conceptual and Comparative Analysis' (2003) 41 *British Journal of Industrial Relations* 557.

23   See, for example, Hall and Soskice, above n. 3.

24   See S. Deakin, R. Hobbs, S. Konzelmann and F. Wilkinson, 'Partnership, Ownership and Control: The Impact of Corporate Governance on Employment Relations' (2002) 24 *Employee Relations* 335; S. Deakin, R. Hobbs, S. Konzelmann and F. Wilkinson, 'Anglo-American Corporate Governance and the Employment Relationship: A Case to Answer?' (2006) 4 *Socio-Economic Review* 155; N. Conway, S. Deakin, S. Konzelmann,

Table 4.6   Comparison of shareholder and employee salience

Statement	Shareholders: % of directors agree	Shareholders mean score	Employees: % of directors agree	Employees mean score
Had the power to influence management	81.2	4.03	78.0	3.74
Were active in pursuing demands or wishes which they felt were important	66.5	3.61	65.4	3.48
Actively sought the attention of our management team	64.6	3.54	70.5	3.60
Urgently communicated their demands or wishes to our company	48.8	3.20	47.0	3.14
Demands or wishes were viewed by our management team as legitimate	78.7	3.88	76.7	3.83
Received a high degree of time and attention from our management team	65.0	3.61	85.9	4.03
Satisfying the demands or wishes of this stakeholder group was important to our management team	83.3	4.02	87.9	4.04

In accordance with our hypothesis, there is some supporting evidence for the view that there is a negative relationship between the idea of 'partnership' relations and a strong 'shareholder-primacy' perspective among directors. A comparison of the responses of directors who indicated that they believed that the relationship between their company and its employees was one of partnership with the responses of those who did not, revealed that directors who rejected the idea of partnership were more likely to characterise their understanding of their legal

H. Petit, A. Reberiouz and F. Wilkinson, 'The Influence of Stock Market Listing on Human Resource Management: Evidence for France and Britain' (2008) 46 *British Journal of Industrial Relations* 631.

obligations as 'I must act in the best interests of the company and this means acting in the long-term interests of shareholders only' than directors who believed that the relationship was one of partnership. Directors who rejected the idea of partnership were also statistically more likely to have ranked shareholders as their number one stakeholder.

We turn now to a closer examination of the salience scales in relation to employees (for detail on these scales see Table 4.2). As Table 4.6 indicates, there were very similar patterns of response regarding both shareholders and employees for the individual scale items. While we noted earlier that shareholder salience was higher overall than employee salience, there are nevertheless some scale items on which employees were more highly rated. In particular, we can see that directors were more inclined to agree that employees received a high degree of time and attention from management (85.9 per cent) than shareholders received (65 per cent). A slightly larger proportion of directors felt that employees had actively sought the attention of management (70.5 per cent regarding employees compared with 64.6 per cent regarding shareholders).

Moving beyond the relative position of shareholders and employees, we examine the effect of a high level of 'shareholder primacy' on the interests of employees. We do this by comparing the responses of directors in companies where shareholder primacy was highly rated (those in which shareholder salience was at the high end of the scale) with those of directors in companies where shareholder primacy was lower (those in the low range of the shareholder salience scale). We compare organisational matters such as the frequency of human resources issues raised at board level, the priorities of directors in the event of a change in company financial performance, and attitudes to partnership relations with employees.

As Table 4.7 indicates the most striking outcome is that directors in companies in the high range of the shareholder salience scale were significantly[25] more likely to report that restructuring and retrenchments concerning employees below executive level had been considered by the board during the previous 12 months (18.9 per cent) than were directors in companies in the low range of the shareholder salience scale (4.8 per cent). A similarly significant, and related, finding (not shown in Table 4.7) is that directors in companies where 'shareholder primacy' was emphasised were more likely to report that staff numbers had decreased in the past year (20.4 per cent) than those in companies in the low range of the shareholder salience scale (7.9 per cent). These outcomes provide some support for the view that where directors manifest a strong shareholder primacy perspective this may be associated with a concern to reduce costs contrary to the interests of employees (through job cutting and so on).

Insofar as other relevant matters are concerned, there were no significant differences. The results show that the four most commonly raised issues concerning

---

25   In this section of the chapter we use the term 'significant' where we have found a statistically significant difference between the groups being compared.

Table 4.7   HR issues raised at the board

HR issues raised at board	% of whole sample raised three or more times	% of high shareholder raised three or more times	% of low shareholder raised three or more times
Remuneration	37.1	37.9	35.5
Productivity	66.3	65.4	68.3
Performance management	64.2	63.0	71.4
Industrial disputes	10	10.2	6.5
Enterprise bargaining	15.4	15.9	14.5
Restructuring or retrenchments	16.1	18.9	4.8**
Employee share schemes	15.8	17.2	14.5
Work organisation	56.9	57.6	61.3
Training	65.0	65.0	63.9
Occupational health and safety	73.3	71.6	74.2

Note: ** significant at 1% level, significant difference is between high and low shareholder groups.

employees below executive level were: occupational health and safety (73.3 per cent of whole sample); productivity (66.3 per cent of whole sample); training (65.0 per cent of whole sample); and performance management (64.2 per cent of whole sample).

To gauge further the extent to which a 'shareholder primacy' conception of the company was likely to result in a lower priority being given to the interests of employees, we asked directors to identify their priorities in the event of an upturn or downturn in the financial performance of the company.[26] Given the demonstrated relationship between high levels of shareholder salience and discussion about retrenchments, we expected to find that there would be differences between the priorities of directors in high shareholder salience companies and those in low shareholder salience companies in the face of change in financial performance of the company.

However, it is evident that the outcomes seen in Table 4.8 do not support this expectation. There are no significant differences between the priorities of directors in times of changed financial performance based on the level of shareholder salience. What is interesting is that while it is clear that shareholders' dividends

---

26   This question was drawn from responses in a 1999 Japanese Ministry of Labour survey of executives in large firms: cited in I. Takeshi, 'From Industrial Relations to Investor Relations? Persistence and Change in Japanese Corporate Governance, Employment Practices and Industrial Relations' (2001) 4 *Social Science Japan Journal* 225.

Table 4.8   Priority in the event of upturn or downturn in financial performance

Priority	Upturn % ranked no. 1[#]		Downturn % ranked no. 1 [#]	
	High shareholder	Low shareholder	High shareholder	Low shareholder
Increase/decrease number of employees	11.1	10.7	14.7	11.9
Increase/decrease executive remuneration or bonuses	6.3	7.1	24.0	33.9
Increase/decrease shareholders dividend	62.6	57.9	59.9	54.1
Increase/decrease employees salaries or bonuses	23.3	25.9	3.2	1.7

Note: # directors were asked to rank in order of priority from 1 to 4 with 1 being highest priority.

are considered to be the first priority in the event of an improvement in the financial performance of the company (62.6 per cent of high shareholder salience directors and 57.9 per cent of low shareholder salience directors), shareholders' dividends are also the first to 'suffer' in the event of a downturn. Some 59.9 per cent of directors in high shareholder salience companies, and 54.1 per cent of directors in low shareholder salience companies, reported that they would prioritise smaller dividends to shareholders in the event of a downturn in the financial performance of the company in preference to decreasing the number of employees or decreasing employee salaries. While nearly one-quarter of directors reported that they would increase employees' salaries or bonuses in the event of an improvement in financial performance, only a very small proportion reported that they would decrease them in the event of a downturn.

Thus to conclude on the nature of relations between companies and their employees, this evidence suggests that, if nothing else, the idea that such relations may be described in partnership terms has a high level of influence among corporate directors. Underlying this idea is the fact that company–employee relations are largely viewed by directors in 'unitary' terms, insofar as employees are regarded as being 'as one' with the company, or at least sharing the same interests in company success. Perhaps for these reasons the expression of support for the idea of partnership, as we have seen, is not generally inconsistent with the 'shareholder-primacy' orientation which is also generally shown up in the survey data. On the other hand, as we have noted, there are further aspects of the data which provide some support for a countering viewpoint; that is, shareholder primacy might also be associated with corporate strategies which are antithetical to the interests of employees.

These inconsistencies point to the potential gap between what 'conception' of the company is held by directors, and what might occur in terms of actual governance strategy and direction in times of financial and economic change. We think it is necessary, therefore, to take into account the outcomes of the detailed examinations of our case study businesses before reaching any major conclusion about the existence and character of any company–employee relations which might be described as relations of 'partners'. This discussion is continued in Chapter 5.

4.5 External Influences on the Priorities of Directors: The Role of Institutional Investors

One major potential source of influence over the outlook of directors, and their approach to different interest groups, lies in the role of institutional investors. This grows out of the marked increase in the proportion of equities owned by institutions, including investment trusts, insurance companies and pension and superannuation funds.[27] This development is common to the UK, the US and to Australia, although in Australia's case the rise in institutional investment, as a proportion of the total listed equities market, has been subdued when compared with the UK in particular.[28]

One argument which flows from the rise of the institutional investor is that this concentration of shareholdings is making the monitoring of corporate governance, and the decisions of directors, less problematical, at least for certain groups of shareholders.[29] In other words it is suggested that groups of institutional shareholders,

---

27   See, for example, G. Stapledon, 'The Structure of Share Ownership and Control: The Potential for Institutional Investor Activism' (1995) 18 *University of New South Wales Law Journal* 250; J. Hawley and A. Williams, *The Rise of Fiduciary Capitalism: How Institutional Investors Can Make Corporate America More Democratic*, University of Pennsylvania Press, Philadelphia, 2000; P. Ali, G. Stapledon and M. Gold, *Corporate Governance and Investment Fiduciaries*, Lawbook Co., Sydney, 2003; S. Deakin, 'The Coming Transformation of Shareholder Value' (2005) 13 *Corporate Governance: An International Review* 11.

28   In Australia, the average percentage of holdings by funds in individual listed companies grew slightly in the 1990s, from 36 per cent in 1991 to 37 per cent in 1999: see Industry Commission, *Industry Commission Inquiry Report: Availability of Capital*, Industry Commission, Canberra, 1991; Australian Securities Exchange, ASX Listed Companies, accessed 30 June 2007 (www.asx.com.au). In the UK, on the other hand, in 1991 institutions held over 60 per cent of the equity market: see G. Stapledon, *Institutional Shareholders and Corporate Governance*, Oxford University Press, Oxford, 1996.

29   See R. Mitchell, A. O'Donnell and I. Ramsay, 'Shareholder Value and Employee Interests: Intersections Between Corporate Governance, Corporate Law and Labor Law' (2005) 23 *Wisconsin International Law Journal* 417; Stapledon, ibid.; P. Davies, 'Institutional Investors in the United Kingdom' in D. Prentice and P. Holland (eds), *Contemporary Issues in Corporate Governance*, Oxford University Press, Oxford, 1993.

by reason of their volume of shareholding, may be both willing and able to exercise or influence control in particular companies. This argument rests upon the supposition that the market options of institutional investors can be somewhat limited: a large shareholding in a particular company can make it difficult for an institutional investor to sell that holding quickly without depressing the share price. Hence there is an incentive to retain holdings and to seek to influence governance policies in other ways.

More specifically some research has suggested that institutional investors may actively seek particularly to influence the human resource management and employment policies and systems of investee companies.[30] Here the argument posits that for various reasons, including those referred to above, institutional investors might prefer to engage in 'relational-insider' relations with companies,[31] and, as part of such a strategy, to encourage or stimulate advanced human resource policies as part of a long-term approach to profitability.

In order to test this proposition we carried out a series of case studies in order to learn about the extent to which institutional investors were actually seeking to influence companies to adopt 'high performance' work practices, or 'partnership style' relations with employees, and, if they were doing so, in what ways. The studies we undertook involved 12 prominent institutional investors with funds held in the Australian equities market, plus a study of the Australian Council of Superannuation Investors, an industry body representing 39 superannuation funds.[32] A complete list of the relevant institutions and their characteristics is seen in Table 4.9.[33]

The study has several limitations. First, the data we collected on the proportion of shares held by institutional investors in investee companies indicates that institutional investors generally hold shares in only a small proportion of all listed and unlisted companies. We would expect the sphere of major market influence of institutional

---

30   See Deakin, above n. 27; P. Waring, 'Institutional Investors and Contemporary Corporate Governance: Prospects for Enhanced Protection of Employee Interests in Liberal Market Economies' (2006) 12 *International Employment Relations Review* 7; R. Johnson and D. Greening, 'The Effects of Corporate Governance and Industrial Ownership Types on Corporate Social Responsibility' (1999) 42 *Academy of Management Journal* 564; S. Graves and S. Waddock, 'Institutional Owners and Corporate Social Performance (1994) 37 *Academy of Management Journal* 1034.

31   See Waring, ibid., p. 19.

32   Most of the superannuation funds examined in our study were 'industry superannuation funds'. The difference between these and other types of institutional investor is significant. This is because under Part 9 of the *Superannuation Industry (Supervision) Act 1993* (Cth), industry superannuation funds are required to have equal representation of members and employers on their boards, usually nominated by employer associations and unions respectively. It is possible that this characteristic of industry superannuation funds might result in different attitudes towards the human resource practices of investee companies.

33   A full report on the case studies, including further information regarding the methodology used and the selection of the studies is available from the authors.

investors to be almost entirely limited to the listed company sector. Second, our study was restricted to the attitudes and strategies of institutional investors in seeking to influence corporate governance. We were unable to draw wider conclusions about the actual impact of the pressure asserted by institutional investors, and the degree to which this had resulted in change to human resource or employment policies in practice.

Leaving these various reservations to one side though, our general finding from the case studies conducted confirmed what the literature suggests; some institutional investors do claim that they seek to influence the human resource and employment policies of investee companies, and they do so because they perceive there to be a link between the volume and duration of their investment, 'good' human resource policies and company performance. For these investors poor labour management practices are commonly seen as a risk to long-term returns.

Overseas research suggests that the desire to monitor and influence the human resource management and industrial relations practices of investee companies is more likely to arise in the case of superannuation funds than with other institutional investors.[34] However, our research did not confirm this expectation. Several of the non-superannuation funds in our case study group demonstrated some activity in relation to this issue. We also found that those institutional investors that directly manage investments have a greater aptitude to act upon their concern regarding human resource management than superannuation funds that outsource the management of investments. Generally speaking superannuation funds engage external fund managers to manage their investment portfolios and, as a consequence, they tend not to intervene in specific share selection strategies or, as a further consequence, in the human resource management of investee companies. Thus those superannuation funds that seek to influence investee companies regarding employment issues usually do so through alternative and complex methods of engagement, which are quite separate from their investment selection strategies.

Since the monitoring of and engagement with labour management policies by the institutional investors in our study is a relatively recent practice, the various strategies adopted are generally embryonic. For some investors, particularly those that engage BT Governance Advisory Service[35] to conduct 'voice' strategies, engagement is on the basis of a complex rating of investment risks following research. For most, however, both monitoring and engagement occurs on an ad hoc and unsystematic basis. Proxy voting does not generally concern human resource issues and enquiries regarding labour management issues are not usually conducted routinely. In the absence of standardised reports on human resource management, institutional investors rely on 'incident based' newspaper reports of labour relations problems or on anecdotal evidence, which cannot provide a complete picture of labour practices.

---

34   Johnson and Greening, above n. 30.

35   For further information, see BT Financial Group, *BT Governance Advisory Service: A Pro-Active Approach to Managing Long Term Risks*, BT Financial Group, Sydney, 2005. BT Governance Advisory Service is now Regnan (see www.regnan.com).

Table 4.9 Summary of case study institutional investor characteristics

Institutional investor	Details#	Take HR into account in investment selection*	Based on systematic analysis of HR^	Use selling pressure re: HR+	Use voice mechanisms re: HR∨
BT Financial	$73 bill Internally managed pooled funds Performance measured in short-term increments	✓ On ad hoc basis	✗	✗	✓ Only when it is perceived to be a concern to realisation of investment
Portfolio Partners	$9 bill Internally managed	✓	✓ Based on survey of companies	✓ Sell investments in companies with poor social performance	✓
Queensland Investment Corporation	$32 bill Internally managed Maintain liquidity in ASX 100 but not smaller companies	✓ On ad hoc basis	✗	✗	✗
Barclays Australia	$41 bill (in Australia) Mixture of indexed and active funds Internally managed	✗	✗	✗	✗
Vanguard	$36 bill (in Australia) 100% indexed Internally managed	✗	✗	✗	✗ Have recently begun proxy voting
Catholic Super Fund	Industry Super Fund $2 bill Externally managed funds	✗	✗	✗	✓ BT GAS

Fund	Details (#)	*	^	+	¥
PSS/CSS	Industry Super Fund $10 bill; Externally managed funds	✓ Stipulated in guidelines for fund managers	✗	✗	✓ BT GAS
Vic Super	Industry Super Fund $3.1 bill; Mainly indexed; Internally managed	✓ 10% of mainstream funds managed according to sustainable approach	✓ (For 10% only)	✓ (For 10% only)	✓ BT GAS
Uni Super	Industry Super Fund $15 bill; 90% externally managed; 10% internally managed	✓	✗	✗	✓
CBus	Industry Super Fund $8.2 bill; 100% externally managed	✗	✗	✗	✗
TWU	Industry Super Fund $1.6 bill; 100% externally managed	✗	✗	✗	✗
Health Super	Industry Super Fund $5.5 bill; 100% of Australian equities investments managed externally (small percentage of cash investments managed internally)	✗ Only in 0.3% of funds (positive and negative screening in SRI product includes HR issues)	✗	✗	✗

Notes: # where dollar figures are noted, this denotes total funds under management as of 2005 or 2006, depending upon the fund; * denotes the use of indicators or information about the HR performance of companies when choosing in which companies to invest; ^ where indicators or information about the HR performance of companies is used when choosing in which companies to invest, this information is collected systematically, using a consistent methodology; + where a company's HR performance is judged not to meet the performance criteria of the institutional investor, this results in selling shares in that company; ¥ denotes engagement with the company through meetings, letters or proxy voting regarding HR matters.

Our evidence suggests that institutional investors are generally reluctant to meddle in 'management issues' and that they only initiate meetings or correspond with company management when they believe a human resource issue poses significant risks to their investment, either because it is a threat to the reputation of the company or because it may expose the company to legal or financial liabilities.

Overall, however, engagement with companies over human relations policies and employment systems among institutional investors seems to be an increasing phenomenon in Australia. The peak body representing superannuation funds, the Australian Council of Superannuation Investors, has commenced engagement with companies in relation to labour management, and has focussed more attention on its corporate social responsibility programme, which includes labour issues. We also found some evidence that these investors are seeking to foster 'high performance/ high commitment' human resource practices among investee companies, which may be associated with a desire by superannuation funds in particular to invest long-term in order to secure the retirement funds of Australian workers.[36]

However, in line with our earlier discussion about the role of regulation, there is little in the Australian institutional framework which facilitates or supports investor monitoring of a company's labour management practices. For example, companies are not compelled to provide information about labour issues to investors in the same way that listed companies are now compelled to provide information about other aspects of their corporate governance.[37] Private mechanisms, such as services that collect data for socially responsible investment,[38] are slowly filling this gap, but it is doubtful that these mechanisms will fully overcome the barriers created by a regulatory framework that assumes that investors are not concerned with the labour policies of investee companies.

Taken together these various pressures and influences which appear to impact on corporate governance and the attitudes of directors to potentially conflicting stakeholder interests suggest complexity rather than straightforward characterisation. Law and regulation appear not as important at grassroots level as might be supposed. Other influences seem more important. Consequently it remains an open question how various legal dimensions of a particular national system, in this case Australia, act together to shape a style of capitalism. This

---

36   For further details see S. Marshall, K. Anderson and I. Ramsay, 'Are Superannuation Funds and Other Institutional Investors in Australia Acting Like "Universal Investors"?' (2009) 51 *Journal of Industrial Relations* 439.

37   For listed companies, Australian Securities Exchange Listing Rule 4.10.3 provides that companies must disclose in their annual reports the extent to which they have followed the ASX best practice corporate governance recommendations.

38   Socially responsible investment (SRI) has been defined 'as an investment management based activity that involves consideration of non-financial factors in investment and related decision-making (e.g. voting of shares)': P. Spathis, 'Corporate Governance and Superannuation Investors' (2001) *Corporate Citizenship: A Newsletter of the Australian Council of Superannuation Investors* 1, p. 23.

question is taken up in greater detail in Chapter 5. For the present, we turn to a more detailed analysis of what our survey data might tell us about the varieties of capitalism issue.

4.6 Varieties of Capitalism and the Research Findings

As we noted in Chapters 1 and 2, Australia is typically characterised as a 'liberal market' economy in the debates over different 'varieties of capitalism'. Associated with this characterisation, it is also said that Australia has a 'market/outsider' system of finance and corporate governance.[39] A further characterisation describes Australia's labour management system in 'liberal market' terms, corresponding with and complementing the other dimensions of the national system (see Chapter 1). In this section our analysis is confined to the financial and corporate governance aspects of the equation.

A finance-centred definition of a 'market/outsider' business system is offered by Gospel and Pendleton in the following terms:

> Market forms of financing are ones where emphasis is placed on finance via public equities and market-based debt. In these systems, equity markets are extensive and there is usually a high turnover of shares and corporate bonds. Investors have diversified portfolios and may easily sell their investments. Under such arrangements, there exists an outsider form of governance based on relatively strong legal rights for investors and on an active market in corporate control (mergers and acquisitions, especially hostile takeovers). This contrasts with relational forms of finance where more reliance is placed on bank and other loans, where securities markets are weak, and where investors are more likely to be long term. This is said to create a form of insider governance, where large owners have a more stable and direct relationship with the management of the firm, but where small investors and the market for corporate control exerts less discipline.[40]

For various reasons which we have touched upon in Chapter 2, and again earlier in this chapter, the extent to which Australia can unequivocally be placed into the

---

39   This terminology is derived from the financial economics literature: see H. Gospel and A. Pendleton (eds), *Corporate Governance and Labour Management: An International Comparison*, Oxford University Press, Oxford, 2005, p. 7. For a quantitative study locating Australia amongst groupings of national systems see G. Jackson, 'Towards a Comparative Perspective on Corporate Governance and Labour Management: Enterprise Coalitions and National Trajectories' in Gospel and Pendleton, ibid., p. 284.

40   Gospel and Pendleton, ibid., p. 7. See also Hall and Soskice, above n. 3.

'market/outsider' category of corporate governance is open to question.[41] But we also have suggested that a similar approach can usefully be applied to an analysis of the character of individual companies within national systems,[42] distinguishing primarily between publicly listed companies with a dispersed ownership structure, and private companies which are necessarily insulated to some degree from the effects of securities markets.[43] Thus the question for us here is whether directors of private and smaller companies have different views from directors of larger, listed companies about priorities and strategies in corporate governance.

In order properly to understand the significance of this question, it is necessary also to understand the composition of the Australian corporate sector. Most companies in Australia are small and privately owned. At 30 June 2009 there were 1,699,830 registered companies in Australia. Of these 98.8 per cent (1,679,547) were proprietary limited (i.e. private) companies, 0.6 per cent (10,801) were companies limited by guarantee, 0.5 per cent (8,483) were public companies limited by shares, and the remaining 0.1 per cent included 243 no liability companies, 269 companies limited both by shares and guarantee and 496 unlimited companies.[44] According to ASX figures in June 2009, listed companies comprised approximately less than 0.13 per cent of total companies registered and 25.9 per cent of public companies.[45] In short, listed companies are a very small proportion of all companies in pure numerical terms. It follows that the vast majority of Australian companies are not open to share market influence and very few of them can be said to be characterised as exhibiting 'diffused ownership patterns'. As we suggested in Chapter 2, this and related data concerning ownership structure at least suggests that one needs to be careful in categorising the Australian system as part of the 'market/outsider' group of nations.

Seventy-five per cent of the companies we surveyed were private companies and 25 per cent were public companies. Some 16.5 per cent were listed on the Australian Securities Exchange, 0.5 per cent of the companies were listed on another Australian exchange and 12.0 per cent were listed on an international exchange. Consequently, the proportion of listed companies in our sample is higher than the proportion of listed companies in Australia generally. This had the advantage of providing a large enough sample of listed companies to be able to comment meaningfully on their

---

41   As we have also noted earlier the same may be said for the categorisation of its labour management systems: see Jones and Mitchell, above n. 1.

42   See the discussion associated with n. 24 above.

43   See also Conway et al., above n. 24. These authors make the point that a focus on individual companies should not be taken as suggesting that discussion of national systems is meaningless. Meaningful cross-national differences will continue to exist, both because of the relative dominance or otherwise of the listed company sector in any national system, and because norms governing business enterprises with the same legal form (e.g. listed companies) may also differ across systems.

44   R. Austin and I. Ramsay, *Ford's Principles of Corporations Law*, LexisNexis Butterworths, Sydney, 14th edn, 2010, at [5.072].

45   Australian Securities Exchange, ASX listed companies (www.asx.com.au).

characteristics and compare them with private companies. The sample comprised a range of company sizes as measured by turnover. Twenty eight per cent of companies had turnover of less than $20 million annually, with a further 28.1 per cent in the $20 million to less than $50 million range and 12.7 per cent in the $50 million to less than $100 million range. Nearly one-third of the sample (30.8 per cent) had turnover of more than $100 million annually.

As Conway et al. point out, private companies tend to correspond with a model of insider-oriented governance in several respects: the exit options of shareholders are limited due to the absence of an organised market in which shares can be traded (thus locking in a semi-closed class of shareholders such as family members and/or founders); and share prices are not assessed by the share market and, consequently, cannot be used as an incentive device for management. The result, it is argued, is to give managers a greater autonomy from capital market discipline, and to give both managers and shareholders a longer-term time horizon compared with managers and shareholders of listed companies.[46] In contrast, in listed companies where shares are bought and sold on a public market, shares can be held by a group of dispersed shareholders 'whose connection with the firm is purely financial'.[47] For these shareholders, the capital market is 'viewed as an information-processing mechanism through which the performance of firms, and their managers, is continuously (and, it is claimed, efficiently) being assessed' whilst a liquid securities market 'also provides shareholders with a low-cost exit option'.[48]

However, rather than simply classifying private companies as 'insider' companies and listed companies as 'outsider' companies, we first tested whether the actual finance structures and ownership and control characteristics of listed and unlisted companies differed in meaningful ways. Table 4.10 shows the particular characteristics of the listed and unlisted companies we examined. These characteristics included the following:

- proportion of shares held by largest shareholder (larger proportions indicate insider/relational characteristic);
- proportion of shares held by staff and managers (larger holdings indicate insider/relational characteristic);
- shareholder representation on board (higher representation indicates insider/relational characteristic);
- proportion of shares held by institutional investors (less institutional investing indicates insider/relational characteristic).

There are a number of statistically significant differences between the two types of companies, thus warranting displaying the characteristics of each separately.

---

46   Conway et al., above n. 24, p. 635.
47   Ibid., p. 634.
48   Ibid., pp. 634–635.

Table 4.10   Ownership and control in sample companies

Ownership Characteristic	Percent of listed companies	Percent of unlisted companies
Largest shareholder holds less than 5 per cent	16.0	4.0**
Largest shareholder holds between 5 per cent and 30 per cent	46.8	13.0**
Largest shareholder holds between 31 per cent and 50 per cent	16.0	31.6**
Largest shareholder holds 51 per cent or more	21.3	51.4**
Largest shareholder is on the board	55.3	92.3**
Other shareholders are on the board	58.5	73.2**
Institutional investors hold less than 10 per cent	34.4	92.3**
Institutional investors hold between 11 per cent and 30 per cent	22.2	2.4**
Institutional investors hold between 31 per cent and 50 per cent	21.1	1.4**
Institutional investors hold 51 per cent or more	22.2	2.9
Directors/managers/staff hold less than 5 per cent	46.2	20.3**
Directors/managers/staff hold between 5 per cent and 30 per cent	40.7	6.8**
Directors/managers/staff hold between 31 per cent and 50 per cent	6.6	5.1
Directors/managers /staff hold more than 50 per cent	6.6	67.8**

Note: ** Significant at the 1 per cent level.

This data partially confirm the distinction made by Conway et al. between the governance structure of listed and unlisted companies. It shows that unlisted companies are more likely to have 'insider'-type ownership and control with more significant block-holdings, shareholder representation on the board, lower proportions of shares held by institutional investors and higher levels of holding by directors, managers and staff. However, and consistent with the point made above, it also shows that even amongst listed companies, it is rare for holdings to be particularly diffuse in Australia. Only in 16 per cent of listed companies did the largest shareholder hold less than 5 per cent of total shares in the company. In 21.3 per cent of listed companies, the largest shareholder held more than 50 per cent of total shares.

On these measures, and consistent with earlier research data,[49] the characterisation of Australian companies as subject to 'diffused ownership patterns' or 'outsider' forms of corporate governance can be questioned.[50] Block-holdings are common, even in listed companies, and medium and small listed companies are more likely to have a 'family' block-holder than a corporate or institutional block-holder, thus leading, in most cases, to a greater propensity to stability in ownership.

Thus empirically it would seem that only a small proportion of Australian companies can properly be said to correspond with the 'market/outsider' descriptor used generally in the varieties of capitalism literature. This is an important issue for an Australian analysis, for if it is the case that the structure of corporate ownership and the patterns of finance 'provide a set of constraints and opportunities which influence managerial choices, including in the labour area'[51] we might expect that outcomes for employees in the vast majority of Australian companies will be different from those in the small minority of companies which correspond with the 'market/outsider' label.[52]

Are directors of those Australian companies corresponding to the 'market/outsider' model more inclined to favour the interests of shareholders over other stakeholders, and employees in particular? As we noted in earlier discussion, a degree of 'shareholder primacy' is indicated among company directors according to a priority ranking order and an analysis of salience scales (see Tables 4.1 and 4.2). But what does our data tell us about the relationship between the existence of the shareholder primacy norm and company type?

In order to analyse these questions, we have attempted to build typologies of companies based on the categories 'market/outsider' and 'relational/insider', derived from the work of Gospel and Pendleton.[53] Based on their analysis of broad company characteristics in market/outsider and relational/insider national systems, we established a set of criteria which would allow us to categorise the companies represented in our sample as belonging either to the market/outsider or relational/insider group.[54] The

49   See, for example, G. Stapledon, 'Australian Sharemarket Ownership' in G. Walker, B. Fisse and I. Ramsay (eds), *Securities Regulation in Australia and New Zealand*, LBC Information Services, Sydney, 2nd edn, 1998; A. Lamba and G. Stapledon, *The Determinants of Corporate Ownership Structure: Australian Evidence*, University of Melbourne, Public Law and Legal Theory Working Paper Number 20, 2001; and further, Chapter 2, nn. 60–66, and associated discussion.

50   This point is also made by others: see A. Dignam and M. Galanis, 'Australia Inside Out: The Corporate Governance System of the Australian Listed Market' (2004) 28 *Melbourne University Law Review* 623.

51   See Gospel and Pendleton, above n. 22.

52   See for a similar analysis Conway et al., above n. 24.

53   See Gospel and Pendleton, above nn. 22 and 39.

54   The model comprises six criteria which are characteristics we would expect to find in a market/outsider company. These are: listed company; largest shareholder not represented on the board; no other shareholders represented on the board; higher level of holding by institutional investors; short-term debt financing; and creditors not represented on the board. For a relational/insider company the criteria are: unlisted company; largest

selected criteria related to particular characteristics such as whether there was shareholder representation on the board, the level of shareholding by institutional investors and whether the company was listed or not, among others. This was done to enable us to compare the responses of directors from these different types of company and thereby 'test' aspects of the theoretical framework offered by these authors.

As can be seen in Table 4.11, both the average rankings and the proportion of directors who ranked shareholders number one among stakeholders are very similar for both company types. There were no statistically significant differences. However, when we compare the mean scores of shareholder importance on the salience scales we do see a significant difference between company types. As shown in Table 4.12, the mean scores on 'the influence of shareholders scales' for companies in the high range of the 'relational/insider' group (3.82) and the high range of the 'market/outsider' group (3.46) differ significantly. In other words, shareholder influence and importance appears to be greater in 'relational/insider' companies than in 'market/outsider' companies.

Table 4.11   Priority ranking of shareholders by company type[#]

Stakeholder	Average ranking		Percentage ranked 1	
	Insider	Outsider	Insider	Outsider
Shareholders	2.21	1.96	43.3	47.4
The company	2.60	2.34	40.3	43.6

Note: # directors were asked to rank a list of nine stakeholders (the nine stakeholders are listed in Table 4.1) in order of priority between 1 and 9, with 1 being the highest priority and 9 the lowest.

Table 4.12   Influence of shareholder scale by company type

Influence of shareholder score	High insider mean score	High outsider mean score
High	3.82	3.46**

Note: ** significant at the 1 per cent level.

shareholder is on the board; other shareholders on the board; lower level of institutional holding; long-term debt financing; and creditors on the board. Each item was given a score 1=present, 0=not and two indexes developed Index.I6 and Index.O6. Those which scored 4 or more on the Index.I6 were categorised as HighIns6 and those that scored 3 or more on the Index.O6 were categorised as HighOut6.

Table 4.13   The influence of shareholders by company type^

Thinking about the relationship between the company and its shareholders over past year ...	% of directors agree#		Mean score	
	Insider	Outsider	Insider	Outsider
Satisfying the demands or wishes of shareholders was important to our management team	87.6	81.5	4.12	3.91
Had the power to influence management	86.9	75.0*	4.17	3.77**
Demands or wishes were viewed by our management team as legitimate	81.8	71.4	3.96	3.67*
Were active in pursuing demands or wishes which they felt were important	75.0	53.3**	3.82	3.18**
Received a high degree of time and attention from our management team	72.1	59.8	3.76	3.43*
Actively sought the attention of our management team	70.1	56.5*	3.66	3.30*
Urgently communicated their demands or wishes to our company	50.4	42.4	3.26	2.98

Notes: ^ the tests between proportions are chi square tests of independence, while the means are t-tests. # Includes responses 'strongly agree' and 'agree'. * Significant at the 5 per cent level. ** Significant at the 1 per cent level.

If we break down the 'influence of shareholders scale' into its composite items as we have in Table 4.13, we see further statistically significant differences between the mean scores for individual items and between the proportion of directors who agree with individual scale items according to company type. Shareholders are perceived as having a significantly greater power to influence management in 'insider-type' companies than in 'outsider-type' companies. Similarly, shareholders are perceived by directors in the 'insider-type' as being more active in pursuing demands and, based on the mean scores, as both receiving a higher degree of time and attention from management and higher degrees of legitimacy. In effect the 'shareholder salience' index captures quite direct forms of shareholder control or 'voice', which might also be indicative of longer-term investment relations. Unable to rely on either a market valuation of share price and limited in their exit options, shareholders in 'insider' companies are able to adopt more direct forms of monitoring and control of management in their longer term interests.

Finally, we compared the responses of directors in 'market/outsider' companies with those in relational/insider companies on the matters of importance to them in their *r*oles as directors as a further test of the relationship between company 'type' and a 'shereholder value' outlook.

Consistent with our findings on shareholder salience in 'relational/insider' companies, we *se*e (Table 4.14) slightly higher proportions of directors in 'insider' types emph*as*ising matters prima facie consistent with a 'shareholder value' corporate strateg*y*, such as 'dividend policy' and 'special dividends'. However, these differences ar*e* not statistically significant. As with the results for the sample overall, these items t*en*d to be less important to directors than items such as 'growing the business', 'ens*ur*ing customers are satisfied' and 'ensuring employees are fairly treated'.

Table 4.14   Importance of matters to director by *co*mpany type#

Item	Insider % important	Outsider % important
Ensuring customers/clients are satisfied	97.9	97.8
Growing the business	95.0	9*3.5*
Ensuring employees are fairly treated	93.6	93.3
Improving productivity	93.5	91.3
Improving employee morale	89.3	83.3
Reducing costs	79.1	80.9
Safeguarding existing employee jobs	67.1	57.8
Ensuring other stakeholders are satisfied	63.0	71.9
Diversifying and expanding into new markets	51.1	46.7
Increasing share price	46.1	50.0
Dividend policy	46.0	38.5
Creating job opportunities within the company	44.2	40.0
Making a contribution to society	31.7	24.7
Special dividends	6.5	4.5

Note: # where rated either most, or very, important.

We next explored whether there was a relationship between various individual company characteristics and shareholder primacy. The characteristics examined were: first whether the company was listed or unlisted; second whether it was a public or private company;[55] and third company size measured by annual turnover. First we looked for statistical correlations through cross-tabulations and chi square

---

55   A private or proprietary company is one that (1) has no more than 50 non-employee shareholders; (2) does not do anything that would require disclosure to investors under the capital raising provisions contained in Chapter 6D of the *Corporations Act 2001* (Cth); and (3) is limited by shares or is an unlimited company with a share capital: s 45A(1) of the *Corporations Act 2001* (Cth).

tests to identify the significance of any differences between the compared groups. Second we employed a regression analysis to examine the same data.

The cross tabulations (not set out in table form) revealed that there were statistically significant differences between listed and unlisted companies, and between private and public companies in the rankings given by directors to shareholders and the company, but no statistically significant differences in the rankings given to employees. Among directors of listed companies, shareholders had a higher average ranking (1.78 compared with 2.39 in unlisted companies) and were ranked first by a greater proportion of directors (55.4 per cent of listed and 39.7 per cent of unlisted). Both these differences were significant at the 5 per cent level. Directors in unlisted companies were more likely than their counterparts in listed companies to rank 'the company' as their first priority (42.3 per cent of directors in unlisted companies did so, compared with 35.1 per cent of directors in listed companies). When we compared the average rank given to shareholders by directors in public and private companies, we found a significant difference: the average rank of shareholders in public companies was 1.89 compared with 2.34 in private companies. Despite this difference, however, shareholders in public and private companies were still ranked as first priority by the largest proportion of directors within each company type (42.5 per cent in private companies and 48.1 per cent in public companies). Company size, as measured by turnover, did not make a difference to the priority ranking of shareholders by directors.

Turning next to the shareholder salience scales set out in Table 4.15, we find again that listing makes a significant difference. 'Shareholder salience' is higher in unlisted companies, both in terms of the overall scale score and in some of the individual scale items. This finding is also consistent with our earlier finding on the higher level of shareholder salience in insider-type companies, and again points to the difference in modes of shareholder monitoring of management as between listed and unlisted companies. Similarly, 'shareholder salience' appears to be stronger in private companies than it does in public companies and also appears stronger in smaller companies than it does in larger companies.

We noted in our earlier discussion of directors' perceptions of shareholder influence that high levels of shareholder power and legitimacy were not necessarily matched by perceptions of similarly high levels of activity or urgency on the part of shareholders.[56] This distinction between types of shareholder salience becomes more important when companies are disaggregated based on some of the company characteristics we have been examining here. For example Table 4.15 reveals that there are significant differences in directors' perceptions of the level of activity or urgency with which demands are conveyed by shareholders that appear related to company size and character. In unlisted companies for example, shareholders are perceived as being more active in seeking the attention of management, having greater urgency in communicating demands and being more active in pursuing demands than they are in listed companies. It appears to be the case that the higher

---

56   See Tables 4.1 and 4.2, and associated discussion.

Table 4.15   **The effect of company characteristics on shareholder salience**

Thinking about the relationship between the company and its shareholders over past year, shareholders ...	Listed/unlisted % agrees#		Private/public % agrees#		Size by turnover % agrees#	
	Listed	Unlisted	Private	Public	Small (less than $50M)	Large (more than $50M)
Had the power to influence management	68.5	85.9**	84.9	68.4**	84.7	75.9*
Were active in pursuing demands or wishes which they felt were important	47.8	73.3**	72.4	48.1**	72.0	60.1*
Actively sought the attention of our management team	56.0	67.7**	68	57	67.2	62.1
Urgently communicated their demands or wishes to our company	33.7	54.4**	55.4	27.8**	53.7	42.8*
Demands or wishes were viewed by our management team as legitimate	74.7	80.2	79.4	74.4	78.4	79.0
Received a high degree of time and attention from our management team	58.1	67.6	67.2	58.8	65.8	64.1
Satisfying the demands or wishes of shareholders was important to our management team	82.8	83.5	83.7	82.5	83.7	83.6
Average score for shareholder salience scale	3.42	3.80**	3.79	3.40**	3.73	3.66

Notes: # includes responses 'strongly agree' and 'agree'. * Significant at the 5 per cent level. ** Significant at the 1 per cent level.

levels of activity and urgency of shareholder demands in unlisted and private companies increase the level of shareholder salience overall.

In addition to looking for correlations between company characteristics and salience rankings, we also employed a multiple regression analysis to identify those individual characteristics which best explained (or predicted) a 'shareholder primacy' corporate strategy (once the effects of all other characteristics have been factored out). The regression analysis showed that there was no significant influence of either the 'relational/insider' or 'market/outsider' model on any other indicators of a high shareholder primacy corporate governance strategy, such as the shareholder salience scales. Further regressions showed that only the 'dummy variable' for 'Private Limited' was significant (t-value 2.1650, significant at the 0.05 level); the significance is positive, implying that the company being a private company would raise (positively influence) the likelihood that the director indicated that the company had a shareholder primacy corporate strategy.

We turn finally to the relationship which exists between those issues of significance to directors and company characteristics. Here, we can note (not shown in table form) that share price appeared to be important to a significantly larger proportion of directors of listed companies than those of unlisted companies (60.4 per cent compared with 38.9 per cent). Similarly, and not surprisingly given the fact that listed companies must be public companies, directors in public companies were more likely to rate the share price as important than were directors of private companies (64.5 per cent compared with 38.7 per cent of directors of private companies).

To sum up, in relation to 'market/outsider' and 'relational/insider' typologies, 'shareholder salience' was higher in companies with characteristics of the 'relational/insider' type such as unlisted and private companies, largely as a result of shareholders' direct monitoring of management: being more active in seeking the attention of management, having greater urgency in communicating demands, and being more active in directly pursuing their demands. For companies with characteristics of the 'market/outsider' type, share price was more important to directors in listed and public companies than directors of unlisted and private companies.

4.7 Discussion and Conclusion

In this chapter we have examined survey and other data on a range of issues associated with the attitudes of directors towards various stakeholders, including shareholders and employees, with a view to finding out what this might tell us about different approaches to corporate governance.

Overall, the data show that greater priority is given by directors to shareholders than to other stakeholders in Australian companies. This is clear from the simple ranking exercise of directors' priorities conducted as part of our survey (see Table 4.1). And when shareholder primacy was tested through more nuanced tests, such as the salience scale, there was clear indication that a large majority of directors regard satisfying shareholder demands as important (83 per cent), regard their demands as legitimate (79 per cent) and view shareholders as having the power to influence management (81 per cent).

However, the outcomes arising from the data also show that an indication of a 'shareholder priority' perspective cannot be reduced to a simple proposition that directors will necessarily pursue shareholders' interests at the expense of other stakeholders. There is very little evidence, for example, that directors see short-term returns to shareholders through share price or other quick gains as a priority at all, and other evidence derived from the survey results indicates that the interests of employees are also ranked highly, and sometimes more highly than the interests of shareholders (see Table 4.4).

We might conclude, therefore, that shareholder primacy appears more of a general outlook than a specific policy based around certain strategies aimed exclusively, or even mainly, at maximising profits for shareholders. For instance dividend policy and increased share price ranked relatively poorly as against job security and employee morale in the list of specific corporate agenda items put to directors. Although there were some outcomes which indicate that shareholder primacy may have a harder edge than this general portrayal would suggest – for example, there is evidence that among directors who were at the higher end of the 'shareholder primacy' scale of perception, job reductions appeared to be more likely to have been considered as part of corporate strategy – we doubt that too much can be read into this finding for two reasons. First, directors who reported having discussed job reductions still only constituted about one-fifth of those who were at the high end of the 'shareholder primacy' oriented group. Second, the finding did not arise consistently when other characteristics were taken into account such as when comparisons were made between listed and unlisted companies or between 'market/outsider' and 'relational/insider' companies.

Our survey also attempted to measure the extent to which the idea of partnership had influence with directors, and to illuminate the policies with which this commitment was positively associated. The data show that the idea of partnership has a high level of resonance with respondent directors, 77 per cent of whom said that 'the relationship between the company and its employees is best described as one of partnership'. While this would not reflect the utilisation of partnership-style policies in practice by the companies, the fact that the idea of partnership enjoys such a high level of resonance among directors is important. The view that employees shared the same interests as the company dominated respondents' understanding of the nature of the relationship between employees and the company, whether the director believed it was one of partnership or not. Of those who said the company was in partnership with its employees, 71 per cent believed that the company and its employees were parties with the same interests working in partnership. It therefore seems that a unitarist conception of the company informed directors' view of partnership relations. In other words, directors most frequently held the view that employees and the company had the same or similar interests.

In Chapter 1, we laid out the broad outlines of the argument about corporate governance and business systems developed in the comparative political economy and 'varieties of capitalism' literature. In Chapter 2 we noted that generally speaking the evidence does not support the proposition that the Australian national system matches a 'market/outsider' model in terms of corporate ownership and financial structures. In this chapter we were concerned with the hypothesised relationship between the shareholder primacy conception of the company and the 'market/outsider' form of corporate governance. The literature tends to assume that companies with 'market/outsider' characteristics will be more oriented toward financial metrics such as share price, current earnings and dividends in the context of a liquid capital market (with investors entering and exiting equity ownership at a rapid rate and holding only small proportions of the shares of companies in which they invest). In contrast, shareholders of unlisted or 'insider' companies will find other, more direct, ways of monitoring management, often in the context of a longer term investment relationship. Our results on several related indicators have revealed a stronger link between shareholder activism and the 'insider/relational' type than between shareholder primacy and the 'market/outsider' model. Given the predominance of unlisted and 'insider' companies in the Australian corporate sector, this reinforces our doubts as to whether, at the level of a national system, Australian corporate governance style matches that of a 'liberal market' model.

Taken together, these outcomes have led us to question whether, at least in the case of Australia, it is a valuable exercise to try to generalise about the form of governance on a broad national basis. We might argue, for example, that institutions may not be as tightly associated or organised as much of the varieties of capitalism and the legal origins literature suggests. It may also be the case that the regulatory dimension of a country, in terms of its governing statutes for example, is not closely related to the practice or behaviour of companies in corporate governance or in the management of employment systems. These are, clearly, important questions which require further research and evaluation. In the following chapter we enlarge upon our findings in general, and what they tell us overall about our key questions – the association between corporate ownership structure, corporate governance and types of employment systems.

Chapter 5

The Interaction of Corporate Governance and Labour Management in Australian Companies: An Analysis

5.1 Introduction

In Chapter 1, we advanced a simplified characterisation of different 'varieties of capitalism' and associated 'styles of regulation' as a means of grounding a study of Australian corporate governance and labour management systems. In particular we were interested in a number of intersecting questions and issues relating to the ownership structure and governance of Australian companies, and what impact these factors had upon how such companies dealt with their employees. One particular concern of our study was to examine the role of law and regulation insofar as it might be seen to impact upon or explain certain corporate practices.

As with other economies around the world, immense transformation occurred in the 1990s and the 2000s in the governance of the Australian economy, and its laws and business systems. This meant that, as part of this study, we were compelled to consider not just how Australia might seem to fit within a particular 'type' or 'family' of economic organisation, but also whether that 'fit' was changing as a result of economic globalisation. In other words we were obliged to examine the responses by Australian businesses to, among other things, regulatory change and the heightened competition created by global economic integration.

When we began this study, it was difficult to see where Australia sat within the broad 'varieties of capitalism' typology or whether trends observed in Australia indicated a convergence towards or a divergence away from one or other of the general models. On the one hand, Australia has a history of strong labour movements, collectively-based industrial relations and strong protective employment rights. On the other hand, Australia has generally been categorised as belonging to the 'liberal market' economic 'block', and had certainly undergone a period of intense economic liberalisation during the 1990s. Institutional reform during the period of our study was universally perceived to have fostered the liberalisation of labour markets aimed at making Australia's economy more competitive. In view of this development it was important for us to see how Australian businesses had availed themselves of the greater freedom provided for managers to organise their labour-management systems. Did Australian businesses respond to heightened global competition by adopting partnership-style, high-performance workplace strategies or more 'low road' systems of labour management? Did Australian businesses become more shareholder-focussed, in the hope, perhaps, that this would drive competitiveness and attract greater investment?

Our general approach to dealing with these research issues is evident in the organisation of this book. Our analysis of the law was set out in Chapter 2, and this included both an indication of how Australian law might have been relevantly 'characterised' in a regulatory sense historically, and the extent to which it might, under the influence of the 'globalising' pressures of the 1990s and 2000s, have been 'converging' towards or 'diverging' from the two opposing 'styles' of regulation anticipated in the varieties of capitalism literature. The evidence about legal change in Australian labour law is uncertain to say the least.[1] In the case of corporate law, we observed in Chapter 2 how legal changes in recent decades have moved Australia more in the direction of the liberal market style of regulation and this is evidenced in particular by the legal changes that have increased shareholder protection.

We also carried out 10 detailed case studies of Australian businesses, and the results of these were presented in Chapter 3. These studies reflect the immense corporate change that occurred in the late 1990s through to the mid-2000s in Australia, as with many other countries that underwent liberalisation. The majority of the companies examined conducted a capital reorganisation of one form or another during this period (see Table 1.5) and in most cases the effect of these changes was still being felt at the time of our investigations. Most of the companies studied had become more exposed to market pressures and heightened competition of one type or another, and this enabled us to study the impact of such changes on unions and employees in particular, and how this related to shareholder interests. Our case study findings helped to refine the sets of issues that we put to company directors through a major survey, the results of which were reported in Chapter 4.

Undoubtedly a key challenge for us in this study has been the question of categorisation. What we have learned about Australian business practices in detail has been less easy to transform into a substantial conclusion. Whether we can conclude that Australia has a persistent and definitive type of 'business system', whether we can show that Australia has a particular 'regulatory style', whether Australia belongs in the 'liberal market' (outsider controlled) or 'co-ordinated market' (insider controlled) set of capitalist countries, are questions which we are unable to answer with exactitude. There are significant sectoral and local differences which inevitably make such exercises difficult. With this note of caution our broad general findings are set out below.

---

1 See R. McCallum, 'Convergences and/or Divergences of Labor Law Systems: The View from Australia' (2007) 28 *Comparative Labor Law and Policy Journal* 455; R. McCallum, 'The New Work Choices Laws: Once Again Australia Borrows Foreign Labour Law Concepts' (2006) 19 *Australian Journal of Labour Law* 98. But see R. Mitchell, P. Gahan, A. Stewart, S. Cooney and S. Marshall, 'The Evolution of Labour Law in Australia: Measuring the Change' (2010) 23 *Australian Journal of Labour Law* 61.

5.2 Corporate Ownership Structure and Governance Orientation

One line of enquiry in our study concerned the hypothesised link between specific types of ownership structures and corporate governance orientation (the broad suppositions lying behind this set of relationships are set out in Chapter 1, Table 1.2). As we noted in Chapter 1 there are arguments in the literature which suggest that companies which are 'widely' (outsider) held (in the sense that they are not under the control of one or more dominant shareholders) are likely to be governed in a way which prioritises the financial interests of shareholders over other stakeholders, whilst those which are more 'closely' (insider) held (in the sense that there are one or more controlling shareholders) may be governed in a way that gives less salience to the short-term interests of shareholders.[2]

We considered this idea of contrasting ownership structures from three different perspectives. First, we asked whether, as a matter of 'regulatory style', Australian law was more sympathetic to one particular type of corporate ownership arrangement and governance over another. For example, we investigated whether the regulatory system appeared to support arm's-length financial arrangements or intermediated financial arrangements, and whether a particular model of corporate governance was prescribed, supported or proscribed. Second, we sought to examine several important issues relevant to the operation of the capital markets such as the extent to which shareholdings in listed companies are concentrated or diffused, the extent to which companies are listed on the securities exchange, and the extent to which there is an active market for corporate control. Third, we examined the issue at the level of the individual company, seeking to understand the extent to which the characteristics evinced within each company reflected the indicators predicted in the literature for 'insider' oriented and 'outsider' oriented models.

Our analysis in relation to the regulatory system, in respect both of company law and labour law, has been detailed in Chapter 2. The conclusion reached as a result of that analysis[3] suggests that in terms of 'regulatory style' Australian law and regulation fits into the general 'market/outsider' category insofar as its listed corporate sector is concerned. That is to say, its general approach to shareholder protection, takeover and disclosure regulation and so on, coupled with a fairly non-interventionist (from a corporate governance point of view) system of labour market regulation is more consistent with the UK and US models than with general European types.[4] However it is also necessary to remember, as we note in the following discussion, that the listed sector in Australia forms only a relatively

---

2   See Chapter 1, nn. 19–27 in particular.

3   See also S. Marshall, R. Mitchell and A. O'Donnell, 'Corporate Governance and Labour Law: Situating Australia's Regulatory Style' (2009) 47 *Asia Pacific Journal of Human Resources* 150.

4   Ibid.

small part of the Australian economy.[5] Any understanding of the Australian 'regulatory style' formed at this level must be seen in this light.

The same types of reservations also applied to our analysis of the general Australian business system model. According to the typology developed by Hall and Soskice, Australia seems only marginally to fall within the 'outsider' group across a set of indicators. For the variable that concerns the extent to which companies are listed on securities exchanges, for example, we seem as close to the Netherlands and Japan (who are in the 'insider' category) as we do to the US (which is in the 'outsider' category), and much closer to them than to the UK (which is also in the 'outsider' category).[6] Only about one-third of Australia's largest companies are stock-exchange listed as compared with two-thirds of the largest companies in the UK and virtually all of the largest companies in the US.[7] And the evidence also suggests continued concentrated ownership patterns in most Australian listed companies.[8] Furthermore, hostile takeovers are relatively rare in Australian corporate dealings.[9] For all of these reasons, and others,[10] it has been suggested that the Australian market for corporate control is not nearly as fluid as that in the UK and the US, and that nationally the Australian corporate sector is perhaps closer to an 'insider' than an 'outsider' type.[11] Similar suggestions have been made about the characterisation of the Australian labour market.[12] At the same time, however, it is necessary to recall that there is also a counter-argument which suggests that more recently in Australia there has been a process of evolution towards the 'outsider' model in relation both to capital and labour market character.[13]

---

5   Ibid., p. 158.

6   See P. Hall and D. Soskice, 'An Introduction to Varieties of Capitalism' in P. Hall and D. Soskice (eds), *Varieties of Capitalism*, Oxford University Press, Oxford, 2001, p. 1.

7   G. Stapledon, 'Australian Sharemarket Ownership' in G. Walker, B. Fisse and I. Ramsay (eds), *Securities Regulation in Australia and New Zealand*, LBC Information Services, Sydney, 2nd edn, 1998, p. 242; A. Dignam and M. Galanis, 'Australia Inside Out: The Corporate Governance System of the Australian Listed Market' (2004) 28 *Melbourne University Law Review* 623.

8   A. Lamba and G. Stapledon, 'The Determinants of Corporate Ownership Structure: Australian Evidence', Public Law and Legal Theory Working Paper No. 20, University of Melbourne, Melbourne, 2001.

9   See B. Buchanan, 'Australian Corporate Casualties' (2004) 9 *Advances in Financial Economics* 55, p. 66.

10   For more complete discussion see Marshall et al., above n. 3.

11   See Dignam and Galanis, above n. 7.

12   See, in particular, M. Jones and R. Mitchell, 'Legal Origin, Legal Families and the Regulation of Labour in Australia' in S. Marshall, R. Mitchell and I. Ramsay (eds), *Varieties of Capitalism, Corporate Governance and Employees*, Melbourne University Press, Melbourne, 2008.

13   See Chapter 2; and see also Marshall et al., above n. 3.

When it came to matching up our abstracted types with actual corporate governance orientation (as perceived through our case studies of Australian companies and our survey of directors) we drew mixed conclusions. In terms of the types of companies which we studied for the survey of directors, some 75.5 per cent were private companies and 24.5 per cent were public companies. Of these, some 16.5 per cent were listed on the Australian Securities Exchange, 0.5 per cent were listed on another Australian exchange, and 12 per cent were listed on an international exchange. Our case study companies also contained a mixture of 'outsider' and 'insider' model companies. We were therefore provided with detail spread across a spectrum of listed/unlisted, insider/outsider types.

Looked at generally, if it were the case that Australian companies matched the standard 'outsider' model suggested in the literature, then, as we indicated in Chapter 1, we might have expected as a consequence a fairly pronounced leaning towards a shareholder-oriented conception of corporate governance. As we have noted in Chapter 4, there is undoubtedly some support for this supposition provided by the outcomes of our survey, but this is by no means unequivocal. Forty four per cent of our respondent directors ranked shareholders as their number one priority, and 40.4 per cent ranked the company as first priority, and only 6.7 per cent of directors ranked employees ahead of all other stakeholders. Yet on the other hand, 55 per cent of directors surveyed understood that in acting 'in the best interests of the company' they were required to balance all stakeholder interests (including employees) as an end in itself. Other findings from the survey revealed that employees were often highly ranked as against shareholders in particular contexts. The findings drawn from our case studies of companies were similarly uneven. Generally it might be said that those case study companies which were publicly listed tended to be more shareholder-oriented, and more market sensitive when compared with those which were not. However, this stance was by no means common to all like cases. In one of our studies, a listed company with extensive international operations nevertheless exhibited a relatively strong leadership/ control influence from some founders, and accordingly constructed more long-term relations with both capital and labour than 'outsider'-types might typically do. And, as the data in Chapter 3 indicated, in most cases the patterns of conduct among this small group of listed companies in times of change was neither uniform, nor at the extreme end of supposed 'shareholder'-oriented governance. Plainly then, there are many intervening factors which moderate the relationship between corporate ownership structure and corporate governance orientation and, as we noted in Chapter 1, this would suggest that the relationship is far more complex, both between and within national contexts, than a simplified 'insider'/'outsider' dichotomy would suppose.

The present study is an examination of law and business practice within the Australian national context. We have sought to investigate the various hypothesised relationships between ownership structure, corporate governance and labour relations not by reference to comparisons between Australia and other nations, but by reference to the structures and behaviours of different types of companies within the country. In this respect the study matches other recent attempts to utilise within-country empirical data to test the 'varieties of capitalism' theories. As Pendleton notes, overall these studies do not match the predicted outcomes,[14] adding weight to the suggestion that perhaps the predicted effects of the 'market/ outsider' model on the prospects for labour needs at least to be revised, if not rejected.[15]

Closer study of the corporate ownership, corporate governance and labour relations connection within national systems suggests, then, greater complexity and uncertainty. But at the same time it may also help to reveal more closely the mechanisms of control and governance in operation.

One example concerns the prioritisation of shareholder interests and how this relates to shareholder control and influence. We saw in Chapter 4 that the results from our survey of directors and their perceptions of responsibilities to various stakeholder groups showed that shareholders were more highly ranked in companies with 'outsider'-style financial arrangements than those with 'insider' arrangements. However, we also found that shareholders were perceived as having a significantly greater power to influence management in 'insider'-type companies than in 'outsider'-types. Similarly, shareholders were perceived by directors in the 'insider'-types as being more active in pursuing demands and, based on the mean scores, as both receiving a higher degree of time and attention from management and as having a higher degree of legitimacy in the eyes of directors when compared with other stakeholders. In particular, in 'outsider'-style companies, shareholders were perceived to be far less active in pursuing demands or wishes which they felt were important as compared with shareholders in 'insider'-style companies.

This general position may correspond with the mechanisms by which control is exercised. In 'outsider'-style companies, where shareholdings are widely diffused, there are fewer opportunities for direct shareholder influence. Rather, influence is generally exercised indirectly, through market mechanisms such as the sale of shares when dissatisfaction is felt (in other words, exiting the company is the strategy to indicate dissatisfaction). Thus, shareholders may be ranked highly by directors, but it does not follow that they have the ability to wield significant power or influence over decision-making. But in 'insider' companies, especially in small ones in which owners may also be managers, it does follow that shareholders have the ability make direct demands using 'voice' mechanisms.

This is consistent with the characterisation of corporate governance in 'insider'-type companies in the varieties of capitalism literature. However, it is difficult to say whether our data from the case study companies confirmed other expected outcomes. The literature suggests that, for 'insider'-type companies, investment is more likely to be patient, and this would have a number of flow-

---

14   A. Pendleton, 'The Liberal Market Model of Finance, Ownership, and Governance: An Evaluation of its Effect on Labour' (2009) 47 *Asia Pacific Journal of Human Resources* 133, pp. 140–141.

15   Ibid., pp. 145 and 147.

on effects in terms of the management of the company, particularly in relation to stakeholders. For instance, such companies could afford to have longer term planning horizons in a number of areas such as greater investment in incremental product enhancement and longer tenure for employees, accompanied by higher levels of internal training. But our survey data does not support any conclusions of this nature when it comes to the attitudes of directors in Australian businesses. The evidence regarding the priorities of directors with regards to shareholders, dividend policy and so on does not sustain the proposition that the owners of 'insider'-owned companies might be inclined to be more patient than those of 'outsider' companies. Nor does the evidence collected through the course of our survey suggest that the policies of 'insider'-type companies are more 'long term' than those of 'outsider'-type companies. For instance, there was no (statistically significant) greater emphasis on increasing share price or on dividend policy in 'outsider' companies when measured against 'insider' companies. There was also no statistically significant greater weight given to reducing costs compared with 'growing' the business, nor to improving employee morale, safeguarding existing jobs or creating job opportunities within the company, regardless of whether the ownership structure was more 'insider' or 'outsider' in character.

Whatever doubt these outcomes might throw upon the utility of the widely drawn characterisations we have utilised in this study, they certainly suggest the possibility of quite distinct characteristics in the relations between Australian shareholders, companies and directors as well the interplay of other factors.

Such complexities are observed in our study of institutional investors, for example. There is an argument that the power of large investors to influence corporate management is influenced by the small size of the Australian stock market: alternative investment options are limited and some institutional investors are therefore, to some extent, locked into investing in some companies that are significant in the Australian market. While some of these institutional investors have grown large due to the compulsory investment by Australian workers in superannuation schemes, they are denied the classic 'exit' option open to the typical 'outsider'-model shareholder in larger markets like those of the UK and the US. As a consequence, there is an important question whether these institutional investors are increasingly resorting to 'voice' mechanisms for influencing company behaviour expected in 'insider'-type companies. These mechanisms include participation in shareholder meetings and voting, as well as investment briefings and individual meetings with company managers.

We interviewed institutional investors to learn about the extent to which the use of 'voice' might be exercised in order to influence the human resource management policies of investee companies. The institutional investors identified a lack of detailed information about company behaviour, particularly in relation to human resource management, as a challenge for any meaningful engagement. Further, institutional investors perceived that it was not the role of shareholders to interfere in the management of the company, regardless of the fact that they felt locked into investment in larger listed companies in the long term. However, institutional investors are engaging companies on what might be regarded as traditional governance issues of concern to shareholders, such as executive remuneration and the structure of the board of directors. Here we see how the views of key investors can potentially act to influence and shape the views of company directors. The reluctance of institutional investors to engage with investee companies on human resource management issues (and presumably other issues that cannot be categorised as falling within a reasonably narrow range of standard governance issues) can in part explain why our survey of company directors found that directors of 'outsider'-type companies (in which institutional investors are shareholders) perceive shareholders to be less active and receive less time and attention from management than is the case with 'insider'-type companies.

Further specific insights into the mechanisms through which owners exercise influence in companies with different ownership structures are seen in our case studies of 10 companies in periods of structural transition.

In the instances where our case study companies had undertaken a capital restructuring which resulted in more arm's-length ownership, a perception was generally noted amongst managers that this was associated with heightened short-term pressure from shareholders. Nevertheless the evidence on this point suggests that this was by no means a uniform response. For instance, in the case of ResourceCo 2, which underwent a dual listed merger, there was great concern before the merger that shareholder influence would be diluted, not strengthened. The Australian component of the merger was an iconic Australian company towards which shareholders, workers and the community felt what can only be described as heightened emotional attachment compared with other listed companies. As a consequence, the company was subjected to sharp scrutiny by all parties and, in particular, by the media. There was a popular feeling that the dual listing would detach the company from its national roots and render it less sensitive to Australian community and shareholder viewpoints. Whether actual shareholder voting power has been diluted is a matter of debate, but concerns of this nature have not continued to be voiced. They may have been muted by consistent, strong returns to investors. It was the view of management that the company's success provided them with considerable autonomy and scope to manage shareholder expectations. In the case of this company – which was an 'outsider' company before and after the merger, but in which relations with investors may have become more arm's length – it cannot be said that the shift resulted in greater pressure for short-term profits.

Some of our other case studies provided evidence that the mechanisms of shareholder influence can be complicated by various factors. For instance, although FinanceCo 2 exhibited market/'outsider' financial arrangements and board of directors composition, broadly speaking, the proportion of shares held by the executive directors, management and staff was estimated at between 30 and 40 per cent at the time of our study. This provided a level of protection against a takeover, reducing the disciplinary impact of the market for corporate control. The company's founder was still in a senior management position, and continued to hold around 10 per cent of the issued shares. Unlike the other companies studied, the dominant business model pursued by FinanceCo 2 appeared to be one of growth rather than profitability passed onto shareholders in the form of strong dividends. Since listing, the company had grown from 40 to 10,000 employees.

Perhaps the starkest contrasts to this scenario were found in the case of FinanceCo 1, which demutualised, and ServiceCo, which went from being a government-owned-and-controlled enterprise to a privately owned business. At the time of our study, the top five shareholders of FinanceCo 1 were institutional investors holding between 3 and 13 per cent of the total shares in the business. To this extent, FinanceCo 1 looked like other 'outsider' companies. However, around 70 per cent of the company's shares were still held by retail or smaller, non-institutional shareholders, with an unusual overlap between shareholders, customers and employees as a result of share distribution to employees and policy holders as part of the demutualisation process. Further, the company was protected by legislation against any threat of a takeover in the first five years of its demutualised existence. Regardless of these exceptional factors, the view of management within FinanceCo 1 was that with demutualisation and share market listing had come a sharper business focus driven by higher levels of accountability and this appeared to be reflected in its general management strategy and relations with investors. In the case of ServiceCo, the shift to 'outsider' financial arrangements had a profound impact upon management's perception of timelines for profitability and investor returns, and thus upon the general management strategy. However, other conflicting requirements for long-term investment in infrastructure militated against this trend, leaving managers feeling squeezed between competing pressures. Nonetheless, these two case studies provide support for the proposition that companies which generally moved toward the characteristics of 'outsider' governance tend to become more shareholder-oriented, market-sensitive, and prone to anti-labour strategies in times of turbulence or downturn (the link between ownership structures and non-stakeholder approaches will be considered further later in this chapter).

'Insider' companies that maintained their 'insider' ownership structures throughout the period of study provided a useful point of comparison. Four of the companies studied fitted this characterisation. Of these, CommCo's board comprised three directors, all appointed by the company's parent organisation. The mechanisms of control and influence by the owners differed from what might be expected of a company which has 'outsider'/market style capital structures. Policy control and business strategy setting by the parent company permeated the Australian subsidiary and, because it was a wholly owned subsidiary, the Australian managers were buffered against direct pressure from shareholders and creditors. Regardless of these factors, during the period of study CommCo displayed a similar transition to management strategies aimed at producing short-term profit. Functions that required long-term investment, such as research and development, were moved out of Australia and centralised internationally. This change in business strategy was the result of major competitive pressures in the international and Australian markets, in particular flow-on effects of deregulation aimed at introducing competition against Australian telecommunications monopoly Telecom, which was CommCo's biggest client prior to its privatisation.

Again speaking very generally, we think that these 'insider' companies did tend more to exhibit the characteristics expected in the literature. In particular they mainly evinced a longer term approach to the development of the business, and a more stakeholder rather than shareholder orientation. But consistent with our findings in relation to the 'outsider' companies studied, the overwhelming impression among this group was the complexity of the outcomes, making straightforward categorisation very problematical. In some instances the private nature of the business seems to have secured the company from market pressures and enabled the pursuit of a long-term strategy. But on the other hand there were also examples where there appeared to be stronger profit-oriented short-term pressures acting upon the company, even though these may not have arisen from external shareholder/market pressure, or from creditors. All of this then, points to the importance of various factors which may compromise the standard classification employed in some of the literature. For example, as we noted in relation to ManufoodCo, the longstanding regional presence of an insider-controlled business may give the business strong local loyalty and workforce commitment, but that does not guarantee a strongly pro-labour strategy. More important in certain respects may be the type of industry involved, and the history of the competitive practices in that industry, which, in the case of ManufoodCo, kept wages and job security low, and fostered little in the way of partnership relations.

It is not clear, then, that 'insider' forms of ownership necessarily correspond with less pressure for short-term profit maximisation and the suite of company policies which are expected to follow from the presence of 'patient' capital. There are two possible explanations for this. The first is that capital is not necessarily 'patient', even where it is stable. The second is that there are many intervening factors which moderate the relationship between corporate ownership structure and the governance orientation of a company.

In companies which are broadly characterised as 'outsider' companies, share market listing and diffused shareholding patterns of themselves do not produce uncomplicated shareholder-oriented management. Issues such as the state of product markets, the need for a company to be seen as responsive to governmental/public expectations (regulatory or otherwise), locality factors, type of industry and workforce are all relevant to the particular outcomes examined in the discussion of our cases in Chapter 3 and discussed further in the next section of this chapter. Overall, the data collected in our case studies supports the conclusion that Australia has a mixed system of ownership structure and corporate governance orientation. The role of regulation in the emergence of this system is also mixed. As we saw in Chapter 2, the listed sector is supported by regulation which would seem to facilitate 'outsider' (or market) forms of corporate ownership and governance. Yet regardless of the fact that they are underpinned by regulation of this type, even amongst listed companies, many of these companies have a reasonably high degree of ownership concentration. Meanwhile, greater regulatory freedom is given to non-listed and private companies to organise capital and corporate governance along 'insider-relational' lines and, indeed, most private companies exhibit characteristics more consistent with 'insider' styles in this respect. As indicated in Chapter 4, the mechanisms of control employed by shareholders in 'insider'-type companies are generally consistent with those suggested in the literature.

5.3 How Does Corporate Governance Orientation Impact Upon the Management of Labour?

Does a particular type of governance orientation or outlook necessarily correspond with particular labour management systems and processes? Our starting point in section 5.2 of this chapter (in keeping with the varieties of capitalism literature) was that companies with an 'outsider' set of characteristics would be relatively more shareholder-oriented in corporate governance than companies with an 'insider' set of characteristics (the broad suppositions underlying these sets of relationships are set out in Table 1.2). This has, as we have seen, numerous implications for the approach a company takes in its dealings with shareholders and other stakeholders. Importantly, for purposes of the present point in the discussion, the varieties of capitalism literature has much to say about the nature of labour relations and the regulation and management of labour systems, both within and outside the boundaries of particular companies.

In section 5.2, we arrived at some very general conclusions about the correspondence between Australian company types and their corporate governance orientation. Our broad conclusions, based upon case study and survey data, were that in some general respects the governance approach of Australian companies and their directors corresponded with what the literature would suggest would be the case in 'outsider' and 'insider' types. At a more specific level, however, we found that there were numerous complexities and inconsistencies in corporate governance outlook which make generalisation difficult and fitting empirical examples into highly simplified and stylised institutional categories highly problematical.[16]

The varieties of capitalism literature would lead us to expect that industrial relations in 'outsider' systems would be characterised by greater managerial prerogative and decentralised or enterprise-based union arrangements, if any. We would expect to see employment relations characterised by arm's-length relationships with labour and unions, recruitment and layoff according to the

---

16   See further on this point, C. Crouch, *Capitalist Diversity and Change: Recombinant Governance and Institutional Entrepreneurs*, Oxford University Press, Oxford, 2005; H. Katz and O. Darbishire, *Converging Divergences: Worldwide Changes in Employment Systems*, Cornell University Press, Ithaca, NY, 1999.

demand for labour, as well as greater use of contingent labour, the fixing of wages based on market principles, leading to more variable pay, less investment in company-specific training and wide wage dispersion between groups of workers.[17] As we noted briefly in section 5.2, it was difficult to draw any clear conclusions from our survey data on these matters. Whilst directors from companies which adhered to the 'insider'-type were marginally more likely to give greater weight to improving employee morale, safeguarding existing jobs or creating job opportunities than those from 'outsider'-type companies, this difference was not statistically significant.

The varieties of capitalism literature would also suggest that in periods of economic downturn, and/or periods of increased market pressure, 'outsider' businesses will be relatively more inclined to reorganise their employment systems with greater emphasis on redundancies, wage cuts and non-partnership practices,[18] whereas, for reasons explained elsewhere, 'insider'-type companies would be under less immediate market and shareholder pressure, and thus be able to take a longer term view. In theory this results in greater protection for labour in the 'insider'-type company.

Our survey data revealed that the majority of directors, whether from 'insider' or 'outsider' companies, even in times of economic downturn, did not immediately think of shoring up shareholder expectations through dismissals and wage cuts. The conclusions we reached from our case studies were more mixed. As we have noted, in many cases the companies examined in this project had been recently subjected to reorganisation and restructuring, exposing them, in many instances, to greater market pressure than had previously been the case. We found that in these conditions there was evidence confirming that overall there were worsened outcomes for labour, in terms of declining influence for unions, and job losses, less employment security and poorer conditions for employees. But again the various complexities in these studies helped paint an interesting picture. On the one hand, we found clear evidence that when companies conducted capital restructuring in an 'outsider' direction, this was most often associated with the major reorganisation of employment relations in the manner expected of 'market/outsider' companies. It would be going too far to suggest, however, that the relationship between the reorganisation of ownership and the changes to the employment systems in these companies was necessarily causal in nature. In the case of the two companies which conducted the most radical restructuring of employment relations (ResourceCo 1 and ResourceCo 2), the changes in employment preceded changes in ownership. In the case of EnergyCo, corporatisation and privatisation was a result of government policy aimed at regulating labour through the provision of employment in state-owned companies, as well as a reflection of a commitment

---

17   For some data on these types of issues across OECD countries see B. Black, H. Gospel and A. Pendleton, 'Finance, Corporate Governance and the Employment Relationship' (2007) 46 *Industrial Relations* 643.

18   Pendleton, above n. 14, pp. 137–138.

to forms of economic governance relying more on market mechanisms. The privatisation of the company and the reduction of its business concerns to what it considered to be its 'core' activities brought about the reduction of its workforce from 27,000 in 1996 to about 9,000 in 2003. In each of these cases, it is possible that the shift to more market oriented and less protected employment relations was the consequence of a generalised commitment to 'market relations', exposing the company to greater competition at different levels.

Among our case-study companies, the systems of employment, labour and work relations cannot be said to have uniformly deteriorated in response to heightened competition and exposure to other market forces. Rather, what we observed was a shift from more uniform conditions to far greater dispersion in the range of conditions and management styles experienced by workers within the one company. The dispersion was associated with a decline in union power and centralised, collectivised wage-setting. Changes in the organisation of work seemed to result in dispersion in the wages and conditions experienced by union members, even when union power remained reasonably high. In the case of EnergyCo, ServiceCo and CommCo, we observed the creation of 'core' and 'peripheral' workforces. In most instances, peripheral workers experienced 'low wage' or 'low road' employment relations entailing managerial discretion, hierarchical work relations and high turnovers.[19] In areas in which labour supply was short, however, contractors sometimes enjoyed high wages and reasonable autonomy, despite receiving 'piece-rate' wages. 'Core' workers enjoyed human resource management strategies, including the propagation of a corporate culture and extensive communication, directed teams, above-average pay with contingent pay and individualised career development. In other companies, such as ResourceCo 2, variations in employment strategies reflected the decentralisation of the business into semi-autonomous business units, resulting in greater variation in employment relations based on local labour market and product market factors. Each of these case studies reflects wider patterns across the Australian economy.[20]

In the counter examples, namely, those that retained 'insider'-style ownership arrangements or corporate governance orientation, it could sometimes be said that the presence of managers with significant ownership stakes provided some protection to labour. For instance, in the case of ManuengCo and possibly also BiotechCo, the presence of owner-managers seemed to have some role in retarding the shift to variable and market-based wage setting (at least for scientific workers, in the case of BiotechCo). In ManufoodCo, on the other hand, the loyalty of employees to an 'insider'-owner – a local family – had perhaps been a factor in locking out unions and maintaining 'low road' employment relations. In each case, 'insider' ownership and corporate governance arrangements seemed to provide

---

19   See Katz and Darbishire, above n. 16 (in particular the descriptions of various types of employment strategies outlined on pp. 10–11).

20   Ibid., ch. 4.

some stability, but they did not result in 'high road' human resource management techniques, or collective partnership-style employment or work relations.

Our studies indicate that the ownership stucture and corporate governance of the company seemed to correlate with the style of employment relations in some way. However, the mechanisms resulting in correlations are complex and not necessarily causal or uniform in nature. 'Insider' arrangements may provide some stability, suggesting long-term capital, but this does not seem to correspond with employment or labour relations of a particular type. In our case study companies, it was not associated with greater investment in training or high engagement work relations. However, shifts to market-oriented and 'outsider' forms of ownership structure often corresponded to more market-oriented relations in the area of employment with deleterious effects for low-skilled and peripheral workers who enjoyed greater protection in the collectivised labour relations of the previous era. The effect here appeared to produce less standardised, more dispersed patterns of employment conditions and protections.

In some of our case studies, then, a structural transformation of the company from an 'insider' to an 'outsider' type led to increased shareholder and market orientation accompanied by quite radical impacts upon the company's employment systems. But in other cases this did not occur – there were factors which moderated the severity with which a restructuring was translated into a new workplace policy. In other words the transformation of a company's ownership structure, and the extent to which it was exposed to the share market and shareholder groups did not exclusively determine the outcomes for labour.[21] Our conclusions in the following section are broadly consistent with this characterisation.

5.4 Partnerships at Work and the Influence of Legal and Economic Contexts

One of our central concerns in this project was to investigate whether or not corporate directors and managers regarded employees as working in 'partnership relations' with the company and, if so, what this might mean for employment relations. As noted in Chapter 1, we adopted a very broad 'indicative' concept of what might be regarded as a partnership between a company and its employees for the purposes of the study. In general we sought to identify working arrangements wherein employees were regarded as 'inside' the business and where they were treated in a relatively balanced way vis-à-vis shareholders. In this context 'partnership' might take on various forms, demonstrating the importance of employee performance, and the relevance of their interests and concerns to the business. This might mean a positive role for trade unions, facilitation of employee 'voice' mechanisms within the decision-making structures of the business, capital

---

21   See also N. Conway, S. Deakin, S. Konzelmann, H. Petit, A. Reberioux and F. Wilkinson, 'The Influence of Stock Market Listing on Human Resources Management: Evidence for France and Britain' (2008) 46 *British Journal of Industrial Relations* 631.

investment by the employees in the business, and various types of employment practices based around operations and supervision (see Table 1.4 in Chapter 1).

In pursuing these concepts, the study sought to understand various objective and subjective elements which might indicate the presence of a 'partnership' culture. One particular element we were interested in was whether company directors themselves regarded their businesses as constituting 'partnerships' between various stakeholders. A second consideration concerned the types of employment systems utilised in business enterprises – whether, and if so to what extent, employees (either individually or through their industrial organisations) had an influence on decision-making within the enterprise, were aligned with organisational performance through various reward systems, were engaged in various 'high performance' style work processes, and had a degree of employment security.[22]

Importantly for the present study each of these elements is, or may be, impacted upon by law and regulation. For example the law may restrict the choices which company directors and managers may make. It may oblige directors and managers to give priority to one set of stakeholders over others. It may oblige businesses to deal with unions. It may necessitate the adoption of particular work practices and systems, or it may allow relative freedom to businesses to decide how to structure their production and employment arrangements. Very detailed labour regulation can limit the conditions under which businesses can operate productions systems and offer services.[23]

In the Australian case there is a degree of tension over the correct interpretation of the law regarding directors' duties towards shareholders. Among corporate lawyers there is a general understanding that the prevailing responsibility of directors in governing companies is to protect the long-term interests of the company and the shareholders. In general this understanding of the legal position clearly provides some cogency for the so-called 'shareholder primacy' view of the company.[24] However, this does not mean that the interests of stakeholders other than shareholders are ignored in the decision-making processes of directors. This would be to ignore the reality of how business decisions are made. It would also

---

22   See generally on the relationship between various high-performance measures, workplace partnerships and workplace outcomes: E. Appelbaum, T. Bailey, P. Berg and A. Kalleberg, *Manufacturing Advantage: Why High-Performance Work Systems Pay Off*, Economic Policy Institute, New York, 2000; D. Guest and R. Peccei, 'Partnership at Work: Mutuality and the Balance of Advantage' (2001) 39 *British Journal of Industrial Relations* 207; M. Huselid, 'The Impact of Human Resource Management Practices on Turnover, Productivity, and Corporate Financial Performance' (1995) 38 *Academy of Management Journal* 635.

23   See, for example, R. Mitchell and M. Rimmer, 'Labor Law, De-Regulation and Flexibility in Australian Industrial Relations' (1990) 12 *Comparative Labor Law Journal* 1.

24   See R. Mitchell, A. O'Donnell and I. Ramsay, 'Shareholder Value and Employee Interests: Intersections Between Corporate Governance, Corporate Law and Labor Law' (2005) 23 *Wisconsin International Law Journal* 417.

ignore the legal position which is that although the Australian *Corporations Act* obliges directors to act in the best interests of the shareholders generally, directors may take into account a range of factors and interests other than the interests of shareholders if this benefits the shareholders as a whole. In addition, there are obligations imposed on directors and companies by many statutes that regulate areas as diverse as occupational health and safety and environmental matters that require directors and companies to consider the interests of stakeholders other than shareholders.[25]

Importantly though, it does not appear from our research data that directors necessarily perceive themselves as limited by law in what decisions they make, nor that they are even principally motivated by legal considerations in how they perceive their duties towards shareholders, employees and other stakeholders. As our survey data show in Chapter 4, more than 90 per cent of company directors hold the view that the law allows them to take account of the interests of stakeholders other than shareholders. A majority of directors believe that acting in the best interests of the company means balancing the interests of all stakeholders, and 38 per cent believe that it means that they must act in the interests of all stakeholders for the purpose of sustaining the long-term interests of shareholders.[26]

On these kinds of interpretations, the idea that the company might be viewed by key actors as a kind of 'partnership' between core stakeholder groups, including employees, is at least tenable. Moreover, other evidence derived from the survey data demonstrates that in practice the interests of employees are ranked quite highly when compared with those of shareholders, and in certain matters (such as fair treatment and employment security) are ranked more highly than shareholder concerns such as increased share price and dividends. On this evidence, directors do not appear particularly inhibited, either in principle or in practice, by corporate law considerations. Nor, for that matter, do they appear particularly influenced by the restrictions set down in labour law. Only about 15 per cent of directors attributed the dominant source of their responsibilities to employees as arising from labour law (and about 17 per cent from corporate law).[27] Far more important in influencing director's minds in how they should exercise their responsibilities towards employees were ethical and social values (about 25 per cent) and business imperatives (about 42 per cent).

It follows from this data that while the law sets parameters on conduct, it does not appear in its own terms, at least on the basis of our survey evidence, overly to

---

25   See S. Marshall and I. Ramsay, 'Shareholders and Directors' Duties: Law, Theory and Evidence', Legal Studies Research Paper No. 411, Melbourne Law School, University of Melbourne, 2009. Two Australian inquiries which have considered this issue are the Corporations and Markets Advisory Committee, *The Social Responsibility of Corporations*, 2006 and the Parliamentary Joint Committee on Corporations and Financial Services, *Corporate Responsibility: Managing Risk and Creating Value*, 2006.

26   See Table 4.5.

27   See Figure 4.1.

influence the shape and operation of employment systems. There is high flexibility for directors to choose which strategy they would like to adopt, and whilst labour law does not appear necessarily to require partnership approaches[28] neither does it exclude them. This suggests that in many respects it is factors beyond legal regulation that determine whether, and if so to what degree, corporate governance exhibits 'shareholder primacy' or 'stakeholder' tendencies, although it is obvious that regulation can both enable particular strategies and send a signal to the relevant actors as to desired policy objectives.

As we noted in Chapter 4, a high proportion of directors (77 per cent) appeared to have some sort of a 'partnership' conception of the relationship between the company and its employees. Most respondent directors also took the view that the company and its employees shared essentially the same interests (71 per cent of those who viewed the relationship between the company and its employees as one of 'partnership'). The evidence further suggests that the interests of employees are considered important by directors, and that their interests and influence are important, even in companies where shareholder primacy is manifested in corporate governance outlook. In other words, even where directors perceive that shareholders are the most important and influential among stakeholders, employees are still seen as a prominent interest group, ranking well above customers, suppliers and creditors.

But does this conception of 'partnership' mean very much in practical terms? And what factors influence whether, and if so to what extent, the idea of partnership is given effect to within companies? The weight of international evidence suggests that in periods of economic downturn, employees are likely to suffer as a consequence of corporate strategies to reduce costs through downsizing, relocation and so on.[29] In Australia there have been numerous examples of these kinds of occurrences, including job shedding and sometimes a failure to meet commitments to employee entitlements.[30] If these cases typify the nature of relations between companies and their employees then it may be argued that the idea that companies are in partnership with their employees is misconceived.

However, the evidence from our research suggests that even in these adverse kinds of contexts notions of 'partnership' may still continue to have some influence, consistent with more recent international findings that even in the 'market/ outsider' model of economic organisation 'labour management practices are often more favourable to labour than is usually claimed'.[31] Beginning again with the expressed views of directors surveyed for this study, it appears that the majority,

---

28   R. Mitchell and A. O'Donnell, 'What Is Labour Law Doing About "Partnership at Work"? British and Australian Developments Compared' in S. Marshall. R. Mitchell and I. Ramsay (eds), *Varieties of Capitalism, Corporate Governance and Employees*, Melbourne University Press, Melbourne, 2008, p. 95.

29   See Chapter 1, and the works cited in nn. 7–9 in particular.

30   For discussion see Buchanan, above n. 9.

31   Pendeleton, above n. 14, p. 146.

even in times of economic downturn, do not immediately think of shoring up shareholder expectations through dismissals and wage cuts. Even if this approach may still be explained as an 'enlightened' shareholder-primacy model, rather than a stakeholder perspective, it is further, if slight, evidence supporting at least a notional partnership conception of the company, in terms of buffering employees in the face of market pressures.

On the other hand, the idea of partnership does not appear, in the context of our case study companies, very often, if at all, to have produced labour management systems which have transformed employment relations into a truly collaborative relationship exhibiting a high level of what have been called 'high performance' workplace practices (characterised, for example, by direct participation of employees and their institutions in workplace decision-making, employee share ownership schemes, performance-based pay, performance management, employment security and so on).

In general the Australian evidence on the adoption of these kinds of practices is quite sparse. But based upon the evidence which is available it would seem that very few Australian workplaces conform to the 'high performance' model, and that where such practices are adopted in isolation they may not always be particularly effective.[32] In the company-based studies carried out for this project we found little in the way of evidence demonstrating any systematic attempt on the part of companies to construct 'partnership' relations around sets of high performance workplace practices, notwithstanding the presence of some such operations (e.g. employee involvement, joint consultative committees, 'work teams', flexible employment and so on) in virtually all of the companies examined (the sorts of things we looked for in our case studies are set out in Chapter 1, Table 1.4). On the whole these generally appeared to be isolated instances of particular ideas rather than systematised and co-ordinated employment models built on co-operation and innovation. In many cases such practices were implemented within non-union or anti-union environments, and sometimes where relations between the company and its employees were problematical at least. Moreover employee share ownership schemes are, on the whole, and for various reasons (including regulatory limitations) poorly developed in Australia among the non-managerial workforce.[33] And the general view on employee participation practices is that where participatory structures such as works councils or joint management-

---

32   See P. Gahan and D. Buttigieg, 'High Performance Workplace Systems and the Social Context of Work: The Role of Workplace Climate' (2008) 19 *Labour and Industry* 1.

33   See I. Landau, R. Mitchell, A. O'Connell and I. Ramsay, 'Employee Share Ownership in Australia: Theory, Evidence, Current Practice and Regulation' (2007) 25 *UCLA Pacific Basin Law Journal* 25; I. Landau, R. Mitchell, A. O'Connell, I. Ramsay and S. Marshall, 'Broad-based Employee Share Ownership in Australian Listed Companies: An Empirical Analysis' (2009) 37 *Australian Business Law Review* 412.

worker committees are established they tend to be management dominated, and marginal in importance.[34]

It follows that if partnership has a worthwhile practical or operational resonance, something beyond mere notional conception, it would most obviously be seen in the more typical general model of collective labour relations where workplaces are governed and regulated by joint management – employee/union bargaining (or some variety of that practice). There have been occasional suggestions that very strong integrated systems of this type, Australia being perhaps the prime example, can provide outcomes which approximate the labour management practices of the less shareholder-oriented, more employee-friendly, systems of co-ordinated market economies, such as those of continental Europe.[35] These are, however, heavily conditioned arguments.[36] Moreover, recent developments in Australian labour law have displayed a crucial and decisive shift away from this conception of 'partnership' relations by reducing the legal pillars of collectivism and trade unionism.[37]

What, then, do our studies tell us about the apparent retreat from widespread collaborative forms of employment, industrial and work arrangements over the past two decades? And what do our studies have to say about the uniformity or otherwise of these developments? One important argument here is based on the regulatory and institutional framework of corporate governance, particularly aspects of both corporate law and labour law. As we saw in Chapter 2, this argument suggests that both corporate and labour law were subject to important change during the 1990s and 2000s in order to produce greater response to shareholder interests, and greater flexibility in the means and costs of employing labour.[38] As noted above, legislative support for the collective determination of wages and other terms and conditions of employment was progressively stripped away between 1996 and 2007.[39] At the

---

34   A. Forsyth, S. Korman and S. Marshall, 'Joint Consultative Committees in Australia: An Empirical Update' (2008) 16 *International Journal of Employment Studies* 99.

35   See, for example, R. Mitchell and P. Scherer, 'Australia: The Search for Fair Employment Contracts Through Tribunals' in J. Hartog and J. Theeuwes (eds), *Labour Market Contracts and Institutions*, Elsevier Science Publishers, Amsterdam, 1993, p. 80; Jones and Mitchell, above n. 12, pp. 64–65.

36   Marshall et al., above n. 3.

37   See, for example, A. Forsyth, 'Arbitration Extinguished: The Impact of the Work Choices Legislation on the Australian Industrial Relations Commission' (2006) 32 *Australian Bulletin of Labour* 27; A. Forsyth, 'Decentralisation and "Deregulation" Through "Ultra-Regulation": Australia's 2005 Labour Law Reforms' in S. Ouchi and T. Araki (eds), *Decentralizing Industrial Relations: The Role of Labour Unions and Employee Representatives*, Kluwer Law International, The Hague, 2007, p. 125; P. Waring and J. Burgess, 'Work Choices: The Privileging of Individualism in Australian Industrial Relations' (2006) 14 *International Journal of Employment Studies* 61.

38   See also Marshall et al., above n. 3.

39   See, for example, the references cited in n. 37 above.

same time formal law encouraging the adoption of co-operative mechanisms in Australian workplaces was also reduced.[40] But as we have also noted, there are uncertainties about how relevant or critical these regulatory changes were, first in enabling labour management change in principle, and second in influencing corporate decision-making over labour management strategies as a matter of fact. As we saw in Chapter 3, our case studies demonstrated that sometimes quite radical corporate responses have occurred without (or perhaps in spite of the absence of) regulatory change, and at other times companies have maintained traditional labour management processes when there is no regulatory obstacle to adopting other strategies. The outcomes have been diverse rather than uniform. There are, for example, several reasons why managers may have more 'strategic choice' options in managing labour than the orthodox account (that shareholders' interests are necessarily prioritised over the interests of employees by managers) would suggest. These include greater acceptance of management leadership on labour management issues and the heightened influence of practices such as corporate social responsibility, sustainable investment and so on.[41]

In accounting for this diversity in corporate response to the challenge of global competition and changing economic conditions it was consequently necessary to look beyond law and regulation for explanation. Other contextual factors obviously were important. For example, the fostering of partnerships at work was viewed by some commentators to be an important strategy in economic competition.[42] Part of our inquiry was thus to investigate whether Australian companies were pursuing a particular employment strategy in response to economic and market pressures rather than legal contexts. The period of our study encompassed an era of substantially heightened international economic pressure as countries reduced tariff- and non-tariff protections and countries with emerging economies entered the global marketplace. Privatisation of public services within some countries, including Australia, also increased competitive pressures. As we saw in Chapter

---

40   See R. Markey, 'The State of Representative Participation in Australia: Where to Next?' (2004) 20 *International Journal of Comparative Labour Law and Industrial Relations* 533.

41   See Pendleton, above n. 14, pp. 142–145; A. Pendleton and S. Deakin, 'Corporate Governance and Workplace Employment Relations: The Potential of WERS 2004' (2007) 38 *Journal of Industrial Relations* 338; K. Anderson, S. Marshall and I. Ramsay, 'Do Australian Institutional Investors Aim to Influence the Human Resource Practices of Investee Companies?' in S. Marshall, R. Mitchell and I. Ramsay (eds), *Varieties of Capitalism, Corporate Governance and Employees*, Melbourne University Press, Melbourne, 2008, p. 245; P. Waring and J. Lewer, 'The Impact of Socially Responsible Investment on Human Resource Management: A Conceptual Framework' (2004) 52 *Journal of Business Ethics* 99; S. Deakin, R. Hobbs, S. Konzelman and F. Wilkinson, 'Anglo-American Corporate Governance and the Employment Relationship: A Case to Answer?' (2006) 4 *Socio-Economic Review* 155.

42   A. Pendleton, *Employee Ownership, Participation and Governance: A Study of ESOPs in the UK*, Routledge, London, 2001.

3, most of the Australian companies examined closely for this project underwent one form or another of ownership reorganisation and in most cases the effect of these changes was still being felt at the time of our investigations. These changes often exposed the companies to more market pressures of various kinds, and the companies responded in ways aimed at improving productivity and profitability. The restructurings were also often aimed at obtaining public investment. The result was not only to access a new source of funds but also to expose company management to the influence of the share market and thereby increase pressure to align company strategy with shareholder expectations.

This type of company restructuring undercut collective styles of partnership in the companies studied. In direct terms, business restructuring often resulted in a decline in union influence as union members lost jobs and employment positions were outsourced or casualised. The reduction in their power and coverage impacted on the ability of unions to insist upon consultation about a range of issues. The case of EnergyCo offers a good example of the undermining of this type of collective partnership. Prior to privatisation and restructuring, unions in that company had permanent offices at various workplaces and intervened in all kinds of workplace matters; there was a collective form of joint determination in place. In due course redundancies reduced the membership base of the various unions which covered the business operations. After the restructuring, unions still had strong coverage of some employee types, but they no longer enjoyed the same standing within the business. The company retained its joint consultative committee, but this appeared to have become far more managerially-driven, as unions lost their day-to-day involvement in the company. The joint consultative committee both involved, and encompassed the interests of, core employees, but not the contractors who now constituted the majority of workers at the company.

Commentators have noted how 'regimes of governance are shaped by sectoral properties, in particular, the contingencies of technology on the one hand and products and product markets on the other'.[43] It might be said that the combination of liberalisation of labour markets and heightened international competition exaggerated sectoral and regional differences in the manner in which labour was managed. A comparison of developments at ResourceCo 1 and ResourceCo 2 showed the importance of both these factors. In Western Australia, where both companies conducted operations, ResourceCo 2 acted as an 'innovator' in labour relations and undertook an aggressive strategy to shift employment relations from collective to individual governance. It did so before changes in labour law

---

43   J. Hollingsworth and W. Streeck, 'Countries and Sectors: Concluding Remarks on Performance Convergence and Competitiveness' in J. Hollingsworth, P. Schmitter and W. Streeck (eds), *Governing Capitalist Economies: Performance and Control of Economic Sectors*, Oxford University Press, Oxford, 1994, p. 270. See also Conway et al., above n. 21.

facilitated the individualisation of employment relations.[44] Because ResourceCo 1 was competing in the same product market, it undertook similar strategies, but only after state labour law reforms provided institutionalised industrial relations instruments of an individualised kind. Although one respondent manager in the company expressed a preference for company-wide individualised employment management, the employment strategies of the company were, at the end of the day, driven by more practical considerations. In New South Wales, where the company operated in a different product market with a long-term contract with a buyer, employment strategies mainly continued as before. Here, agreements were collective with most workplaces governed and regulated by joint management and union bargaining, which might be characterised as collective-style partnerships.

Regional differences were also at play in this and other case studies. Viewed generally our studies bore out the observation made by Hollingsworth and Streeck that: '[r]egimes of economic governance vary with spatial-territorial location as well as between functional-economic sectors. Variation in territory occurs because social institutions are rooted in local, regional, or national political communities and their shared beliefs, experiences and traditions.'[45] Thus in the case of ResourceCo 1, differences in employee management were shaped not only by sectoral or product market factors, but also by the strength of community ties, which supported strong unionism. In Western Australia, in contrast, workers were generally immigrants to the area and the local community factor was less of an issue. In the case of ManuengCo, on the other hand, the situation of the company in the local, regional environment seemed to shelter it to some degree from the business and management trends which impacted adversely upon a number of our other case study companies.

The experience at ManuengCo further illustrates the potential influence of sectoral factors. As Hollingsworth and Streeck have argued, specific industry standards can lead to a standardisation of production styles within particular sectors,

---

44   For discussion see W. Ford, 'Reinventing the Contract of Employment: The Workplace Agreements Act 1993 (WA)' (1996) 9 *Australian Journal of Labour Law* 259; B. Ford, 'Changing the Dynamics of Bargaining: Individualisation and Employment Agreements in Western Australia' in S. Deery and R. Mitchell (eds), *Employment Relations: Individualisation and Union Exclusion*, Federation Press, Sydney, 1999, p. 88; R. McCallum, 'Australian Workplace Agreements: An Analysis' (1997) 10 *Australian Journal of Labour Law* 50; R. Mitchell, 'Juridification and Labour Law: A Legal Response to the Flexibility Debate in Australia' (1998) 14 *International Journal of Comparative Labour Law and Industrial Relations* 113.

45   Hollingsworth and Streeck, above n. 43, p. 271. See further on this issue generally M. Jones, S. Marshall and R. Mitchell, 'Corporate Social Responsibility and the Management of Labour in Two Australian Mining Industry Companies' (2007) 15 *Corporate Governance: An International Review* 57; R. Markey and A. Hodgkinson, 'The Impact of the *Workplace Relations Act* on Regional Patterns of Industrial Relations: The Illawarra Region of Australia, 1996–2004' (2008) 50 *Journal of Industrial Relations* 752.

but across national boundaries.[46] These standards, the authors argue, are becoming as important, if not more important, than national regulation, because they are internationally recognised indicators of high quality, safe production methods. Products manufactured under the control of nationally-based regulation, on the other hand, particularly in countries with relatively unregulated labour market and production systems, may not induce the same confidence in buyers in the global market. As our discussion in Chapter 3 indicates, ManuengCo had been largely immune to national industrial relations influences over a very lengthy period. Located in a country town, and controlled through family ownership, it complied with awards, but pursued only very basic human resource management practices, largely unfettered by union involvement. The introduction of the internationally recognised ISO 9001 standard[47] signalled a major change in management style in response to perceived customer demand in relation to 'employee engagement'. The introduction of this measure resulted in a form of employee consultation in production management which might be classed as a 'high performance' work system. On the other hand the changed management approach fell well short of genuine engagement with employees and unions of a 'partnership' type.

Similarly, in other cases the introduction of partnership-style practices appeared to have been made for reputational or other reasons, rather than pursuit of the measures themselves.[48] In more than one case, corporate social responsibility appeared to be a factor which on the one hand seemed to enhance employee consultation, but which on the other was unable to provide balance against the various countervailing forces which were at the same time reducing employee influence.[49]

Our conclusion, drawn from the evidence gathered for this project, is that there was a decisive shift in influence away from workers and unions towards managerial authority during the 1990s and into the 2000s, and this is consistent with the great weight of published research in the field.[50] This shift towards managerial authority occurred in tandem with radical changes to corporate structures in the case of many of the larger companies which we studied, which in turn was brought about in response to, and in order to become more responsive to, heightened competition in the markets in which those companies operated. The reduction in the power

---

46   See Hollingsworth and Streeck, above n. 43.

47   International Organization for Standardization, *ISO 9001 – Quality Management Systems – Requirements*.

48   See S. Marshall, K. Anderson and I. Ramsay, 'Are Superannuation Funds and Other Institutional Investors in Australia Acting like "Universal Investors"?' (2009) 51 *Journal of Industrial Relations* 439.

49   K. Anderson, S. Marshall, R. Mitchell and I. Ramsay, 'Union Shareholder Activism in the Context of Declining Labour Law Protection: Four Australian Case Studies' (2007) 15 *Corporate Governance: An International Review* 45; Jones et al., above n. 45.

50   R. Mitchell, D. Taft, A. Forsyth, P. Gahan and C. Sutherland, 'Assessing the Impact of Employment Legislation: The Coalition Government's Labour Law Programme 1996–2007' (2010) 23 *Australian Journal of Labour Law* 61.

of employees and unions, and the consequent withdrawal by some companies from longstanding 'partnership-style' employment relations, was assisted in general terms by an evolving, more sympathetic, regulatory framework. Legal change undoubtedly provided a context within which less co-operative and less consultative employment practices could be adopted, even if that regulation was not always crucial in specific terms to whether and, if so, how companies adjusted their employment systems in actual practice. And again speaking generally, the shift in control seemed to signal objectively an overall decline in 'partnership' relations, notwithstanding a continued subjective conception by most directors that businesses work in partnership with their employees.

But at the same time there was a diversity of corporate responses, and sometimes a degree of continuity in partnership relations. Not all employers hastened to exploit more liberal employment laws,[51] and again this confirms a point made earlier: '[l]abour management is more complex and often more "benign" to workers than is predicted in the market model'.[52] In some cases, as noted, location, or regional, variation proved to be an important factor in determining whether or not companies reacted to certain market pressures and, if so, how they reacted. In other cases contrary regulatory pressures also entered the equation. In the case of at least one privatised company (EnergyCo) the continued state regulation of its quality standards meant that it was circumscribed, to a degree, in how it could readjust its employment systems and as a consequence something of a joint regulatory system persisted in this company.

5.5 Varieties of Capitalism and the Role of Law

While for the purposes of this project we have adopted the 'bipolar typology', distinguishing two varieties of capitalism as a starting point, we have also acknowledged from the outset in Chapter 1 that there are numerous problems with such an approach. When we commenced our research, we expected that our empirical studies of Australian companies and analysis of business outlooks and practices might enable us to contribute to the debate about how Australia appears to match up against its supposed 'ideal-type' of capitalism, the 'liberal market/ outsider' category (as we have labelled it in this book), or how far it deviates from it. We have noted that in general terms Australia is typically located among the Anglo-American group as a liberal market/outsider-governed type of capitalism, but also that there are important and meaningful differences in the Australian case, and that perhaps there is a case to be made out for Australian exceptionalism. We have asked whether Australia should be more properly identified as a member of the co-ordinated market/'insider'-governed group, or whether it seems to be

---

See A. Frazer, 'Industrial Relations and the Sociological Study of Labour Law' (2009) 19 *Labour and Industry* 73, p. 89.
Pendleton, above n. 14, p. 134.

a hybrid and to exhibit mixed characteristics. Most significantly, our study was concerned with the mechanisms by which change occurred in business priorities and practices, and the role of regulation in shaping that change.

The 'varieties of capitalism' schema is based on national contexts of corporate governance, ownership structures, and labour management systems. These derive from the way in which employers are seen to co-ordinate their activities: either through market mechanisms or through more co-operative means. In understanding how these sets of 'institutional configurations'[53] interrelate to produce national 'styles' of market regulation, it is necessary to have regard to both regulatory and empirical dimensions of a national political economy. These include the main source of finance of major companies within a particular national system; whether it is mainly equity or debt finance; whether markets for finance are deep or shallow; whether shareholdings are generally consolidated or diffusely held; whether the legal protections extended to minority shareholders are strong or weak; how secure companies are against takeover and merger activity in a particular national market; how shareholder-oriented decision making is within particular companies; whether labour is strongly integrated into decision-making within companies; whether there is co-ordinated collective bargaining; whether employees have strong protections against dismissals, and so on.

Among these various factors, the law, particularly corporate and labour law, is a crucial component (though by no means the only one) in setting the 'regulatory style' of a particular national system. Legal dimensions set a boundary between the 'liberal market/outsider governed', and the 'co-ordinated market/insider governed' systems, as exemplified in Chapter 1, Table 1.1. However, the major works in the varieties of capitalism and comparative business systems literature, from which our theoretical approach is largely drawn, do not deal with law and legal systems in specific detail, nor do they deal with questions of change through legal reform.[54] One of our purposes in this book, as indicated in the preceding section, has been to expand attention on that dimension of the Australian data to enable more specific legal factors to be explored and absorbed into the analysis (see Chapter 2). We drew also upon the 'legal origins' literature, as a major source

---

53   See R. Deeg and G. Jackson, 'Towards a More Dynamic Theory of Capitalist Variety' (2007) 5 *Socio-Economic Review* 149.

54   See, for example, H. Gospel and A. Pendleton (eds), *Corporate Governance and Labour Management: An International Comparison*, Oxford University Press, Oxford, 2005. Two contributions to Hall and Soskice, above n. 6, examine the role of legal regulation in some detail (S. Casper, 'The Legal Framework for Corporate Governance: The Influence of Contract Law on Company Strategies in Germany and the United States' and S. Vittols, 'Varieties of Corporate Governance: Comparing Germany and the UK'), but as Stryker has argued, law occupies a peripheral status in most institutionalist scholarship: 'Law is there but not there – mentioned in passing yet not a sustained object of inquiry in its own right': R. Stryker, 'Mind the Gap: Law, Institutional Analysis and Socioeconomics' (2003) 1 *Socio-Economic Review* 335, p. 340.

of debate concerning the relationship between regulatory style and business practice (see section 5.6 following).

One of the most important governing contexts of the varieties of capitalism literature is that it is presumptively generally based on what happens in the major/ large company sector (however that may be defined). This has particular implications for our analysis of the Australian position. As we noted in Chapter 1, and again in Chapters 2 and 4, Australia has tended to display a more concentrated pattern of share ownership in large companies than most of the other leading countries categorised in the liberal market/outsider group. That is to say, the evidence suggests that in certain respects the Australian corporate sector has as much in common with some of the continental European countries as it does with the US and the UK. This had led some scholars to suggest that Australia is incorrectly classified.[55] And, as noted earlier, on other data relating to the comparative levels of share market capitalisation, there is scope for an argument that Australia is at least as close to 'insider' types such as Japan and the Netherlands as it is to those in the 'outsider' category.[56] But as we have pointed out in Chapter 2, there are other, perhaps counterbalancing, factors which also need to be considered in any characterisation.

Quite apart from these matters of ownership structure and control, there are other issues which bear upon the characterisation of the Australian 'regulatory style'. For example, in our survey of corporate law and labour law in Chapter 2, various questions were raised about the nature of that regulation and whether it could be said to match that of other liberal market countries. Our conclusions arising from those accounts were that, in historical terms, much of the Australian regulation dealing with minority shareholder protection and with the 'market for corporate control' was relatively weak. However, in recent decades there has been systematic reform that has resulted in considerable strengthening of the rights of shareholders.[57] At the same time, the analysis of the regulation of the Australian labour market, considering a wide body of secondary and empirical detail, seemed to point to various ways in which, for a significant period of its history, the Australian system was closer to the 'integrative' and 'universalist' approach typical of co-ordinated market economies as outlined in Chapter 1.[58] However, some developments point to a degree of alignment with the style of regulation typical of liberal market economies.

---

55   See Dignam and Galanis, above n. 7.

56   Hall and Soskice, above n. 6, p. 19.

57   See the discussion in Chapter 2 and also H. Anderson, M. Welsh, I. Ramsay and P. Gahan, 'The Evolution of Shareholder and Creditor Protection in Australia: An International Comparison', Legal Studies Research Paper No. 539, Melbourne Law School, University of Melbourne, 2011.

58   See Jones and Mitchell, above n. 12; Marshall et al., above n. 3.

These are interesting points of reservation or qualification which need to be considered in the process of 'situating'[59] Australia's regulatory style. In Chapter 1 we noted that detailed examination and analyses of single countries are likely to privilege national idiosyncrasies and differences over structural similarities between countries and so complicate any rigidly dichotomous characterisation between, say, 'liberal market' and 'co-ordinated market' economies.[60] Having said that, though, our broad conclusion, as indicated throughout this chapter, remains generally on the side of the established characterisation of Australia as a 'liberal market' rather than a 'co-ordinated market' type in terms of regulatory style. First, whilst Australian labour law does throw up some interesting inconsistencies if considered alongside others in the liberal market model, there are some core reasons, particularly the exclusion of labour from decision-making over crucial workplace issues, which suggest that the Australian position is more consistent with the 'liberal market' model than might appear to be the case at first glance. Second, and more importantly, in more recent decades, both in respect of corporate law and labour market regulation, there has been a decisive shift in Australia towards the liberal market/'outsider' model, which strengthens the argument for Australian inclusion in that group of systems in the contemporary period.

Over the years in which changes in the case study companies occurred, the regulatory style in Australia arguably underwent significant change in a number of areas, contributing to it fitting more decisively with the 'liberal market' group. It has been argued that both corporate and labour law were subject to important change during the 1990s in order to produce greater accord with shareholder interests, and greater flexibility in the means and costs of employing labour.[61] The two areas of regulation were reformed in different ways, although they may have contributed to the same shift to the liberal market model. The law governing companies, as we saw in Chapter 2, saw the introduction of more mandatory standards regulating the governance of corporations and greater scope for shareholder participation. Labour law reduced the level of mandatory standards regulating labour markets. The purpose of corporate law reforms was to strengthen shareholder power and disclosure.[62] The aim of labour law reform was to provide businesses with a greater range of instruments through which to govern employment relations, and more flexibility in rewarding and firing labour. Both sets of reforms were

---

59 Marshall et al., above n. 3.

60 Compare K. Thelen, 'Beyond Comparative Statics: Historical Institutional Approaches to Stability and Change in the Political Economy of Labor' in G. Morgan, J. Campbell, C. Crouch, O.K. Pedersen and R. Whitley (eds), *The Oxford Handbook of Comparative Institutional Analysis*, Oxford University Press, Oxford, 2010, p. 55.

61 Marshall et al., above n. 3.

62 Although, as we noted in Chapter 2, Australia has utilised regulatory methods which more closely track UK reform approaches in this area than they do US approaches, suggesting scope for a recognition of 'varieties of liberalism': see Chapter 1 at n. 22.

based on ideas concerning economic governance which promoted free, rather than regulated, markets.

We sought to evaluate the effect of these regulatory reforms on company behaviour: whether companies were more or less shareholder-focussed and whether they perceived that the law was an important source of influence in that regard. Our survey data suggested that directors were shareholder-focussed – they generally ranked shareholders ahead of the company and other stakeholders – but not to the same extent as is found in the US or in Australia in the mid-1990s (based on an earlier survey). They did not perceive their duties to the company as requiring them to pursue the short-term interests of shareholders, but rather saw their legal obligation to act 'in the best interests of the company' as either to act in the long-term interests of shareholders or to balance the interests of all stakeholders. They perceived that the law gave them considerable freedom to take account of interests other than those of shareholders. Our survey findings also revealed that neither labour law nor corporate law were regarded as the dominant source of obligation to employees for the majority of directors. Directors were far more likely to see either business imperatives or ethical and social responsibilities as the major source of their obligations to employees. Indeed, the survey suggested that directors felt relatively unimpeded by the law with regards to shareholders or employees, the two key stakeholders we were concerned with based on the varieties of capitalism literature.

What happened, in practical terms, when companies perceived themselves to be freed from strong legal impediments in the area of the management of labour? Based upon our case study findings, the most observable impact of the period of labour market liberalisation was the diversification of practices, and the more noticeable relevance of other influences such as sectoral and regional factors. Certainly, the fact that labour arbitration was no longer compulsory had a significant impact upon union power, and this had a general negative flow-on effect for the ability of unions to influence the governance of companies in most cases. But in other respects, labour market liberalisation impacted so as to create less uniformity in the ways in which employment relations were managed. This diversity was observed within companies in the great differences established in the wages, conditions and management of different types of workers. For example, among the companies we studied the incomes of skilled workers increased, and these workers were also more likely to enjoy consultative employee relations than less skilled workers, whose incomes sometimes decreased and who were less likely to be engaged in co-operative, partnership-like mechanisms. This company-level effect was reflected in national wage dispersion and increased income inequality patterns in the period of our study.[63]

As labour market regulation became a less important factor governing the labour relations of our case study companies, other market features seemed to have

---

63   R. Fincher and P. Saunders (eds), *Creating Unequal Futures? Rethinking Poverty, Inequality and Disadvantage*, Allen & Unwin, Crows Nest, 2001.

acquired heightened impact. Regional or local factors were strong determinants. We saw that labour markets could be embedded in community structures moderated by associational bargains such as good will on the part of the local community, familial relations, and ties between unions and local populations.[64] Likewise, product markets, industry and sectoral factors had a strong impact on labour relations. As might be expected, for instance, whether a company was providing a product to a secure and long-term business partner or, alternatively, was selling it in a highly competitive market, was seen to have had a significant impact on how that company might manage its labour and employment relations systems. It is likely that these determinants often had a greater impact due to other forms of market deregulation and creation. Thus the breaking up of former state-owned monopolies had flow-on effects for the companies that had previously provided them with services or goods on secure terms. The lowering of tariffs and non-tariff barriers is also likely to have been an important determinant, although we have not been able to explore these factors in any detail here.

Although we witnessed the fostering of more market-based relations through liberalisation in the area of labour market regulation, during the 1990s the law created markets in far more prescriptive terms in other areas. This was seen most starkly in the companies which moved from state ownership to private sector control. In these cases, the laws which brought about the privatisation and corporatisation of state-owned monopolies were only one step in the process. More far-reaching regulatory measures were taken in order to create competitive markets. In the case of ServiceCo, for instance, this was engineered through regulatory changes which allowed competitors to enter the Australian market. In the case of EnergyCo, market pressure was created not only through privatisation and breaking up the state monopoly into multiple parts, but also through the intricate regulatory system associated with its licensing. In both cases, new forms of market governance were accompanied by major restructuring of employment away from what would previously have been characterised as 'insider', partnership-style management based both on collective bargaining and internal joint consultative mechanisms.

What we can conclude is that, in terms of national data, there is a fair degree of correspondence between the Australian system and the 'liberal market' model, allowing for some inconsistencies and historical change. In particular, we can say that in the 1990s and into the 2000s, there may have been a general shift towards the liberal market type, facilitated by legal reform. But as we have noted earlier in this chapter, when it comes to closer examination of particular companies, there are further complexities and inconsistencies which make the stylised exercise we are attempting to carry out very problematical. It has been suggested there is a 'need to move away from the simple, abstract notion of markets found in the market model, as well as moving beyond the simplistic view of the managerial-investor relationship found in agency theory'.[65] Perhaps a better way forward is to

---

64 Hollingsworth and Streeck, above n. 43, p. 271.
65 Pendleton, above n. 14, p. 147.

recognise that there is much diversity within, as well as between, national systems, and to start from that point rather than adopting the simplified duality of parts of the varieties of capitalism discourse.[66]

5.6 Legal Origins

This brings us finally to the general issue of the 'legal origins' debate. As we noted in Chapter 1, a broad general argument about the nature of business regulation is that a particular national 'regulatory style' is largely set by the legal origins of a country. This theory suggests that the way an economic or business system is constructed and regulated depends principally upon whether that country's legal system is based in the common law or civil law, or perhaps one or more variants of these fundamental categories. The supposition in this argument is that legal origin sets in place a certain style of regulation from which it is difficult, if not impossible, to depart in a fundamental 'systemic' fashion. The different systems are, therefore, 'path dependent', and do not necessarily evolve according to efficiency demands of markets and market actors. The influence of legal origins is subsequently transported (by colonisation or conquest) to foreign jurisdictions, and impacts in those jurisdictions accordingly. As Katharina Pistor has noted, the 'legal origins' idea maps quite neatly on to the 'varieties of capitalism' discourse: common law origin countries are most associated with the 'liberal market/ outsider' model of capitalism (the Anglo/American model), while the civil law origin countries are associated with the co-ordinated market/insider model of capitalism.[67] Yet while some of the varieties of capitalism literature does recognise law and legal systems as important institutional elements effecting distinctive modes of economic organisation,[68] the legal origins literature posits law as the defining factor in accounting for the diversity of economic organisation across countries, in particular differences in corporate ownership structures.

The primacy of law with respect to diversity in national systems of corporate ownership relates to the degree of legal protection given to minority shareholders. La Porta et al. argue that deep or liquid share markets correlate with an index of basic minority shareholder protections. Absent these protections, concentrated shareholdings will persist. A potential buyer will not buy into the share market if he or she feels the value of a company is going to be disproportionately siphoned off by a majority shareholder, or such a potential buyer will offer such a substantially reduced price for shares that the shareholder will not sell and the concentrated

---

66   For some suggestions on different approaches, see Crouch, above n. 16.

67   K. Pistor, 'Legal Ground Rules in Coordinated and Liberal Market Economies' in K. Hopt (ed.), *Corporate Governance in Context: Corporations, States, and Markets in Europe, Japan and the US*, Oxford University Press, Oxford, 2006.

68   See above, at n. 54.

holdings remain intact.[69] Key protections for minority shareholders range from an independent and efficient judiciary, through to mandatory disclosure rules, the fiduciary duties of directors, proxy voting and one-share-one-vote rules. La Porta et al. found that the jurisdictions that scored highly in terms of minority shareholder protections tended to be common law origin countries. It is not immediately clear why this is the case and, being interested largely in empirical analysis, the authors of these studies did not offer a strong theorisation of the link between minority shareholder protection and common law origin. They claimed their results:

> Support the view that the benefit of common law in this area comes from its emphasis on market discipline and private litigation. The benefits of common law appear to lie in its emphasis on private contracting and standardised disclosure, and in its reliance on private dispute resolution using market-friendly standards of liability.[70]

Scholars have adopted this 'legal families' categorisation to explain a broad range of economic differences between countries. Notably for our study, a group of scholars, including La Porta, have made a study of comparative labour market laws.[71] They looked at employment laws, the regulation of collective bargaining and social security laws across 85 countries and concluded that legal traditions – that is, whether a country's legal system fell into the common law or civil law tradition – were 'a strikingly important determinant of various aspects of statutory worker protection'.[72]

---

69   R. La Porta, F. Lopez-De-Silanes, A. Shleifer and R.W. Vishny, 'Investor Protection and Corporate Governance' (2000) 58 *Journal of Financial Economics* 3.

70   R. La Porta, F. Lopez-De-Silanes and A. Shleifer, 'What Works in Securities Law?' (2006) 61 *Journal of Finance* 1, p. 24.

71   J. Botero, S. Djankov, R. La Porta, F. Lopez-De-Silanes and A. Shleifer, 'The Regulation of Labor' (2004) 119 *Quarterly Journal of Economics* 1339. Subsequent studies in this area can be found in D. Pozen, 'The Regulation of Labor and the Relevance of Legal Origin' (2007) 27 *Comparative Labor Law & Policy Journal* 43; B. Ahlering and S. Deakin, 'Labour Regulation, Corporate Governance and Legal Origin: A Case of Institutional Complementarity?' (2007) 41 *Law and Society Review* 865; S. Djankov and R. Ramalho, 'Employment Laws in Developing Countries' (2009) 37 *Journal of Comparative Economics* 3; S. Deakin and P. Sarkar, 'Assessing the Long-Run Economic Impact of Labour Law Systems: A Theoretical Reappraisal and Analysis of New Time Series Data' (2008) 39 *Industrial Relations Journal* 453.

72   Botero et al., ibid., p. 1365. The study also found that common law style of regulation led to better economic efficiency outcomes than the civil law style, which has important policy implications and was taken up by the World Bank in its *Doing Business* project to promote 'business friendly' regulation: see, e.g., World Bank, *Doing Business in 2010*, World Bank, Washington, DC, 2009. See further, R. La Porta, F. Lopez-de-Silanes and A. Shleifer, 'The Economic Consequences of Legal Origins' (2008) 46 *Journal of Economic Literature* 285.

There have been a number of critiques levelled at the legal origins literature. Some of these question the method used by legal origins scholars in the major empirical studies.[73] The studies tend to take a set of laws or rules within a given area of regulation and assign each rule a numerical value according to, for example, the level of protection provided to minority shareholders, or the level of protection given by the labour law system to persons who are engaged under non-standard contracts of employment. But these approaches may often mean that important forms of regulation are overlooked,[74] or may fail to deal with the distinction between 'law on the books' and 'law in action', the latter focussing on actual implementation and enforcement of rules.[75] Other critiques point to the ahistoricity of some of the legal origins studies, which rely on cross-sectional data rather than time-series data. In the area of corporate governance, the purported stability of legal systems in fact contrasts with changes in ownership structure in some advanced capitalist countries across the twentieth century.[76] Related to this are critiques that stress the role of politics over and above legal origins, that current differences between countries owe more to relatively recent political decisions than to legal variables going back perhaps centuries.[77] One final problem with the legal origins approach is that it relies on a fairly stylised distinction between common law and civil law traditions that is open to question. For example, the distinction between systems based on judge-made law and those based on statutory codes is becoming blurred, including in the area of corporate law and regulation.[78] In any case, many comparative lawyers are sceptical of taxonomies based on 'legal families', suggesting many national legal systems are actually hybrid systems that defy easy classification.[79]

---

73   See, e.g., S. Deakin, P. Lele and M. Siems, 'The Evolution of Labour Law: Calibrating and Comparing Regulatory Regimes' (2007) 146 *International Labour Review* 133; Pozen, above n. 71.

74   For example, in many countries labour markets are not merely regulated by statute but also by collective agreements: if the latter are excluded a country may be incorrectly coded.

75   S. Cooney, P. Gahan and R. Mitchell, 'Legal Origins, Labour Law and the Regulation of Employment Relations' in M. Barry and A. Wilkinson (eds), *Handbook of Comparative Employment Relations*, Edward Elgar, Cheltenham, 2011.

76   M. Goyer, 'Corporate Governance' in Morgan et al., above n. 60, pp. 427–428; See also B. Cheffins, 'Does Law Matter? The Separation of Ownership and Control in the United Kingdom' (2001) *Journal of Legal Studies* 30; G. Herrigel, 'Corporate Governance: History Without Historians' in G. Jones and J. Zeitlin (eds), *Oxford Handbook of Business History*, Oxford University Press, Oxford, 2008; R. Rajan and L. Zingales, 'The Great Reversals: The Politics of Financial Development in the Twentieth Century' (2003) 69 *Journal of Financial Economics* 5.

77   Goyer, ibid., p. 430. See also M. Roe, 'Legal Origins, Politics, and Stock Markets' (2006) 120 *Harvard Law Review* 460.

78   Deakin et al., above n. 73.

79   Cooney et al., above n. 75.

As we observe below, much of our research does not support a legal origins effect. However, some of our research identifies what Deakin et al. refer to as a 'weak' legal origins effect, rather than a strong, functionalist effect.[80] These authors accept that there are 'significant differences in regulatory style between the common law and civil law', and that these may 'hamper the flow of ideas from one system to another' and, conversely, that they may 'facilitate the exchange of legal models *within* the main legal families'.[81] However, the strength of a legal origins effect 'would differ from one context to another', and it cannot be assumed a priori. Thus, the impact of legal origins is a matter for empirical analysis.[82] Important issues to be taken into account include the extent to which foreign legal rules may be adapted to local economic, cultural and political conditions (endogenisation), the strength of 'opposing tendencies for the convergence of legal rules' deriving from various harmonising and transnationalising influences, and particularly the timing and nature of legal innovations in relation to the process of industrialisation.[83]

Having inherited its legal system from the UK, Australia clearly falls in the 'common law' legal family for the purposes of the legal origins hypothesis. However, Australian corporate law and labour law has received little explicit attention from a legal origins perspective.[84] In the light of our study, how does the Australian experience measure up?

Our survey of regulation in Chapter 2 suggested that Australian corporate law, both as it evolved and in terms of its recent form, did indeed generally bear strong resemblance to that of the UK. However, we would make two observations in this regard. First, in taking a historical approach, it is clear that the nature of the UK's corporate law and hence, by implication, Australia's corporate law was not, for much of its evolution, particularly protective of minority shareholders. This runs counter to legal origins theory.[85] However, this has changed significantly in recent decades with law reform focussed on protecting shareholders. Second, there is no

---

80   Deakin et al., above n. 73, p. 141.

81   Ibid., p. 137, emphasis in original.

82   Ibid., pp. 137–141; Jones and Mitchell, above n. 12.

83   For a recent critique of legal origins theory, particularly as it applies to the development of financial markets and labour protection, see J. Cioffi, 'Legal Regimes and Political Particularism: An Assessment of the "Legal Families" Theory from the Perspectives of Comparative Law and Political Economy' [2009] *Brigham Young University Law Review* 1501. See also C. Milhaupt 'Beyond Legal Origin: Rethinking Law's Relationship to the Economy – Implications for Policy' (2009) 57 *American Journal of Comparative Law* 831.

84   But note Jones and Mitchell, above n. 12; Marshall et al., above n. 3; Mitchell et al., above n. 1.

85   Cheffins, above n. 76. The fact that the UK saw the emergence of dispersed ownership structures and deep securities market *despite* there being little by way of minority shareholder protection is taken by Cheffins as indicating law's fairly marginal contribution to an outsider/arm's-length system of ownership and control, again at odds with the legal origins hypothesis.

clear empirical evidence that Australia has fully made the transition to the dispersed 'outsider' system of corporate ownership and control that would rank it alongside some other common law jurisdictions such as the UK and the US. As indicated in Chapter 2, for reasons to do with market structure and the relatively small size of the listed sector, various aspects of corporate governance in Australia appear to mark it out as something of an exception among the common law family. Despite the legal origins of its corporate law, there are grounds to suppose that it may in some respects resemble an 'insider' system of corporate control.[86]

Recent research that compares the evolution of shareholder and creditor protection in six countries (Australia, France, Germany, India, the UK and the US) over the period 1970 to 2005 does not find support for legal origins theory.[87] For example, over the period of the study Australia generally had the highest level of shareholder protection and the US the lowest level of shareholder protection, despite both countries being in the same legal origin category. The authors identify other findings from their research that do not support legal origins theory.

What this suggests is that the note of caution in what we have said about the varieties of capitalism approach in the previous section has also to be applied here: that is to say, the need to be alive to complexity in assessing the status of nations in major categorising exercises such as legal origins. National cases will often reveal a more layered or historically contingent mix of laws and institutions and outcomes than the legal origins account suggests.[88]

In labour law we also noted possible exceptionalism, although in this case more specifically with respect to the legal framework and regulatory content itself. It was argued that on some important indicators Australia might look, for a significant period of its history, more like a 'co-ordinated market' system than a 'liberal market' system (Chapter 1, Table 1.1) on some important (perhaps fundamental) indicators. Thus employee representation in Australia was more or less 'integrative', at least to the extent of imposed trade union recognition, extensive union rights, de facto compulsory bargaining; and also more 'universalist' in terms of award coverage, and the range and levels of minimum conditions provided through regulation.[89] Put in terms of the legal origins debate, on this basis it might be argued that Australia deviated from the common law system and adopted forms

---

86   See Chapter 2 at nn. 60–70. Pendleton, above n. 14, makes a similar point about New Zealand exceptionalism, based on that country's low market capitalisation of listed companies relative to GDP.

87   Anderson et al., above n. 57.

88   For a more nuanced account of the interaction between laws and markets, see C. Milhaupt and K. Pistor, *Law and Capitalism: What Corporate Crises Reveal about Legal Systems and Economic Development Around the World*, University of Chicago Press, Chicago, 2008.

89   Jones and Mitchell, above n. 12.

of regulation which brought it closer to the civil law family style of labour market regulation.[90]

However, there are two main arguments which reduce the force of this 'Australian exceptionalism' argument to a degree. First, there is a counterbalancing proposition to the effect that (despite appearances) the 'essence' of Australian labour law has preserved what legal origins theory would suppose about the common law model: that in terms of regulatory style, Australian labour law has not interfered historically with capital's right to manage the enterprise, nor empowered labour or its institutions with important decision-making rights. Second, recent legal change has moved Australian labour law more towards the 'liberal' model exemplified by the UK and the US: that is, greater reliance on contracts, less state regulation in substantive matters, and a vastly diminished role for arbitral intervention. This would match the supposition in much of the labour law literature that Australian labour law is converging on the common law Anglo-American model.[91]

But this counterbalancing argument, itself, also comes with two notes of reservation. First, in this area we are able to directly engage with the legal origins hypothesis as there has been an attempt to adapt the coding method used by legal origins scholars in their empirical surveys of national labour laws to the Australian case.[92] The findings indicate that in terms of actual protective strength, Australian labour law does not appear to have altered very much over the past 40 years.[93] As a bald finding this suggests that the argument of an evolving labour law – in the direction of a more liberal, less protective, more common law family model – is mistaken.[94] Second, data from the same exercise do not show the kind of convergence on a common law model which might be supposed from the legal origins literature. Whilst Australian labour law has remained relatively unchanged as regards its protective strength, and there is more recently some convergence with UK labour law, Australian labour law diverges notably from some other common law systems. That is, it has remained markedly more protective than US labour law, yet less protective than Indian labour law. Although Australia clusters more closely with two of the common law countries within the study than it does with the two civil law countries – France and Germany – the divergence between Australia and the US and the anomalous position of India – which by the mid-1980s begins to approach German labour law in protective strength – suggests

---

90   Mitchell et al., above n. 1, p. 87.

91   McCallum, above n. 1; L. Bennett, 'The American Model of Labour Law in Australia' (1992) 25 *Australian Journal of Labour Law* 135.

92   See Mitchell et al., above n. 1.

93   Ibid., particularly Figure 6, p. 80.

94   We refer to this as a 'bald finding' as there may be potential weaknesses in the way the index which attempted to measure change over time was constructed, and that such an index measured change at a general or national level rather than at State level or at the level of particular labour market sectors, such as low-paid workers in small businesses: ibid., p. 81.

at best a 'weak' legal origins effect.[95] The longitudinal nature of the data further confirms the 'weakness' of the legal origins effect as it does not unambiguously support the legal origins claim concerning the path dependency of laws and institutions. In the one instance we can discern a notable shift in Australian labour law's protective strength in the past 40 years – that is, an incline and then decline in the level of protection between 1993 and 1997 – this is clearly referable to political change. More generally, both UK and French labour law have exhibited a marked degree of volatility in terms of their protective strength, a volatility that again seems referable to changes in political administration.[96]

5.7 Conclusion

In this chapter we have presented our analysis of the interaction of corporate ownership, corporate governance and labour management in Australian companies. Our study has used two different types of analytical approaches. First, we drew upon data derived from our case studies of companies, a survey of company directors and interviews with institutional investors to investigate the relationship between ownership structure, corporate governance and labour management within companies, and how the regulation of that relationship is perceived by leading decision-makers in the companies concerned. Second, we employed a legal and historical approach to the development of regulatory policy in order to investigate what role corporate law and labour law appear to have played in the shaping of the Australian 'style' of capitalism.

Our analysis has questioned the dual model classification that underpins much of the varieties of capitalism literature. The analysis has also provided no significant support for legal origins theory (noting that legal origins theory maps onto the varieties of capitalism literature because common law origin countries are associated with the liberal market/outsider model of capitalism while civil law origin countries are associated with the co-ordinated market/insider model of capitalism).

One part of our analysis considered links between specific types of ownership structure and corporate governance orientation. An issue for investigation was whether there was evidence to support the argument that market outsider companies (that have widely held ownership structures) have a corporate governance orientation that prioritises the financial interests of shareholders over the interests of other stakeholders such as employees. This argument is advanced in the varieties of capitalism literature. Our investigation of the 'regulatory style' of Australian corporate law and labour law found there are aspects of both areas

95   Mitchell et al., above n. 1, p. 84 (Figure 7). The comparative measures were constructed by integrating the Australian data with that obtained by Deakin et al., above n. 73.

96   Deakin et al., above n. 73, pp. 145–146. See further, Roe, above n. 77.

of law that fit the market/outsider category. In general terms we consider that the regulatory style of Australian corporate law and labour law can be characterised more as liberal market than co-ordinated market. In particular, an important focus of corporate law reform has been to increase the protection of shareholders. In the case of labour law, management has been granted greater flexibility in the means and costs of employing labour. Yet our analysis also reveals that the classification depends on the period of time under consideration and also the specific aspects of the law being investigated.

Our study of the business practices of the case study companies and the survey of company directors also revealed findings that do not lend themselves to ready classification in terms of the models of capitalism presented in the varieties of capitalism literature. Some of our findings indicate a degree of alignment between the business practices of some of the case study companies and the predictions of the varieties of capitalism literature in terms of models of capitalism. For example, several of the case study companies which underwent ownership changes that reflected a shift to an outsider form of ownership and governance tended to become more shareholder oriented and also engaged in strategies that had negative consequences for employees. However, this trend was not uniform and the findings from our research revealed a complex interplay of various factors (including the competition that companies face for their products or services, legal regulation, industry standards that regulate the quality of products or services, and the location of the company's business) that were all shown to influence management strategies depending upon the particular company being studied.

Our research has found considerable diversity in the way in which corporate ownership, corporate governance and labour management intersect in Australian companies. We also found considerable diversity in the outcomes of this intersection in terms of management strategies adopted by the companies. Such diversity defies easy classification in terms of the theories advanced in the varieties of capitalism literature and in the legal origins literature. Rather, our research reveals the value that lies in a study grounded in a detailed investigation and analysis of companies that have undergone major changes in their ownership structure and the implications of those changes for the corporate governance orientation and labour management of those companies.

Chapter 6
Postscript

The genesis of the research reported in this book lies in developments in Anglo-American human resource management and corporate governance across the last decades of the twentieth century. In the realm of human resource management, there was an increasing emphasis on 'high trust', 'high commitment' and 'co-operative' workplace management strategies.[1] In corporate governance, the triumph of agency theory elevated the delivery of 'shareholder value' to an overarching corporate goal.[2] As legal academics, we were particularly interested in the extent to which law and regulation had contributed to these developments. At first glance, though, these two trends appeared potentially incompatible: the long-term commitment called for in the human resources literature seemed at odds with the emphasis on short-term financial metrics in much of the corporate governance literature.[3] This suggested that the favoured form of corporate governance in Anglo-American economies – at least as advocated by many academic commentators and others forming part of the burgeoning corporate governance 'industry' – would operate as a constraint on the adoption of what the organisational literature was promoting as 'best practice' labour management.

By the beginning of the twenty-first century a range of scholars were starting to explore more closely the relationship between corporate governance and labour management. We were initially inspired by those who focussed primarily on the intersections of corporate governance, ownership structure and labour management.[4] In doing so they pointed to a wider literature regarding hypothesized 'complementarities' between sets of institutions – that is, between collective bargaining structures, corporate ownership, vocational training, product market regulation and so on – in varieties of capitalism more generally.[5] Related to this was the emerging literature on legal origins, whereby the distinction between 'liberal market economies' and

1   R. Mitchell and J. Fetter, 'Human Resource Management and Individualisation in Australian Labour Law' (2003) 45 *Journal of Industrial Relations* 292.

2   R. Mitchell, A. O'Donnell and I. Ramsay, 'Shareholder Value and Employee Interests: Intersections Between Corporate Governance, Corporate Law and Labor Law' (2005) 23 *Wisconsin International Law Journal* 417.

3   S. Konzelmann, 'Corporate Governance and Employment Relations: The Competing Logic of Markets and the Management of Production' (2009) 22 *Australian Journal of Labour Law* 109.

4   H. Gospel and A. Pendleton (eds), *Corporate Governance and Labour Management: An International Comparison*, Oxford University Press, Oxford, 2005.

5   P. Hall and D. Soskice, 'An Introduction to Varieties of Capitalism' in P. Hall and D. Soskice (eds), *Varieties of Capitalism*, Oxford University Press, Oxford, 2001.

'co-ordinated market economies' mapped rather neatly onto the distinction between common law legal systems and civil law systems and which also attempted to say something about national varieties of corporate law and labour law.[6] This literature is reviewed in Chapter 1.

Informed by this scholarship, most of our research was undertaken in a time of economic growth, albeit at times punctuated by various intermittent corporate scandals in many countries. In Australia, the first decade of the twenty-first century saw the collapse of significant companies in industries including airlines, financial services and telecommunications. A key regulatory response to these local and overseas corporate collapses was to reinforce the dominant model of granting increased protection to minority shareholders.[7] Since the conclusion of our empirical research, however, a far more systemic crisis has manifested itself by way of the global financial crisis. Its origins lie in the rapid growth of subprime home lending in the US (i.e. lending to high risk borrowers), the development of high risk financial products that were complex, lacked transparency and were mispriced in the terms of their risk, and significant increases in leverage in the financial system. Whilst Australian labour law has undergone a major legislative redrafting since we conducted our empirical research that, to some extent, alters the balance of power between employees and employers towards employees,[8] in Australia, as in many other 'liberal' economies, the financial crisis has put new pressures on companies' labour management strategies, justifying the adoption of 'low cost' employee relations rather than co-operative or 'high trust' labour relations.

Interestingly, though, the financial crisis has played out in Australia in a relatively subdued way compared with other 'liberal' economies, such as the US and UK.[9] This

---

6   See, for example, R. La Porta, F. Lopez-de-Silanes, A. Shleifer and R. Vishny, 'Investor Protection and Corporate Governance' (2000) 58 *Journal of Financial Economics* 3; J. Botero, S. Djankov, R. La Porta and F. Lopez-de-Silanes, 'The Regulation of Labor' (2004) 119 *Quarterly Journal of Economics* 1339.

7   J. Hill, 'Regulatory Responses to Global Corporate Scandals' (2005) 23 *Wisconsin International Law Journal* 367.

8   *Fair Work Act 2009* (Cth).

9   Although the case study and survey research for this book was completed before the recent global financial crisis we have not found it necessary to alter our major conclusions as a result of that event. There is now a great deal of evidence to suggest that legal developments around the world in the two decades leading up to the crisis have by no means accorded with the legal origins formula: see, for example, J. Cioffi, 'Legal Regimes and Political Particularism: An Assessment of the "Legal Families" Theory from the Perspectives of Comparative Law and Political Economy' [2009] *Brigham Young University Law Review* 1501. And as a result of various economic crises, countries of various political and legal backgrounds have often adopted quite similar regulatory solutions: see, for example, C. Milhaupt, 'Beyond Legal Origin: Rethinking Law's Relationship to the Economy – Implications for Policy' (2009) 57 *American Journal of Comparative Law* 831. This point is evident in the growing number of reports and other publications from different countries and international organisations that document the causes of the recent financial crisis and

leads us to reiterate a theme that has become apparent in our research. That is, we need to differentiate *between* liberal economies. The differential impact on the Australian economy of the global financial crisis suggests that the Australian model of capitalism and business systems cannot be unproblematically collapsed into the same 'liberal' model of countries such as the US and UK – or, for that matter, Canada, Ireland and New Zealand. This is a point that is increasingly recognised as scholars evaluate the usefulness of the varieties of capitalism literature.[10] However, the fact that easy categorisation of national economies into either a 'liberal' model or a 'co-ordinated' model (or any one of the other proliferating models[11]) appears less and less likely as more detailed country studies are undertaken should not be seen as invalidating the type of inquiry we have embarked upon here. As other researchers in this area have recently argued, typologies of capitalist diversity make a valuable contribution 'by focussing attention on important interactions across institutional domains'.[12] It was the relatively neglected question in the Australian context of the interaction between corporate governance and labour law that initially prompted our research.

Our focus on the particular national case of Australia also drew attention to the considerable diversity within capitalist economies. Again, this is consistent with a growing body of empirical literature showing national forms of capitalism to 'be more institutionally fragmented, internally diverse and [to] display greater "plasticity" with regard to the combinations of institutional forms and functions'.[13] Internal diversity within national settings – such as we have found in our study – is not necessarily incompatible with a notion of comparative capitalist typologies, but it means greater attention needs to be paid to accounting for such diversity and considering, for

---

propose common solutions to the crisis. Some of these reports include: United Nations Conference on Trade and Development, *Corporate Governance in the Wake of the Financial Crisis: Selected International Views*, 2011; *Report of the High Level Group on Financial Supervision in the EU*, 2009 (chaired by Jacques de Larosiere); *A Regulatory Response to the Global Banking Crisis*, 2009 (chaired by Lord Turner); *A Review of Corporate Governance in UK Banks and Other Financial Industry Entities*, 2009 (chaired by David Walker); US Government Accountability Office, *Financial Regulation: A Framework for Crafting and Assessing Proposals to Modernize the Outdated US Financial Regulatory System*, 2009, and see the various reports published by the International Organization of Securities Commissions and the Financial Stability Board.

10 See R. Mahon, 'Varieties of Liberalism: Canadian Social Policy from the "Golden Age" to the Present' (2008) 42 *Social Policy and Administration* 343; S. Konzelmann, M. Fovargue-Davis and G. Schnyder, *Varieties of Liberalism: Anglo-Saxon Capitalism in Crisis?* Working Paper No. 403, Centre for Business Research, University of Cambridge, 2010.

11 See Chapter 1 at n. 20.

12 R. Deeg and G. Jackson, 'Towards a More Dynamic Theory of Capitalist Variety' (2007) 5 *Socio-Economic Review* 149, p. 172. Such a focus may include a strong view of 'complementarity' between domains (that is, each institution operates better in concert with the other than each would operating alone) or a weaker view of institutions 'reinforcing' each other across domains, or having similar historical roots and so on.

13 Ibid., p. 157.

example, whether different types of capitalism produce different types of diversity. That is, whether we are witnessing what some scholars are labelling as 'bounded diversity' within what can still be meaningfully labelled a particular type of capitalist system.[14]

One final aspect of our research which may seem at odds with the varieties of capitalism literature as originally propounded a decade ago is our focus on the trajectory of regulatory change in the areas under review. Our analysis of the law in Chapter 2 and the case studies in Chapter 3 highlighted the way in which laws and institutions change. In contrast, the varieties of capitalism literature focuses on national types of capitalism as comprising coherent and complementary sets of institutions, and hence they tend to be viewed as stable across time and immune to large scale change. We would suggest that greater attention be given to explaining regulatory and institutional change within national systems, and linking such change both to politics and to actors – including labour and capital – who view established institutions as resources that can legitimately be manipulated to achieve their ends rather than as simply a 'matrix of incentives or constraints'.[15] More recent contributions to the comparative capitalism literature have begun to explore precisely this point[16] and could usefully inform an understanding of the trajectory of Australian law.

Since we commenced this study, and particularly since the mid-2000s, the debate over the relevance of legal origins, and the division of countries into different legal families, has grown considerably as scholars have begun to examine the claims of the early research carried out by La Porta and his colleagues.[17] In the legal origins literature various criticisms have emerged about the theory itself, and its quantitative methodology, to such an extent that the general trend of opinion seems to be moving decisively away from legal origins as an explanation for economic development towards a different explanation. In particular, the idea that a legal system can be treated as an exogenous variable predicting a priori an evolution in market formation and economic institutions within nation states appears largely discredited. Rather it seems to be the case that scholars are pointing to the need for an analysis of legal

---

14   G. Wood, R. Croucher, C. Brewster, M. Brookes and D. Collings, 'Varieties of Firm: Complementarity and Bounded Diversity' (2009) 43 *Journal of Economic Issues* 239.

15   Deeg and Jackson, above n. 12, p. 159. On law more particularly as offering a set of resources, see R. Stryker, 'Mind the Gap: Law, Institutional Analysis and Socioeconomics' (2003) 1 *Socio-Economic Review* 335.

16   See, for example, P. Hall and K. Thelen, 'Institutional Change in Varieties of Capitalism' (2009) 7 *Socio-Economic Review* 7.

17   See, for example, J. Armour, S. Deakin, V. Mollica and M. Siems, 'Law and Financial Development: What We Are Learning from Time Series Evidence' [2009] *Brigham Young University Law Review* 1435; J. Armour, S. Deakin, P. Lele and M. Siems, 'How Do Legal Rules Evolve? Evidence from a Cross-Country Comparison of Shareholder, Creditor, and Worker Protection' (2009) 57 *American Journal of Comparative Law* 579; Cioffi, above n. 9; C. Milhaupt and K. Pistor, *Law and Capitalism: What Corporate Crises Reveal About Legal Systems and Economic Development Around the World*, University of Chicago Press, Chicago, 2008.

origin and evolution more deeply grounded in the political and social contexts of each country in order to understand how law evolves and its relationship with economic development.

As our study and other recent legal origins work shows, there is considerable force in these arguments. Recent published work on legal origins theory and labour and corporate law in Australia suggests that the theory is at best a weak indicator of legal development over a 40-year period.[18] Importantly there are indications in this research that political change may be a more potent factor than legal origins in accounting for development in legal systems, and this provides some support for the recent critiques of the theory itself. Cioffi (among others) has argued strongly that while legal origins may provide some limited insights into 'broad patterns of legal, institutional and economic organization and development'[19] there is a strong need for more 'fine grained qualitative and historically empirical research to the study of relationships among law, politics and economic institutions'.[20]

Our study does not purport to investigate the theory of legal origins in any formal way. However, we noted in Chapter 2 that the account of legal developments in corporate law and labour law, and their relationship with the development of economic institutions raises questions about the legal families typology in relation to Australia – nominally a common law/'liberal market' example – suggesting that further empirical work on the long-run historical evolution of the Australian system is warranted. While it might be the case that developments in the later part of the twentieth century eventually brought Australia more into line with the regulatory style of other common law countries, that is not the point. For legal origin and path dependence to have some traction one would have expected the Australian legal system from the time of colonisation onwards to have followed a broadly similar path in shaping labour and capital markets to that of the UK. As noted earlier in this book there are at least strong doubts that it did so, at least in relation to some important Australian legal and economic institutions. Consequently, if scholars like Cioffi, and Milhaupt and Pistor are correct, we might expect to learn more from a detailed historical analysis exploring the endogenous relationship between law, politics and economic organisation, than we do from legal origins.[21]

The explanatory value of legal origins, it has been argued, appears to hold up better for the origin countries themselves than it does for transplant countries.[22] And

---

18 R. Mitchell, P. Gahan, A. Stewart, S. Cooney and S. Marshall, 'The Evolution of Labour Law in Australia: Measuring the Change' (2010) 23 *Australian Journal of Labour Law* 61; H. Anderson, M. Welsh, I. Ramsay and P. Gahan, 'The Evolution of Shareholder and Creditor Protection in Australia: An International Comparison', Legal Studies Research Paper No. 539, Melbourne Law School, University of Melbourne, 2011.

19 See Cioffi, above n. 9, p. 1550.

20 Ibid., p. 1552.

21 Ibid.; Milhaupt, above n. 9; Milhaupt and Pistor, above n. 17.

22 K. Pistor, 'Rethinking the "Law and Finance" Paradigm' [2009] *Brigham Young University Law Review* 1647, p. 1659.

if explanations are more grounded in the relationship of socio-political structures and legal and economic institutions in particular countries, we might equally expect there to be a serious disparity in the impact of legal origins across and between countries at different points of development.[23]

A further important point to note is that generally speaking law does not appear to take the central role in works of comparative political economy that perhaps its importance requires.[24] Self-evidently this makes it difficult to explore fully the role that law plays in constructing the institutions which are central to political economy accounts. In this book we have attempted to look more closely at the role of law, by providing both a detailed account of the evolution of labour and corporate law and regulation in Chapter 2, and examining empirically the role that specific legal developments have had on corporate decision-making in relation to employment systems and the interests of shareholders.

The fact that 'law matters'[25] is a critical supposition, central to legal origins theory, and by and large those critical of the theory are not intending to refute this supposition, merely to temper it. Thus in this branch of scholarship, law is important in setting a regulatory style and shaping economic institutions and activity, but it is *how* law functions, and whether it is an independent, or intermediate, variable that matters.[26] At the very least the empirical studies collected for this book raise important questions about how relevant the law is to corporate governance. They question whether company directors consider the law in general as an important guide to corporate decision making (as compared with other values) and also question the extent to which the law in its specifics necessarily sets the boundaries for appropriate strategies in relation to stakeholders. Company directors and managers may find themselves motivated not to fully exploit or utilise legal powers available to them. This can be for a variety of factors, in Australia as elsewhere,[27] but the point is that our studies show that while we might assume that law matters, why it does, when it does, and how it does are matters that need teasing out more carefully in particular instances of corporate change and economic development. In other words understanding the impact of law and its interaction with other social and economic forces requires detailed empirical study.

---

23   See Cioffi, above n. 9.

24   Ibid., p. 1527.

25   See Chapter 1 at nn. 28–66.

26   See Cioffi, above n. 9, p. 1533.

27   See C. Arup, A. Forsyth, P. Gahan, M. Michelotti, R. Mitchell, C. Sutherland and D. Taft, *Assessing the Impact of Employment Legislation: The Coalition Government's Labour Law Programme 1996–2007 and the Challenge for Research*, Research Report, Workplace and Corporate Law Research Group, Department of Business Law and Taxation, Monash University, Melbourne, 2009.

Index

Australian employment models 69
'Australian exceptionalism' arguments 197
'Australian experience' 195
Australian Fair Pay and Conditions
    Standards 57
Australian Federal Coalition 55
Australian government 54, 59, 77–78, 94,
    125, 134
Australian government inquiries 134
Australian Journal of Labour Law 46n,
    48n
Australian labour laws 12, 17, 49, 51, 53,
    56–60, 64, 66–67, 121, 150, 164,
    181, 188–189, 197, 201–202
    contracts of employment 45
    and deregulation 55–59
    labour markets 55
    'legal origins' theory 197–198
    nineteenth century comparisons 46
    origins and evolution 45, 48
Australian labour management systems
    149
Australian labour market, characterisation
    of 166
Australian labour market regulation 22,
    49–50, 54, 56, 121
Australian laws 32, 40, 51, 66, 164–165,
    204 *see also* Australian labour laws
Australian legislatures (1863-1874) 30
Australian 'liberal market' economy 149
Australian markets 91, 166, 169, 171, 191
    see also markets
Australian regulation of companies 34,
    188
Australian regulatory agencies 125
Australian regulatory reforms 43
Australian regulatory style 29, 188
Australian Securities Commission 36
Australian Securities Exchange *see* ASX
Australian Securities Exchange Corporate
    Governance Council 72, 104, 121,
    125
Australian shareholders (*see also*
    shareholders) 4–6, 16–17, 30–38,
    40–44, 71–72, 94–96, 104, 106–
    108, 116–118, 128–137, 139–143,
    151–155, 157–161, 167–171,
    176–179

Australian stock exchange listings 150,
    167
Australian telecommunication companies
    91
Australian telecommunications monopoly
    91, 172
Australian workplace 5, 20, 47, 51–52,
    54, 60, 62–63, 65, 90, 93–94, 121,
    123–124, 180–182
*Australian Workplace Industrial Relations
    Surveys* (1990 and 1995) 52, 54
autonomy
    of the board 32, 40
    determining agreements 76
    enjoyed by contractors 175
    managing shareholder expectations
        170
    principle of 77, 151
award provisions 62, 65
award restructuring 54, 121
awards 23, 50, 54, 59, 62, 65, 73, 105,
    108, 113, 121–123, 185

banks 5, 29, 96, 149
bargained agreements 15
bids, hostile takeover 43, 45
bids, rejection or modifying of 35, 40, 45
BiotechCo 99–103, 116, 118, 175
    diffused capital structure 103
    experience of venture capital 100
    human resources strategy 100–101
    stock market listing 99
    work organisation 102, 122
blue collar employees 74, 93
board composition 36
Board of Trade (UK) 30
boards 18, 32, 34–36, 37n, 38, 42,
    71–72, 82–83, 85–86, 95, 134, 140,
    151–152, 154, 170
    advisory 87
    chairman of 40
    corporate 5
    hostile target 45
    independent 107
    members of 39, 99
    over-powerful 16
    representation of shareholders
        151–152, 154

For Product Safety Concerns and Information please contact our
EU representative GPSR@taylorandfrancis.com or Taylor & Francis
Verlag GmbH, Kaufingerstraße 24, 80331 München, Germany